EXPLORATIONS IN METAPHYSICS

EXPLORATIONS IN METAPHYSICS
Being—God—Person

W. NORRIS CLARKE, S.J.

UNIVERSITY OF NOTRE DAME PRESS
Notre Dame

University of Notre Dame Press
Notre Dame, Indiana 46556
All Rights Reserved
Published in the United States of America
Copyright © 1994 by University of Notre Dame
The author gratefully acknowledges permission to reprint his articles from the following sources:
"What Is Most and Least Relevant in the Metaphysics of St. Thomas Today" from *International Philosophical Quarterly* 14 (1974), 411–34.
"The 'We Are' of Interpersonal Dialogue as the Starting Point of Metaphysics" from *Modern Schoolman* 59 (1992), 357–68.
"Action as the Self-Revelation of Being: A Central Theme in the Thought of St. Thomas" from *History of Philosophy in the Making: Essays in Honor of James Collins* (Lanham, Md.: University Press of America, 1982), 63–83.
"The Limitation of Act by Potency in St. Thomas: Aristotelianism or Neoplatonism?" from *New Scholasticism* 26 (1952), 167–94.
"The Meaning of Participation in St. Thomas" from *Proceedings of American Catholic Philosophical Association* 26 (1952), 147–57.
"To Be Is to Be Substance-in-Relation" from *Metaphysics as Foundation: Essays in Honor of Ivor Leclerc*, ed. P. Bogaard and G. Treash (Albany: SUNY Press, 1993), 164–83, by permission of the State University of New York Press, copyright 1993.
"Analogy and the Meaningfulness of Language about God" from *The Thomist* 40 (1976), 61–95.
"Is a Natural Theology Still Viable Today?" from *Prospects for Natural Theology*, ed. E. Long (Washington, D.C.: Catholic University of America Press, 1992), 151–81. The original of this extensively revised and reworked version appeared in the symposium sponsored by the Vatican Observatory: *Physics, Philosophy, and Theology: A Common Quest for Understanding*, ed. R. Russell, W. Stoeger, G. Coyne (Rome: Vatican Observatory, 1988—distributed by University of Notre Dame Press.).
"A New Look at the Immutability of God" from *God Knowable and Unknowable*, ed. Robert Roth (New York: Fordham University Press, 1973), pp. 43–72.
"Person, Being, and St. Thomas" from *Communio* 19 (1992), 601–18.

Reprinted in 2008

Library of Congress Cataloging-in-Publication Data

Clarke, W. Norris (William Norris), 1915–
Explorations in metaphysics: being—god—person/W. Norris Clarke.
p.   cm.
ISBN 13: 978-0-268-00696-9 (alk. paper) ISBN 10: 0-268-00696-2 (alk. paper)
1. Metaphysics.   2. God.   3. Thomas, Aquinas, Saint, 1225?–1274.
4. Thomists.   I. Title.
B945.C483B45 1994
110—dc20   94–15469
                                                         CIP

∞ This book is printed on acid-free paper.

To Gerald McCool, S.J., for his insightful inspiration, and to Cary Lynch and Sara Penella for their constant support and encouragement, as well as to many others along the way too numerous to mention, with deep appreciation and gratitude.

CONTENTS

	Introduction	ix
1.	What Is Most and Least Relevant in the Metaphysics of St. Thomas Today	1
2.	The "We Are" of Interpersonal Dialogue as the Starting Point of Metaphysics	31
3.	Action as the Self-Revelation of Being: A Central Theme in the Thought of St. Thomas	45
4.	The Limitation of Act by Potency in St. Thomas: Aristotelianism or Neoplatonism?	65
5.	The Meaning of Participation in St. Thomas	89
6.	To Be Is to Be Substance-in-Relation	102
7.	Analogy and the Meaningfulness of Language about God	123
8.	Is a Natural Theology Still Viable Today?	150
9.	A New Look at the Immutability of God	183
10.	Person, Being, and St. Thomas	211

Introduction

I have brought together this collection of essays—articles, chapters in books, etc.—at the urgent suggestion of my many colleagues, friends, and fellow philosophers with whom I have happily shared philosophical discussion over the last forty-six years—thirty-one teaching at Fordham University, six in Jesuit seminaries before that, and nine on the road as Visiting Professor around the country. Not a few of these essays, I am told, have had significant impact in influencing the flow of ideas, especially in the American Catholic philosophical community, the main—but by no means the only—theater of my own professional activity. Yet I am also told that, scattered as they are in diverse periodicals and especially in collections of essays on various themes or in *Festchrifts*, they are hard to find and follow up systematically.

So it seemed appropriate, now that I am Professor Emeritus, to make it easier for those interested to examine my work as a whole, for what it is worth, by bringing together in one place what I consider the most significant of my philosophical essays. I was further disposed to do so because it seemed to me that with several of my most recent publications I had finally completed the circle by expressing my views on most of the great central themes of Thomistic metaphysics and my own creative reappropriation of them, so that some kind of rounded picture of the systematic unity of the whole could be discerned by others. There are indeed a number of other essays I would have dearly loved to include, both because of their significance and influence, but publishing wisdom forbade it. Perhaps at some future time. . . .

My Own Work as Thomistically Inspired Metaphysician

A word now about the central focus of my own work as a Thomistically inspired metaphysician spread over some forty-six years of teaching and writing, and how each of the essays chosen here illustrates some facet of this still ongoing effort.

I say "Thomistically inspired" metaphysician, rather than simply "Thomistic," because the focus of my effort has not been purely or primarily historical scholarship for its own sake—though I have the highest esteem for the latter, consider it indispensable for any well-grounded systematic thought, and am deeply grateful for all that I have learned from it. My concern, building on the results of historical scholarship, has rather been to operate what I might call a "creative retrieval" (in the Heideggerian sense) of the great seminal ideas of St. Thomas in metaphysics and philosophy of the person, under the stimulus of what seem to me some of the authentic contributions of later, especially twentieth-century, philosophy, and also, where there seems to me a definite lacuna in Aquinas's own thought, to suggest a "creative completion" of his own expressed ideas, in the line, I think, of the intrinsic dynamism of his own basic insights. One of the places where I have tried to do the latter most explicitly is in my recent little book, *Person and Being* (the expansion of my 1993 Aquinas Lecture at Marquette University), which should be taken together with the present collection to adequately express where I have arrived at present on my philosophical "journey."

The central inspiration of my philosophical vision has been from the beginning what I take—with most contemporary Thomists—to be the great central metaphysical insight of St. Thomas: being as *existential act* (what he calls *esse*: the "to be" or act of existing of real beings), seen as the ground and central core of all the positive qualities or "perfection" of all real things. Here God is seen as the ultimate Source of all being and perfection, as the pure Subsistent Act of Existence, uncontracted by any limiting essence, whereas all other beings distinct from God are "participations" or imperfect images of the infinite perfection of God, through a metaphysical composition of an act of existence with a limiting essence.

The reader will recognize here the general approach to Thomistic metaphysics known commonly as "existential Thomism," or by some as "Thomistic existentialism," though there are dangers of misunderstanding in using such a historically conditioned term as "existentialism." My understanding of what I take to be existential Thomism focuses on three main points:

1) *Real being understood as grounded in existential act*, with the act of existence (*esse*) constituting the central core of all positive perfection, composed with limiting essence in all beings but God. Etienne Gilson is largely responsible for introducing this interpretation into this country, through his own writings and those of his numerous disciples, and into European Thomistic circles together with Joseph de Finance, Cornelio Fabro, and L. B. Geiger. It was through the writings of Gilson, mediated through perhaps his most famous and articulate disciple on this side of the ocean, Anton Pegis, that I first came to

Introduction

appreciate fully this aspect of St. Thomas during my M.A. in philosophy at Fordham University in 1940.

2) The appreciation of the role of *Neoplatonic participation metaphysics*, taken over and adapted by St. Thomas as the conceptual framework for expressing his doctrine of the limitation of existence by essence, as well as the limitation of form by matter. This I picked up in Europe during my doctorate in Louvain (1947–49) from such Thomistic metaphysicians as Geiger, Fabro, de Finance, and De Raeymaeker, and did my own Ph.D. dissertation on the topic. Gilson and his immediate disciples tended to be reluctant and uneasy over allowing such a central role to Platonic sources in Aquinas's thought, based on Gilson's firm conviction that St. Thomas had made a fundamental option for Aristotle and against Plato. In fact, when I consulted Gilson in Paris during my dissertation, he told me with jovial frankness that in trying to trace St. Thomas to his sources I was doing "the work of a madman," that it couldn't be done. This "anti-Platonist option" of St. Thomas can indeed be defended, for the most part, in Aquinas's theory of knowledge; but this does not do justice to the rich complexity of his metaphysical system precisely as an original synthesis of the strong points of both Aristotelianism and Neoplatonism, under the powerful influence of Pseudo-Dionysius in particular. I believe this interpretation of St. Thomas's metaphysics as a synthesis of both Aristotelian and Neoplatonic elements has now come to be fairly widely accepted by most contemporary Thomists.

3) *The central role of action* as the natural overflow of the act of existence in all real beings, so that all existential being is intrinsically self-communicative and self-expressing, self-revealing, through action. This highly dynamic and relational notion of being—not yet fully exploited, it seems to me, by American Thomists—I have found highly fruitful in applications to epistemology, the metaphysics of being as constituting an interrelated universe with God as its source, and the philosophy of the person, where it has helped to illuminate St. Thomas's profound insight that the final goal of the whole universe is the communion of persons. The principal source for my recognition of the centrality of action in St. Thomas's metaphysics was the seminal work of Joseph de Finance, S. J., *Etre et agir dans la philosophie de S. Thomas*, first published in 1939 but never translated into English.

Three early influences that I must mention as playing a decisive role in helping me to integrate all this into a unified metaphysical system that I could call my own were the following:

1) My first exposure to *systematic Thomistic metaphysics* under the tutelage of the brilliant young French Thomist, André Marc, S.J.,

who taught me in my first philosophical studies at the French Jesuit house of philosophy on the island of Jersey in the English Channel, during the years 1936–39, just before the Second World War. His powerful and original systemization of Thomistic metaphysics was an eye-opener to my young mind, already groping for something of the sort.

2) The influence of *Transcendental Thomism* through the work of Joseph Maréchal, S.J., just completing his great work, *Le point de départ de la métaphysique*, on the radical dynamism of the mind toward the whole of being and implicitly toward the Infinite at its core, plus the complementary work of Maurice Blondel, *L'Action* (1893), on the dynamism of the will toward the Infinite Good. Though I have not bought into all the technical details of this school as a school, chiefly because I did not think they had given sufficient emphasis to the existential dimension of Thomistic metaphysics, the notion of the unrestricted innate dynamism of the mind and the will toward the fullness of being, hence implicitly toward God, has had a profound effect as underlying all my thinking ever since, not only in philosophy but in theology and spirituality as well.

3) The notion of *interpersonal dialogue* through language as the privileged and most epistemologically efficacious instance of the contact of the human mind with the order of real being and its natural aptitude for knowing both the existence and nature of real beings, hence as the privileged starting point of metaphysics. The initial suggestion for this aproach I owe to another professor on the island of Jersey, Auguste Brunner, S.J., who had been forced to flee from Germany during the Nazi ascendancy and who proposed reflection on linguistic dialogue as the starting point for philosophy (*La personne incarnée*, 1947). Father Gerald McCool, S.J., in his essay on my place in contemporary Thomistic thought, "William Norris Clarke, S.J., An Alert and Independent Thomist" (*International Philosophical Quarterly*, March 1986), maintains that this approach to being through interpersonal dialogue is distinctive and unique among contemporary Thomists, or indeed Thomists of any age. I express this approach in the second essay of this collection.

So much for the Thomistic background of my thought. The most significant modern influences (in addition to meeting the challenges of Kant and contemporary theoretical physics, which has always fascinated me and stimulated my metaphysical reflection) have been the contributions of contemporary phenomenology along the lines of interpersonal existentialism—the person seen as relational and dialogical in its very being. I owe a considerable debt here to thinkers like

Introduction

Martin Buber, Gabriel Marcel, Maurice Nédoncelle, Emmanuel Mounier and the Christian Personalist movement, whose work was in full flower just at the time I was studying in Louvain in 1947. The incorporation of their insights on the person into my own Thomistic synthesis did not appear till fairly recent years and did not reach full articulation till my 1993 publication of *Person and Being*. My ongoing dialogue with Process philosophy has also significantly influenced my philosophy of God.

THE PRESENT COLLECTION OF ESSAYS

The first one, "What Is Most and Least Relevant in the Metaphysics of St. Thomas Today" (1976), is self-explanatory. It outlines the content of my basic project of retrieving and re-presenting the perenially seminal insights of St. Thomas in metaphysics.

The second one, "The 'We Are' of Interpersonal Dialogue as the Starting Point of Metaphysics" (1992), presents my own distinctive approach to the philosophical discovery of being through the realm of the personal, as the place where the meaning of being and our openness to it shine through most luminously and incontrovertibly.

The third one, "Action as the Self-Revelation of Being: A Central Theme in the Thought of St. Thomas" (1982), is also self-explanatory and seems to me one of my most important contributions to the retrieval of a dynamic Thomism. The implications for what it means to be a person are profound.

The fourth, "The Limitation of Act by Potency in St. Thomas: Aristotelianism or Neoplatonism?" (1952), has been one of the most widely influential of the articles I have written. Despite its apparently narrow technical title, it is actually the place where I develop most explicitly the essential lines of St. Thomas's unique synthesis of Aristotelianism, Neoplatonism, and his own original insight into the act of existence as the root of all perfection and action, all laid out in historical context.

The fifth, "The Meaning of Participation in St. Thomas" (1952), is a condensed exposition of the basic systematic structure of participation metaphysics as used by St. Thomas, for which the historical roots are given in the preceding article.

The sixth, "To Be Is to Be Substance-in-Relation" (1992), spells out my retrieval of the dynamic notion of substance as a central piece in St. Thomas's metaphysics, as contrasted with the various distortions the notion underwent in modern philosophy since Descartes.

The seventh, "Analogy and the Meaningfulness of Language about God" (1976), explicates my understanding of the basic structure of analogical language and its application to God by St. Thomas, following the recent analyses of analogy as fully meaningful only in terms of a participation metaphysics.

The eighth, "Is a Natural Theology Still Viable Today?" (1992), presents my best effort—so far—to construct a natural theology, or philosophy of God, in a contemporary context of difficulties against it. It is certainly Thomistically inspired in a general sense, but puts together the elements in my own way that cannot be found as such in Aquinas himself and avoids the many lacunae and difficulties for modern readers found in the famous Five Ways, which I do not consider at all the best efforts of St. Thomas. I have laid out a more historically faithful reconstruction of what I consider his most adequate strictly metaphysical approach to God in my book *The Philosophical Approach to God* (1979).

The ninth, "A New Look at the Immutability of God" (1973), presents my own adaptation and "creative completion" of what seems to me too incomplete and unqualified a position in Thomas himself. This is one fruit of my dialogue with contemporary American Process thinkers, Whitehead, Hartshorne, Ford, etc., which has been an important part of my effort at creative completion of St. Thomas. I have rewritten the last part of this essay to reflect a recent shift of my position, which in fact brings it back a little closer to that of St. Thomas himself.

The tenth, "Person, Being, and St. Thomas" (1993), is significant as an example of my turn in recent years more toward the philosophy of the person, as nourished both by deep roots in the metaphysics of existence of St. Thomas (not always made explicit by Aquinas himself) and by the rich contributions of contemporary personalist phenomenology. This essay contains some of the key ideas later developed more amply in my book *Person and Being* (1993). I have here rewritten the last part of the article in order to cope more adequately with the problem of the divine freedom in creation.

I have left the above essays for the most part in the state in which they were originally written, save for an occasional minor correction of some inaccuracy or an addition to fill an obvious lacuna. The whole text has also been slightly revised to conform to gender-inclusive language, in accordance with the policy of the Press, except where this would have required extensive rewriting, as is the case in chapter 9 on the philosophy of God. My purpose—and hope—in the publication of this collection is that the essays contained therein may help to

Introduction

awaken in my readers, either anew or for the first time, an appreciation of the seminal riches in St. Thomas's own metaphysical thought, and stimulate them, critically and creatively, to go beyond the text of the Master to draw out the hidden implications of what is already there, or complete what is missing, in the light of our own partially richer perspectives and insights of today.

1

What Is Most and Least Relevant in the Metaphysics of St. Thomas Today

My purpose in this paper, written for a symposium at Fordham University commemorating the 700th anniversary of the death of St. Thomas Aquinas (1274), is to attempt a critical sifting and reassessment of the rich metaphysical heritage handed down by St. Thomas in order to discern what is most relevant and fruitful in it for the philosophical thinking of our own day. Such an attempt also implies, inevitably, a negative discernment as to what is less relevant, less fruitful, less accessible for contemporary thought—if indeed still valid at all—in this heritage. Both facets of this enterprise are bound to be controversial, but more especially the second.

Yet I think the risk must be taken. The substantive content of St. Thomas's metaphysical vision is extremely rich and profound, as I think those will agree who have been willing to take the time and effort to make themselves at home in it. But it also seems to me a fact, as a teacher, that there is a serious block to the accessibility of this content for the ordinary educated contemporary thinker, even Christian, who has not been exposed to long scholarly specialization in the texts of St. Thomas, the history of medieval philosophy, and the subsequent history of Thomism. Thus students ordinarily find St. Thomas one of the most difficult of Western philosophers to approach directly on their own in his own texts, without the help of very ample introduction and detailed commentary.

This arises from the fact that St. Thomas's thought comes to us encased in a whole tightly knit technical framework of Aristotelian logic, terminology, methodology of scientific knowledge (in the Aristotelian meaning of science), and scientific worldview (philosophy of nature), which was once the common patrimony of the thinking West but is now so difficult of access without a long apprenticeship that few contemporary thinkers are willing to invest the time and effort required, especially since the limitations of the technical framework are now more evident. What is needed, therefore, if the substance of the thought of St. Thomas is to enter in any significant way into the bloodstream of contemporary philosophical reflection, is an operation of "detechnicalizing" this thought, i.e., of lifting it out of its forbidding technical armature to put it in simpler terms more directly accessible to the ordinary lived experience and language of reflective Western thinkers today. I am well aware that the profound rethinking and retranslating necessary to carry out this detechnicalizing successfully is itself quite a difficult and tricky business and one that might be rejected in principle by those who believe on philosophical grounds that content and a given technical methodology and language are in principle interdependent and inseparable. Still, I think the risk is worth taking and that something like it has been going on in fact with most of the great thinkers of the past whose thoughts have become part of our intellectual heritage, like Plato, Aristotle, Kant, etc. I do not mean by this, however, that the thought of St. Thomas can ever become easy to assimilate without a profound effort of rigorous and systematic thinking or that his *general* methodology of proceeding from observable experience to hidden explanatory principles and causes, guided by first principles, should be laid aside—this is in fact one of its greatest strengths. I mean rather that the technical apparatus required should be revised or built up anew in simpler and more streamlined terms, as arising more naturally out of our own contemporary experience and language. For all conceptual frameworks must be embedded in some concrete cultural form of life, and such forms of life are bound to change significantly over a period of centuries. The present essay is a modest attempt to assist along this difficult but, I think, highly fruitful enterprise, from the viewpoint of one who has meditated on both Thomistic and modern thought for some forty-five years.

The main themes I would like to single out as the most relevant and fruitful for nourishing our philosophical thought today are the following:

1) The intrinsic correlativity, or connaturality, that exists between the human spirit, in its two main facets of intellect and will, on the one hand, and the realm of being, on the other. This correlativity is summed up in the two first principles of the *intelligibility of being* and the *goodness of being*, and constitutes a basic matrix of harmony within which the destinies both of man and of the material universe take on their full meaning.

2) The *existential meaning of being*, focused on actual existence conceived as an inner act and the immanent source of all perfection in any being, an act diversified in different beings according to diverse

modes of essence. Stemming from this is the close relation between *being and action*, where action is seen as flowing from real being as its natural self-manifestation and therefore becomes the criterion for distinguishing real from merely mental or merely possible being.

3) The explanation of the *one and the many* within being, which is solidary with the above conception of being, namely, the theory that all finite beings participate in the act of existence as central unifying perfection of the universe, through composition with diverse limiting modes of essence, all deriving from a single ultimate Source, which is pure unlimited plenitude of existence.

4) The notion of *person as the highest mode of being*, being become *self-possessing* through self-consciousness and self-determination (freedom).

5) The *dynamic notion of substance* as unifying center of attributes and operations and active principle of self-identity through change.

6) The notion of *substantial potency* as the condition of possibility of the intrinsic unity of complex wholes in nature.

7) The theory of *efficient and final causality*, which binds together the universe into a system of interacting, goal-oriented agents, giving to and receiving from each other by means of the central bond of all communication, which is action.

8) The *relation to God*, the *ultimate Source and Goal of all being*, the keystone which holds the whole universe together in a unity of being, intelligibility, and goodness.

In the brief time at my disposal I shall obviously not be able to develop all these themes in detail. I shall be content to call your attention to their centrality and point out some key implications.

I. THE NATURAL CORRELATIVITY OF SPIRIT AND BEING

At the root of the whole Thomistic vision of the universe and its systematic articulation are the dual principles of the intelligibility and the goodness of being. This means that spirit—all spirit, and therefore human spirit too in its modest analogous way—is intrinsically oriented by its very nature toward being, i.e., has a natural aptitude and drive to know all being (being as intelligible) and to be fulfilled by it (being as good). It means also that the reciprocal is true: being itself has a natural intrinsic aptitude to unveil itself to mind, to be brought into the light of consciousness, and to fulfill the drive of the spirit towards its self-actualization or self-perfection. This double correlative aptitude, this connaturality between spirit and being, is the fundamental matrix of harmony which makes possible the unfolding of the entire *intellec-*

tual life in all its forms, including the whole enterprise of science, and the entire *practical and moral life* in the human search for happiness. "Being is intelligible" is the first dynamic principle of the intellectual life, and "The good is to be done and evil avoided" is the first principle of the moral life, presupposing of course as its implicit foundation that being itself is good. In what follows we shall focus on the first principle of the intellectual life, the intelligibility of being, as more immediately germane to our purposes of the construction of a metaphysics.

There is no doubt that St. Thomas holds this basic principle and that it is the secret dynamo energizing the whole movement of his thought to work out a systematic explanation of the world, as the transcendental Thomist movement has so convincingly shown. And in this he shows a profound kinship with St. Bonaventure and most, if not all, other medieval thinkers. But there are two main difficulties which modern thinkers run into in trying to get at and critically evaluate this doctrine when they approach him through his own texts. The first is that he rarely lays out the whole doctrine and its implications formally in a single synthetic presentation for its own sake. Rather he presupposes it as a common background already known and lived out of, constantly using it as a supporting principle, which he formulates often enough but usually piecemeal in the form of technical expressions such as "Being is the formal object of the intellect," "Truth (i.e, ontological truth, or intrinsic intelligibility) is a transcendental property of all being," etc., with an occasional synthetic sweep such as in the splendid article 1 of the *De Veritate*. What is needed for our day is to lay out this whole underlying doctrine clearly and as a unit, and in more general and easily accessible terms than the technical vocabulary of St. Thomas, which does not always allow the vast scope of the doctrine and its dynamic view of intelligence to shine through.

But once one attempts to do this from a strictly philosophical point of view a second difficulty arises. This is a methodological problem which St. Thomas himself, writing as a theologian *using* an already presupposed underlying metaphysics, did not have to face and in any case did not face explicitly, although he gives many indirect hints. How does one establish *philosophically* such a radical a priori as the correlative aptitude of mind for being and being for mind, which is the presupposed condition for the whole quest of philosophy itself and indeed for any meaningful use of intelligence, whether theoretical or practical? St. Thomas himself, writing as theologian able to draw upon all of philosophy as he wishes, grounds it in the doctrine of the creation of all things by God as *Logos*: all being is intelligible because the Source of all being is identically both the fullness of being and the fullness of intelligence, and all other beings proceed from God by an act of free creative intelligence and love. Thus there is nothing in their being which has not been first thought through and through by this divine intelligence, making them apt to be rethought, however imperfectly, by all finite intelligences. This doctrine is available to St. Thomas both from Christian Revelation and as the final conclusion of metaphysics. But neither source is available to philosophers to help them validate this principle as the a priori condition of all philosophy at the *beginning* of their quest. And formal proof is obviously out of the question, since all proof presupposes it.

The only way left is the way that St. Thomas himself seems at times to be practicing but never formally expounds, that is, the way of unveiling, uncovering, what is already present or accepted as existentially lived, as a "form of life," the commitment to which is an indispensable condition for rational human living and the denial of which involves one in implicit or "lived" contradictions. This method was occasionally practiced by the ancients and medievals, in particular by Aristotle and St. Thomas in defending the principle of contradiction against would-be deniers. But the generalization of this method, especially the linking it up with the notion of a form of life, has come into clearer focus in our own day, through the work of Wittgenstein, Heidegger, Merleau-Ponty, and other existential phenomenologists, and in particular by the school of Transcendental Thomism, initiated by Joseph Maréchal in the 1930s and followed up by Rahner, Coreth, Lonergan, Donceel, etc. To sum up, the strength of St. Thomas's thought here lies in the recognition and content of the principles of the intelligibility and goodness of being as the dynamic lived a priori of the human mind and will; its weakness lies in his own mode of presentation and justification.

II. The Existential Analysis of Being

Under this heading I would like to single out two main points that render St. Thomas's conception of being distinctive in the history of metaphysics and also highly relevant today. The first is its uncompromisingly *existential character*, which has given rise to the term "existential Thomism," coined in the 1940s when Gilson and others first brought into the open this long-neglected aspect.[1] The second is the close link of *action* with being, so that action (in the widest sense) flows naturally from any actually existing being—and only from such—and hence serves as the necessary and sufficient criterion for distinguishing real from merely mental or possible being.

By the existential analysis of being I mean St. Thomas's interpretation of the immanent constitutive structure of real being as a synthesis of essence as determining mode and the act of existence (*esse*, the "to-be" of a thing) as the central core of perfection in every being and the bond of similarity that links it in community with every other being in the universe. The stress on the act of existence as ultimate immanent or intrinsic principle of perfection in every being, including God, is what is distinctively new in the doctrine: "Ens dicitur ab actu essendi" (being receives its name and meaning from the act of existence).[2]

Other notions of being in the history of metaphysics have tended—and outside of the existentialists still tend—to analyze the positive perfection of being and its intelligibility almost exclusively in term of form and essence, the *what*-it-is of a being. The aspect of actual existence, or actual *presence*, of things, if given any explicit attention at all, is treated as a kind of indispensable but intellectually opaque fact impervious to any further intrinsic analysis. If any further analysis is offered, it usually proceeds from what I might call an extrinsic point of view, i.e., either (1) from the point of view of the relation of a being to a knower who affirms the *fact* of its existence as "outside" or independent of the knower's own knowledge of it; or (2) from the point of view of the relation of a being to its *cause*: something is real if it exists as a fact "outside of its cause(s)," or, in the case of God, if it exists "of its own essence, as uncaused," to cite traditional scholastic expressions. I might add that it is a source of endless wonder to me to observe how this apparently obvious dimension of actual presence has been either ignored, or acknowledged and then brushed under the rug without further development, or reduced to essence, intelligibility, or some other attribute, by most of the great metaphysicians in the history of thought. Even Aristotle, committed realist that he is, after clearly affirming that the prime analogate of being is singular, existing, active substance, proceeds to carry on his entire explicit analysis of being in terms of substance, form and matter, change, and efficient and final causes. Existence plays no further technical role in his metaphysics.

The two main advantages of St. Thomas's existential interpretation of being which seem to me most significant for us today are the following: 1) In penetrating beyond the mere *fact* of existence of some being, affirmed by a knower distinct from it, to the inner *act* of existence *within* the being itself, which objectively grounds the true affirmation about it, he has provided a far more intrinsic analysis than hitherto available in more essence-oriented, essence-dominated, conceptions. For the first time the fact of actual existence as immanent act and perfection is formally and technically integrated into the metaphysical analysis of the constitutive structure of being, being thereby "unveiled" as constituting the very root of all the ontological perfection within a being, including its intelligibility. The latter now appears as the very light of existence itself shining through the manifold prism of essences recognized as diverse modes of active presence.

Such a conception of being is required, it seems to me, if we are to do justice to the legitimate insights and exigencies of the personalist and existentialist movements, which quite justly insist on the unique concrete individuality of every real thing—especially persons—as actually existing centers of action and irreducible to anything universal or abstract or merely intelligible. At the same time, since this conception of being includes form and essence as interior modes determining the act of existence, hence as also intrinsically constitutive of the real, it avoids the sharp dichotomy between essence as principle of intelligibility, on the one hand, and existence as irrational brute fact, on the other, which we find in so many forms of existentialism. In a word, what St. Thomas has succeeded in doing is to shift the center of gravity in the constitution of the real from form and essence to actual existence as inner act, without thereby letting go of the intelligibility of being; for existence itself, as the direct participation in God's own essential perfection, has now become the root of intelligibility itself, mediated to our finite intelligences through the spectrum of finite forms.

2) In focusing on the supra-formal, supra-essential factor of the act of existence as the root of all perfection and the all-pervasive bond of unity in all beings, St. Thomas has also made it possible to include the entire range of reality—from the most evanescent subatomic particle, that burns out its being in a micro-second flash, to the infinite and eternal plenitude of God—under one completely positive viewpoint, yet without being forced to constrict the mystery of the divine Infinity into our own limited categorical concepts. For the notion of God as pure Subsistent Act of Existence, transcending all limited forms and essential modes, is by that very fact clearly *understood* as transcending all our limited categories which allow of direct conceptual representation, yet at the same time without breaking the bond of similarity between the divine Being as Source and all finite beings as diverse participations in the one all-pervasive perfection of existence.

In a word, this allows God to remain at once radical Mystery but yet not "Wholly Other," as the various traditions of the so-called "negative theology" have been forced to characterize the divine. Without in any way denying the rich and fruitful insights which these various negative theology traditions have contributed to metaphysical and religious thought, I still submit that one of the main reasons why they have felt it necessary to characterize the Transcendent as "beyond being," and hence in primarily negative terms, is their insufficiently critical presupposition—quite explicit in the West, more vague and implicit, though still at work, in the East—that all positive attributes, including being itself, must be understood as somehow implying determinate essence or form. Once this position is adopted, it follows inevitably that Ultimate Reality, as Infinite, can only be characterized negatively, as "Beyond Being," or "Non-Being," or the "Void," or, perhaps even more consistently, simply pointed to, as the Buddhists do, in utter silence, as the Goal of all longing. St. Thomas, with his notion of *esse* as a supra-formal, yet, positive, perfection, is not caught in quite the same bind, though he too still stresses strongly the mystery aspect of this positive knowledge of God and the need for an accompanying negative corrective.

The Self-Revelation of Being through Action

The second main point I would like to single out in St. Thomas's existential conception of being is the close connection between being and action, so that action becomes the natural self-manifestation of a being, both of its presence (its act of existence) and its mode of presence (its essence). As he never tires of repeating, *agere sequitur esse* (to act follows upon, or naturally flows out of, to be). Here real being is conceived as a dynamic inner act of presence, which has a natural aptitude and tendency to flow over into activity proportionate to and expressive of its nature. Every act, he says, is naturally communicative of its own perfection, according to the degree in which it is in act.[3] Since *esse* is the supreme act, the higher and more intense is the act of existence in a being, the more it is connatural to it to pour out and express its perfection more richly and generously, both within itself and to others.

What St. Thomas has actually done here is to incorporate into his metaphysics of being as act the basic thrust of the whole Neoplatonic tradition of the self-diffusiveness of the Good: *bonum est diffusivum sui*. But he has reversed the order of priority of the terms. For Neoplatonism the Good is primary and being is a derivative of the Good. For St. Thomas goodness cannot be absolutely primary, since it implicitly presupposes the actual existence of what is good. Goodness is an intrinsically relative term—goodness *of* ——— and *for* ———, hence it must be grounded in the most radically immanent, ultimate act that grounds all else, the act of existence itself. But the same inner dynamism of self-diffusiveness, self-communication, self-sharing, is incorporated here, not as a strict law of metaphysical necessity but as a connatural aptitude under the control of freedom, if the being in question is a person.

Let me point out two highly significant consequences which flow from this conception of being as naturally self-communicative through action. First, we now have a decisive *criterion*, both necessary and sufficient, for *recognizing real being* and distinguishing it from merely mental, possible, or ideal being. If a being acts in some way (interpreting activity in the widest possible sense, as including both immanent and transient activity), this is a sure sign, the primary sign, of its real presence as an actual existent, both to itself and to others.[4] If it does not act at all, there is no way of knowing that it is actually present at all rather than a mere content of thought, no sufficient grounds for affirming it as real. Even the non-active elements in a being can be known only as inferred from the kind of nature it has, which in turn is known only as manifested by its characteristic activities. Something that would be totally non-active in any way at all would be totally unmanifested, either to itself or to others, and the totally unmanifested, as such, cannot be affirmed at all, would remain totally unknowable, would make no difference to itself or anything else whether it were present or not, and hence would be literally indistinguishable from nothing.

Action thus reveals itself as the primary communication system of the universe: all communication of any kind is linked to action, and all action, since it flows from and is also manifestive of the particular being from which it emanates, is intrinsically and necessarily a communication, a revelation, of this being. All action is communication, and all communication is action. This opens up a magnificent metaphysical vision of the universe as a vast communication system, linked together precisely as a universe by the universal dynamic bond of action and interaction, through which the inner act of presence of one being is made known, or makes a difference, to another while leaving intact the distinct identity of each.

Let me remind you that all through the history of metaphysics this has been a central and thorny problem, even when a thinker does not formally and explicitly come to grips with it: what does a philosopher take as the criterion for recognizing the *authentically real*? I know of few more challenging and illuminating questions to put to a metaphysician, for the answer given will shed a unique light on the sources of inspiration and the general lines of orientation of his whole system.

Thus the whole Platonic tradition has been plagued with ambiguity, to my mind, once Plato made the fateful step of choosing self-identity and immutability as the criterion of the really real. Since ideas qualify eminently over agents as the really real in terms of this criterion, the whole Platonic tradition, including Christian Platonists, has always had trouble distinguishing the logical and conceptual from the ontological order. And it becomes quite a dilemma for a Christian Platonist to hold, on the one hand, that the divine ideas are real, and many, and in the mind of God, and yet on the other hand that the ontological being of God is absolutely simple (aside from the unique multiplicity of the divine Persons). Whitehead, on the other hand, is here very close to Aristotle and St. Thomas in his stress on activity as the mark of any actual entity and in his consequent refusal to classify his eternal objects as real in themselves, although he differs from them in not identifying actual entity with perduring *substance*.

The second significant consequence of this linking of action with being as its natural manifestation is that it provides the basic *grounding for a realistic epistemology*, especially to the key question: "How can I know the existence and nature of anything real outside my own mind, as it is in itself?" The only possible link between two distinct beings across which knowledge can pass is that of action. One being can know another only if it either actively produces the other or consciously receives the action of the other. Indeed, if pushed hard, we might sum up the whole of Thomistic epistemology as resting on this one principle: "All knowledge of real being is an interpretation of action," whether through direct awareness of a being's action on the knower, or through inference to causes through observed effects.

It is the failure to take into account this basic communication channel of action that has caused so much of the trouble which modern epistemologists since Descartes have had in holding onto, let alone justifying, the ability of the human mind truly to know, albeit imperfectly, the real world outside of its own thoughts. Once we take human knowledge to be a set of images and representations already given within the mind like a collection of paintings hanging on the walls of a museum, and try to reconstruct their relation to the real merely in term of their immanent content within the mind, the problem has become insoluble. It is only by being aware of other beings as actively expressing themselves within us and to us as knowers, by acting on us in determinate ways varying characteristically with each agent, that we can discern not only the *presence* but the *natures* of the real beings that surround us. No single action, it is true, at least of a finite being, can reveal exhaustively its whole essence or nature, and in addition each action, with its immanent message-content, can be received in the knower only according to the mode and capacity of the receiver. Hence the necessarily limited, incomplete, and perspectival character of all human knowing. But still, no matter how much an action-message is coded and recoded within the receiving system, there is no action which of its very nature as action is not in some way genuinely communicative of both the existence and nature of the source from which it flows. Non-communicative action is a contradiction in terms.

Hence we genuinely know the other in its own reality, as the proportioned source from which flows this particular, determinately structured self-expression that is its action. What more, in fact, do we know, or *need* to know, about the real natures of the so-called "things-in-themselves" than that they are the *perduring centers* of such-and-such characteristic actions on me, and on the surrounding world as manifested to me—centers which must be proportioned in their "private" inner perfection to the kind and degree of perfection they express in their actions? What else in fact does a nature *mean* than *this kind of actor*? The conception of being, therefore, as self-expressive through action lies at the very root of the Thomistic theory of knowledge—and must, I submit, lie at the root of any realistic theory of human or divine knowledge.

I have outlined above what seem to me the most relevant and fruitful aspects of the Thomistic understanding of being: its focus on the immanent act of existence as the root of perfection in every being and its linking of being with action as the natural overflow and self-expression of being. But before passing on to the next point I must balance the picture by calling attention to what seem to me serious weaknesses in St. Thomas's own presentation of this doctrine, at least from our perspective today as highly sensitized to philosophical method and to the psychological genesis of basic concepts.

The first weakness is St. Thomas's almost casual brevity and reticence on how we actually come to psychological awareness of existential being as such, in a word, the *phenomenology* of *our discovery* of being as such. He seems to take this for granted as a pre-philosophical acquisition which he can refer to as already familiar to his readers. The roots of his own discovery of being seem to lie hidden in his meditative reflection as a Christian on the mystery of creation as the gift of being and on the name of God as revealed in Exodus: "I am Who am," interpreted as a metaphysical statement that God is pure being. This may have been enough in his own day, when the notion of creation lived so vividly in the habitual consciousness of a religious culture (Christian, Jewish, Moslem). But with the disappearance of such a religious culture in our own day, we need a new propaideutic to metaphysics to help us reawaken to an explicit awareness of the depth and density and wonder of being as actual existential presence standing out from the nothingness that all finite things might have been. Since we cannot find this propaideutic in St. Thomas himself, we must reconstruct it for ourselves out of the rich materials available in contemporary thought, e.g., in Kierkegaard, Buber, Heidegger, Marcel, Transcendental Thomism, etc., as well as in art and literature.

The second main weakness in St. Thomas's presentation of how we come to the metaphysical notion of being as the object of metaphysics is the use of the schema of the so-called Three Degrees of Abstraction. This schema implies that we come to the metaphysical notion of being as transcendental and analogous by passing through three levels of abstraction: (1) being considered as changeable (the perspective of the philosophy of nature), (2) being considered under the aspect of pure quantitative extension (the perspective of mathematics), and finally (3) being considered as abstracting from all matter and motion (the perspective of metaphysics). Although it may be possible with considerable explanation and rather profound adaptation to render this classical Thomistic doctrine meaningful, still it seems to me that as it stands it is not only one of the least relevant parts of historical Thomistic metaphysics but is positively misleading if not false, because, if for no other reason, it builds upon a radically defective theory of the nature of mathematics as the result of abstraction from the concrete material world. In fact I see no methodological reason even for passing through the philosophy of nature, let alone the science of mathematics, to arrive at the metaphysical notion of being; a much more simple and direct elaboration of the notion of being seems to me not only possible but desirable, although I am aware that the contemporary followers of the more classical Dominican Thomistic school would disagree with me here.[5]

III. PARTICIPATION IN BEING: ESSENCE AND EXISTENCE

The third doctrine I shall single out is the celebrated Thomistic solution to the problem of the one and the many in terms of the participation of all finite beings in existence as the central unifying perfection of the universe, "the act of all acts, the perfection of all perfections," as St. Thomas calls it. This participation is mediated through the metaphysical composition of *esse*, the act of existence, and essence as particular limiting mode—a composition found in all

The Metaphysics of St. Thomas Today

beings save one, the Infinite Source, who alone possesses this perfection in unlimited intensive plenitude as pure Subsistent Act of Existence. This undoubtedly is at once the most central and the most original doctrine of St. Thomas's metaphysics, put forward by him as his response to what metaphysicians generally agree is *the* central problem of all metaphysics, the problem of the one and the many: i.e., how to reconcile the two apparently antinomical truths, that on the one hand the universe is undeniably multiple and diverse in the *kinds* and *instances* of being that force their reality upon us from all sides, and that on the other there must be some underlying bond of unity which all must somehow share as being *actually present* to each other in the real order, standing out together from nothingness. Since my remarks on St. Thomas's conception of being as existential have already overlapped deeply into his doctrine of universal participation in existence through essence, I will not attempt to develop in further detail here this position that is already so well known to most of you.[6] Let me content myself with a few selective observations.

If we leave out radical monisms, which eliminate half of the problem, all metaphysical systems which attempt to come to grips with the problem of the one and the many are either non-participation doctrines or participation doctrines. The former undertake to unify the universe in terms of what I might call an "extrinsic" bond of *origin* from some common source. But such theories are forced to leave unexplained or in the shadow any intrinsic bond of *similarity* which binds all together in terms of something common that is immanent in all at once, in addition to and perhaps flowing from, their common source. All theories which admit and try to explain an immanent bond of similarity can be reduced down to some form of participation theory, i.e., a theory of participation in some unifying perfection common to all. Let us divide such theories into those which identify existence itself as the basic perfection, as St. Thomas does, and those which select some other attribute, such as goodness, unity, form, matter, consciousness, etc., as is the case with most non-Thomistic systems. The difficulty that all explanations of the latter type run into is that they are left at the end of their analysis with an unreduced residue of duality: the basic perfection they have chosen, say goodness, plus the affirmation of actual existence about this perfection: "The good *is*, is real. All things *are* truly good." Since unreduced duality cannot be an ultimate explanation of the bond of similarity that links all things, one must finally either reduce existence to a mode or property of goodness, or reduce goodness to a property or dimension of existence. As St. Thomas saw it, it is impossible to reduce existence to anything more radical and ultimate than itself, since all other attributes implicitly presuppose the act of existential presence by which they stand out from nothingness or from mere idea. The genius of St. Thomas is to have concluded that if you can't reduce existence to anything else more basic, why not turn the tables completely and reduce all other perfections to that apparently so lowly and easily overlooked, yet strangely unbanishable, "is" of existence, conceived now not as a minimum brute fact but as the intensive plenitude of all perfections? The result is one of the most radically unified and daringly simple metaphysical visions of the unity of the universe, short of monism, that one can find anywhere in the history of thought, whether in the West or the East.

What seems to me most fruitful and relevant in this essence-existence doctrine is the notion of diverse participation in the central perfection of existence through the varied limiting modes of essence. Essence and its primary constituent, form, here no longer play the role of primary respositories of perfection, as in essentialist metaphysical systems like that of Aristotle himself, but take on rather the secondary, derivative role of principles of limitation and hence of partial negation of a deeper, supra-formal perfection: "Omnis determinatio est negatio," as Spinoza has so well said. Diverse participation in existence according to limiting modes of essence, all derived from a single supra-essential Source that is pure unparticipated, hence unlimited, Act of Existence: this seems to me the irreducible positive core of St. Thomas's vision.

What seems to me less relevant and crucial for our day, though still an important problem for specialized technical discussion, is whether or not the best way to express this participation-through-limitation doctrine is by the technical theory of a *real* composition or distinction between essence and the act of existence in each finite being. Such an expression tends to say too much by implying that essence is somehow a positive principle in its own right added on to existence, whereas all positivity resides in the act of existence. On the other hand, there is an objective irreducibility of some kind in the real order between a limiting principle and the real perfection which it limits, mirrored in the intractable irreducibility of our concepts and words expressing the two aspects. Hence to say that existence and its limiting mode of essence are simply identical would be saying too little. But what precisely is the reality of limit as such (and I mean here the kind of limit that brings about a *qualitative restriction* in a perfection capable of higher degrees of intensity, not limit merely as the coming-to-an-end of a purely quantitative extension)? It may be that our concepts are incapable of grasping more closely the being of limit as such, and it would be wiser to content ourselves with speaking of a real limited participation in existence through essence as limiting mode, without trying to press further and determine what is the precise "reality" of this "composition" between the act of existence and its limiting essence.[7] But I am willing to admit that I may be running the risk of letting go something essential in thus playing down the traditional "real distinction" aspect of St. Thomas's doctrine and the role of essence as positive subject distinct from the act of existence that is traditionally said to "receive and limit." I am still open on the question.

IV. THE PERSON AS THE PRIMARY MODEL OF BEING

This is a typical case of a central underlying theme in St. Thomas's metaphysics which clearly permeates his thought when we carefully analyze it, but which is rarely thematized with full explicitness as a central doctrine. Hence it can easily escape the notice of those who are not on the watch for it. One of the main reasons for the unobtrusiveness of this theme is that the principal technical categories which St. Thomas uses to elaborate his thought are drawn originally not from the inner personal world but from the outer world of nature—and principally biological nature—following the lead of Aristotle. Yet Father Johannes Metz has written a whole book on person as the basic "thought-form" (*Denkform*) underlying St. Thomas's entire thought. There is much truth in what he says, but he himself admits that it is a thought-form which has not yet found its adequate vocabulary of expression.[8] Hence, unless it is highlighted and reformulated in more explicitly personalist terms by contemporary Thomists, it will not be able to enter effectively into the bloodstream of our contemporary thought.

The principal point I would like to single out here is the relation of person to being. For St. Thomas, the person is not a peculiar mode of being added on from the outside, so to speak, to what would be the normal non-personal mode of being. On the contrary, if being is allowed to be itself above a certain level of limitation, which disperses its act of presence into parts external to each other (matter), it naturally flowers out into the perfection of a person, i.e., its act of presence becomes luminous and transparent to itself, it becomes presence to and for itself (self-consciousness), and master of its own actions (freedom). Thus the fullness of being, which is act of presence, is of its very nature personal, or self-possessing presence, and the nature of the person, on its side, is nothing else than to be an active self-possessing presence, present both to itself and to others—to the whole world, in fact, if its act of presence is intense enough.[9] "The person is that which is the most perfect in all of nature,"[10] St. Thomas tells us; and since the act of existence is the root of all perfection for him, being naturally turns into person wherever its restricting level of essence allows it to *be* intensely enough, transcending the dispersal of matter. Once this perspective of the correlativity (though not full co-extensivity) of being and person is achieved, the human person can be taken as the primary model or analogue for us of all the basic metaphysical concepts, such as unity, activity, efficient causality, act and potency, etc.—the privileged vantage point from which we know *from within* what each concept stands for and from which we extend it by analogy both below and above us. But it is only honest to admit that the richness and fruitfulness of this personalist viewpoint on being has not been given adequate thematized treatment by St. Thomas himself. This remains one of the major tasks for contemporary Thomists.[11]

V. The Dynamic Notion of Substance

By this I mean the notion of substance as the principle of perduring self-identity of a being throughout the succession of its changes—a traditional Aristotelian doctrine—yet substance understood not as an inert underlying substratum in the manner of the later Lockean conception, but as a dynamic center of activity and receptivity. Substance has gotten quite a bad name for itself in modern philosophy, principally because of the Cartesian and Lockean conceptions of it which were commonly accepted as the primary models of this so-called traditional doctrine. The Cartesian notion is that of a self-enclosed entity needing only God in order to exist. The Lockean notion is that of an inert, static, unknowable, "pin-cushion"-like substratum in which the changing accidents are inserted for support.

Both of these conceptions have been the butt of strong attack by process philosophers such as Whitehead—and quite justly so. For in fact every finite substance we know or can conceive of is intrinsically relational, set in the matrix of the world-system as a whole. And nothing real that we know or can conceive of is purely static and inert. But most modern philosophers, especially process thinkers, seem unaware of an older tradition of substance, lost for the most part from Ockham on, which is not burdened with either of the above deficiencies. This is the authentic Aristotelian one of dynamic substance, highlighted considerably more clearly by St. Thomas himself. Here substance is conceived precisely as the integrating center of a being's activities, a center which is constantly pouring over into self-expression through its characteristic actions and at the same time constantly integrating or actively assimilating all that it receives from the action of other substances on it. St. Thomas is not afraid to say that the substance is totally oriented towards its operations.[12]

It must be clearly affirmed that such a perduring active center in a changing being is *not* without qualification unchanging, though it *is* self-identical. Of course the substance itself changes, otherwise it would be totally unaffected by and indifferent to all that it does and receives—which does not make sense. But it does not change so radically that it loses its active self-identity. In a word, in technical language, the substance itself changes, but not substantially, only accidentally (or non-essentially). This is not the same as to say, according to a common misinterpretation, that only the accidents change. Substance and accident, as metaphysical co-principles, ontologically interpenetrate each other, each affecting the other more or less profoundly, as the case may be. The Thomistic substance remains self-identical only by constantly being at work, so to speak, actively expressing itself through its own actions and actively assimilating and transmuting into itself—i.e., imposing its own characteristic unity on—whatever else the surrounding world of agents presents to it in the vast interacting system which is the real world. Thus reality is indeed "through and through togetherness," as Whitehead so well puts it and as any alert Thomist should be glad to accept.

Such a notion of substance as perduring principle of dynamic self-identity in an interacting system can go far in our day, it seems to me, toward making contact with the process philosophy tradition and assimilating much of its richness. Yet it stops well short of dissolving all centers of perduring identity into the flux of momentary actual occasions, which to my mind ends up by throwing the baby out with the bath.[13]

VI. Substantial Potency as Necessary Condition of Possibility for Any Complex Whole

You are all familiar enough, I hope, with the classic Thomistic notion of potency, or potential principle, as the correlative opposite pole of act in the act-potency couplet that expresses the general structure of any inner metaphysical composition within a being. The two main roles of potency for St. Thomas are, first, that of *limitation* of some higher perfection, in a situation where no change is involved—e.g., the limitation of the act of existing by essence, or the limiting individuation of form by matter. This is the new dimension of potency not in Aristotle but introduced by Neoplatonism and taken over by St. Thomas. I am not here concerned with this role of potency in a participation structure. The second role is the original one given it by Aristotle and preserved by St. Thomas: namely, potency as *the subject of continuity in change*, possessing the real inner aptitude or capacity to take on some new mode of being and form an intrinsic unity with it. It is the significance of this role of potency, especially at the profoundest substantial level, that I would like to highlight here.

What precisely is the significance of acknowledging this admittedly elusive, because never directly observable, mode of being that we call "potentiality," i.e., a real aptitude for some mode of being that is not now actualized but could be? Ivor Leclerc in a brilliant and challenging recent study, *The Nature of Physical Existence* (New York: Humanities Press, 1972), has traced the fortunes of the Aristotelian notion of potency with respect to the efforts of modern science and philosophy to explain our world of complex material wholes. Modern science began, in the sixteenth and seventeenth centuries, by rejecting the Aristotelian potency-and-act theory, whereby lower elements have the potency to be taken over by unifying higher acts and made into new wholes in which the original elements no longer exist autonomously as such. It substituted instead a theory of the make-up of all bodies by discrete atomic actualities which combine to form aggregates according to mathematical laws, while remaining essentially intact all through their transformations. Our contemporary physics, however, has finally come back again, especially in quantum theory, to admit the necessity of the potential in order to make sense out of the behavior of subatomic particles. Thus we have the notions of potential energy, potential location of subatomic particles, not to mention the many applications to the biological and human worlds. Much logical and linguistic analysis has made it abundantly clear, it seems to me, that it is impossible to reduce the "can," "could," or "-able" aspects of our description of the world to any combination of simply actual "is," "was," or "will be." Hence "potency" must refer to some irreducible ingredient of the real world.

But in addition to this general point, which I think is important enough in itself, I would like to call your attention to the very specific point highlighted so well by Leclerc, namely, the indispensable role of potency as a condition of possibility for the existence of any complex *whole* that is not a mere aggregate. The point is a simple but profound one, laid down first clearly by Aristotle, but elaborated much more explicitly by St. Thomas, namely, to use his own words, that "out of two entities in act it is impossible to make a natural or intrinsic unity (an *unum per se*)."[14] Such a combination can only be an *aggregate*, a society, with a unity of order perhaps, but not coalescing to form a genuine new being.

In order to form a *per se* unity, without which of course there cannot be *one* being present in any meaningful sense of the term, all the lower elements in a composite must have the potentiality to be taken over and unified by a single higher act. This means that all these lower components must have an innate "plasticity" or determinability at the substantial (not merely accidental) level, by which they are intrinsically apt to be taken over by a higher principle of unity, without being totally destroyed but nonetheless losing their normal autonomy of being and action. If they do not undergo this profound modification of surrendering their inner autonomy to a higher unifying principle, then there is no reason at all to assert that there is present anything more than an aggregate or society of many beings. One cannot have it both ways. If the components do not lose their autonomy, then they can only form an aggregate. If they do form a genuine intrinsic unity, then they must have surrendered their autonomy to a higher unity. Their independent actuality has dropped back into latent potency (not simply non-being, of course) and their previously existing latent potentiality to be taken over by a higher has now been actualized by a new higher act.

Without this ingredient of substantial plasticity there can be no adequate metaphysical theory of the unity of complex beings, and we are at the mercy of a radical reductionism of all higher levels of material being to the lowest level of the most elementary particles, grouped in accidentally unified aggregates. There will then be no such *being* as man, but only a complex chemical factory, directed, if you wish, by a single "engineer," the soul or mind, which becomes an autonomous entity in its own right. The issue is clear-cut, although all too many philosophers, especially scientist-philosophers, have either failed to see it or tried to blur the lines: either radical reductionistic atomism must be accepted, or the reality of potency at the deepest substantial or essential level, what I prefer to call "substantial potency." In the light of our new stress today on "holistic thinking," i.e., the recognition of organic wholes in nature as essentially different from machines and other aggregates, this ancient notion of substantial potency must come—and I believe is coming—back into honor in philosophical circles today. A metaphysics which holds the ingredients of the real to be nothing more than actualities plus relations is incapable of making sense out of ontological wholes. Such a metaphysics, I submit, has shown itself incapable of being an adequate instrument for contemporary thought in any area touching the real.

The alert reader will not have failed to notice that I have not used the traditional Aristotelian-Thomistic term of "pure potency" or "primary matter." This is the notion of a potency, or potential subject, that is pure or unqualified potentiality, lacking any determination whatsoever. My reason is that I am not sure it is necessary to go this far in order to do justice to the intelligibility of substantial change, which was the basic reason for positing this mysterious and endlessly controverted principle of primary matter in the first place. The traditional argument is simple, clear-cut, and apparently impregnable. Since in any single being with a single nature or essence there can be only one actual substantial or essential form at any one time, both at the beginning and the end of a substantial change there is present only one substantial form. Since by the very definition of a substantial change the first form is replaced by the second, then what passes over as the potential principle providing the continuity cannot be another substantial form but only some real subject entirely lacking any substantial form. This is the principle of pure potency, totally lacking form, hence called "primary matter." It is therefore of itself unintelligible, but indirectly known through forms as what underlies form in beings capable of substantial change. Yet it is clear enough that in all the organic wholes we know which emerge out of transformation processes, the component elements which are integrated into the new higher unity do not have their characteristic structures and activities entirely wiped out down to pure indetermination, but abide somehow in a latent subordinate way, which St. Thomas himself describes as a "virtual presence," such that they can reappear again if the higher complex breaks down. This virtual presence, which St. Thomas admits under pressure of answering objections, is not simply pure potency with no qualification at all. It includes many determinate potencies, not merely one totally indeterminate one, abiding within the new unity, even though at the same time St. Thomas is quite correct in insisting that there can only be one fully actual substantial form at one time in a complex whole that is a true intrinsic ontological unity.[15]

Hence it seems to me that there remains considerable ambiguity in the traditional doctrine of pure indeterminate matter underlying change. If "pure potency" means only that there is no *properly actual* substantial form in what passes over in a substantial change and abides within the new whole, then this claim seems to me an impregnable one. If "pure potency" means that what passes over is totally denuded of any determination whatever, then it seems to me it goes beyond what is required to handle the problem. But if "pure potency" does not mean the latter, then the term is dangerously misleading. That is why I prefer the terms "substantial potency," or "determinability at the substantial level." This more restrained term implies that reality is not quite that susceptible of being fitted into clearly distinct categories as we would wish. We cannot lay down absolute alternatives, such as that the unity of a genuine complex whole is *either* an unqualified unity allowing of no ontological plurality of component elements remaining within the whole, *or* else the unity is merely accidental and the lower elements continue present as actually existing and operating substances in their own right. Each alternative goes too far. What reality seems to present us with is rather a spectrum of more or less imperfect but still substantial unities. Complex unities are so strong that the lower elements integrated within them are not merely accidentally united; the unifying substantial form penetrates deep into the very substances of the components, so that they lose their *autonomy* of being and action. Yet these components can still retain some latent plural presence, not totally dominated and integrated, which is precisely "in between" pure indetermination (or pure determinability) and merely accidental determinability. There seems to be no adequate term for this somewhat messy, but I believe more realistic, "in-between" state in the Thomistic system, although Thomas's term "virtual presence" can do the job.

I must, however, add in all honesty that Father Joseph Donceel, in a very penetrating critique of my attempt to dispense with pure primary matter understood in an absolutely unqualified sense, has given me serious second thoughts as to whether such a principle is not still needed, not so much to explain substantial change, as from the point of view of human *cognitional theory*. Following the Maréchalian school of Transcendental Thomism, he points out the undeniable fact that there is always in our cognition of material things some kind of opaque residue that seems in principle never directly accessible to intelligence. All our intellectual knowledge of material things is in terms of forms, or intelligible structures, *of* something underlying beyond form that we can only identify indirectly as extended-matter-stuff, quantitative spatial extension, or the like. This "other-than-form" can be known only through contact with our material senses in sensible images, in which in virtue of the substantial union of soul and body, hence of intellect and sense, the intellect can discern the immanent formal intelligibilities and know *that* these are structures of an ultimate non-formal "something," not susceptible of further analysis in terms of form. From this point of view we might well have to posit an ultimate dimension or ingredient of the material world that is pure non-formal, indeterminate "matter," not reducible to form but never without some form. This principle, however, would not necessarily have to be identified as the ultimate *subject* by itself of all substantial change, but only a *dimension* of radical potentiality or determinability characterizing all lower entities that can be taken over into large intrinsic unities. Such substantial determinability, in fact, would be one way of defining what we mean by a "material being," since such an aptitude is lacking in spiritual beings. Spirits can indeed join together to form very intimate societies, but they cannot surrender their ontological autonomy of being and action to become non-autonomous—hence non-personal—parts of any larger whole. To be a person is necessarily to exist as a *whole*, possessing its own being in itself, not as a part of any other. And any existing spiritual being must be a personal being.

On reflection, when rereading in 1993 what I had written in 1974, I have come to the conclusion that I must agree with Father Donceel, not merely for epistemological but for independent ontological reasons. It seems that science is revealing today that far down in the world of subatomic particles, as portrayed by quantum physics, there are tiny particles that change back and forth into each other, enduring for only infinitesimal lengths of time, and it is not clear that they are composed of smaller particles which might pass over in the change. Since something must pass over in every change—lest we be faced with total annihilation and total creation in each case—it can only be a substratum of some radical formless "matter." And it seems more probable, in the light of contemporary physics, to conceive this formless principle, not as some kind of inert, passive stuff, as St. Thomas, following Aristotle, seemed to do, but as the radical raw *energy* of the material (space-time extended) universe, which has no form of its own, but is captured in part now by this form, now by that. Thus the entire process of the material universe can now be described by physicists as "transformations of energy." The sum total of this energy is constant, quantitatively—according to the law of conservation of energy—but the transformations are endless. These transformations correspond to successive forms, but they are transformations *of* something that is not itself form.

This seems to me a much more illuminating interpretation of the classical form/matter doctrine, and one that is equally faithful to the original metaphysical insight grounding it. For the insight grounding the *argument* for primary matter in Aristotle and St. Thomas is that there must be some radically *indeterminate* principle (without any form of its own) that passes over in substantial change. But it does not stipulate that this must be passive or inert stuff rather than formless energy. The passivity of matter was not required by the exigencies of the argument, but seems rather to have been taken for granted by the scientific presuppositions of the time. Thus it is more probable that there is indeed in the very depths of the material world a radically formless principle, never without some form but with none of its own, which functions just as the classical primary matter did, yet is much more in harmony with the worldview of contemporary physics.

VII. Efficient and Final Causality

There is neither time nor need to develop here these basic and well enough known notions. They are simply the fuller elaboration of the conception of the world as a vast system of interacting agents, actively communicating to each other out of their richness and passively receiving from, or dependent on each other out of their poverty, their lack of self-sufficiency—all under the universal influx (i.e., the communication of existence) of the one self-sufficient Source of all existence. Let me just mention a few key points: (1) Efficient causality is understood by St. Thomas not merely as the causing of *change*, as was the case for Aristotle, for whom the existence of the world was given eternally and only its transformations required explanation, but more profoundly as the causing of *being*, the *communication of existence* according to a certain mode or form. (2) Efficient causality is not, as for Hume and for so many modern philosophers after him, even non-empiricists such as Kant, Paul Weiss, etc., a succession of two events in time, linked by some bond of necessity, mental or real. It is a *single event*, which is precisely the production-of-the-effect as by the agent. This takes place, not back in the cause, but *in* the effect as *from* the cause (*actio est in passo*). Causing and being caused constitute one single reality with two distinct relations, one to the effect and the other to the cause. The important corollaries follow that cause *as such* and effect are simultaneous, and that to cause implies of itself no change in the cause, but only in the effect.[16]

3) Final causality is simply the inner orientation of every agent toward some determinate effect-to-be-produced. And since such orientation or dynamic predetermination of the agent at the moment of beginning its action is toward a not-yet-existent future, the ultimate sufficient reason or ground for any final causality (hence for any action whatsoever in the universe) must be sought in an intelligence; for intelligence is the only power that can make the non-existent pos-

sible or future *present* as a guide for action now. Thus all final causality and therefore all action requires either a consciously thought idea-goal in the agent itself, or a participation in idea, imprinted by intelligence somewhere along the line, in agents which do not themselves possess intelligence. At the beginning of all action, therefore, is the Word. All action in the universe is ultimately the expression, direct or mediated, of a *Logos*, an ordering Mind.

VIII. THE NATURE OF GOD AS PURE SUBSISTENT ACT OF EXISTENCE

The crown of the entire Thomistic vision of the universe is the notion of God as infinitely perfect pure Plenitude of Existence, ultimate Source and Goal of all other being. This notion of God receives its philosophical meaning as the keystone of a universal participation structure, in which all finite beings participate the basic common perfection of the universe, existence as intensive act, in diverse limited degrees, according to the modes of their respective essences, all deriving from a single ultimate infinite Source, which possesses the perfection of existence in pure unlimited, unparticipated plenitude. There is no need for me to develop this aspect of St. Thomas's metaphysics at length, since it is already so well known. I shall content myself with calling attention to a few key points.

1) This participation doctrine centered around the act of existence allows for a radically unified vision of the universe, with no ultimate unreduced dualities left around as loose ends, such as happens when one chooses any perfection less ultimate than existence as universal unifying principle.

2) Since it places God beyond all form and limiting essence, it permits at once a doctrine of God in positive terms, yet one that leaves intact the full mystery of God as ineffable and beyond any direct representation of His *mode* of being (or essence) by our limited concepts and categories. Since this positive knowledge is so vague, St. Thomas can say that the most perfect knowledge of God we can have in this life is to realize that while we can know *that* God is, and is infinite plenitude of perfection, we cannot know at all *what* God is, his own proper essence or infinite mode of being. Hence St. Thomas's notion of God is one of the very few in the West that are not simply "negative theologies" but yet allow for a profound rapport with Hindu, Buddhist, and other Eastern notions of God as the utterly Ineffable beyond all form and concept. Despite the latter's characteristic negative descriptions of the Ultimate in terms of "Void," "Non-Being," etc., St. Thomas's supra-formal Pure Act of *Esse* functions

in his system in a highly analogous way to the Void in theirs. His notion also serves as a very illuminating metaphysical grounding for the typical mystical experience of God in all traditions as pure Presence beyond all form, and hence beyond all conceptual grasp or expression.

3) Let me call brief attention now to the main point in St. Thomas's doctrine of God which seems to me to arouse so much misunderstanding and instinctive repugnance on the part of religious-minded people today that it may well be judged no longer fruitful or relevant for us today, at least in the way St. Thomas is content to express his position and then take us no further. This is the interpretation of the immutability of God in so absolute and uncompromising a way as to exclude any "real relation" on God's part toward us, whereas every creature has a non-symmetrical real relation of dependence on God. This non-symmetrical relation seems to negate on the metaphysical level one of the most cherished of our religious—at least Judaeo-Christian—notions of God: namely God's deep loving concern for us, inviting us into an authentic interpersonal dialogue of love.[17]

St. Thomas's reason for this highly technical doctrine of real relation is his theory of efficient causality. To cause means to make something happen in *another*; it does not of itself imply that the cause loses or gains anything. Hence for God as perfect cause, already infinite in perfection, to create the world does not for that reason imply any increase or loss of his own intrinsic perfection. If he cannot thus change in his own real perfection, then no new real relation can accrue to his eternal being when he makes the created universe appear in time.

The reasoning is impeccable as far as it goes. But it does not say enough. While it is quite true that sharing his goodness with others in creation does not increase or decrease the *intrinsic* plenitude of the divine ontological perfection, which is already infinite—and how could one strictly speaking add or subtract a finite amount from an infinite?—still it is the case that in the order of the divine knowledge and love, which is the order of *intentionality* (*esse intentionale* as opposed to *esse naturale*, in St. Thomas's words) as focused on *others* than himself, it makes a *distinct difference* in the divine consciousness whether he creates or not, and what are the specific mutual relations between himself and his creatures, especially created persons. This specific focusing of his knowledge and love on the created participations of his own goodness certainly does not add to the plenitude of his own intrinsic perfection which he is sharing. Hence there is no change or real relation in the strict and strong *Aristotelian* meaning of change. But this does make a highly significant difference in *personal relations*. For it is precisely in the intentional order of knowledge and love that interpersonal relations are located. This whole domain of being simply escapes or transcends the entire set of Aristotelian categories of change, immutability, and real relation. Hence I believe we can truly say that without doing violence to his own basic metaphysical positions St. Thomas could and should say that God does have authentic mutual *personal relations* with all created persons, even though he himself would not call these by the strong technical term of "real relation."

Though one can indeed make this defense of St. Thomas, I have nonetheless found it too laborious and unfruitful an enterprise to try and explain convincingly to contemporary people that we should not say God has real relations with the world. The return is no longer worth the investment of effort. This means that a technical concept, while still theoretically defensible in itself, has outlived its effective accessibility and fruitfulness for the minds of contemporaries. Hence I think one could also follow another and much simpler strategy in handling this question of God's immutability and relations with the world. This would be to distinguish two senses of immutability. God remains immutable in the intrinsic intensity and fullness of his own being and faithful love of us—to which, it must be remembered, he has committed himself freely but *eternally*, in his eternal *now* (i.e., he was not *first* uncommitted, then changed to commitment). This is the kind of immutability that we judge appropriate and necessary for a perfect *Person* (or Personal Being). But there is another sense of immutability that we cannot help but judge inappropriate for a perfect Person, i.e., that interpersonal relations of love would make no difference at all in the consciousness of the Lover. Ongoing sensitive adaptation to the mutual relations of an interpersonal dialogue is appropriate and necessary for the perfection proper to a person. But this does not imply that God must "change." Speaking more accurately, since God is eternally present to all that goes on in time, we should rather say that God is eternally and contingently (freely) *different* in his consciousness directed toward us because of our responses in time than he would have been had we responded otherwise; but this does not mean any *change* in God, i.e., first being one way and later another. "Different" and "changing" are not identical concepts. It is not easy, however, to get Process thinkers to grapple with this crucial distinction. "Difference" and "mutability" seem inseparably linked for them, so that a God who is immutable *must* be indifferent toward us. A Thomist need not be caught in such a dilemma.

The Metaphysics of St. Thomas Today

Furthermore, there is no good reason why the *human categories* in which we express the divine perfections should always remain immutable. What remains fixed in all conceptions of God is the formal notion of *plenitude of perfection*. Also for us in the Judaeo-Christian tradition the notion of God as loving Person(s) remains stable. But precisely what we judge as most *appropriate* to describe the perfection proper to a loving Person can indeed change, slowly or sometimes rapidly, as our understanding of person and personal life evolves and, hopefully, matures. Thus we have the fruitful paradox that in our philosophy of God the notion of *perfect Person* remains immutable, but the notion of *immutability* is itself a relative term not sharing the same privilege of immutability.

Let me hasten to add that St. Thomas himself did not make this "creative readjustment" of the interlocking network of our description of God. But I submit that without doing any damaging violence to the spirit and key doctrines of his own metaphysical system, this adaptation could be made, and that without this it is too difficult to make the great richness of the rest of his doctrine truly accessible, relevant, and fruitful for serious and well-disposed thinkers of our own day, in particular for the large number who are at present attracted by the positive contributions they find in the process philosophy tradition.

Let me add, as a final word on the doctrine of God, that the famous Five Ways of St. Thomas for proving the existence of God seem to me, *in their present textual form*, the least adequate part of his metaphysics and certainly the least relevant for the contemporary philosopher. The first two, from motion and causality, are formally valid if the proper latent premises are supplied, but have no literal application to our world since there are no *simultaneous* causal chains in our material cosmos. The third, from contingency, is formally invalid as it stands, based on the logically invalid principle, uncritically taken over from Aristotle, that all logical possibilities must come true, given infinite time—a dubious principle, difficult if not impossible to ground. The fourth, from degrees in being, argues that wherever there are degrees of perfection, this implies a maximum, and then goes on to argue that this maximum must be the efficient cause of all those which possess the perfection in limited degrees. This is the reverse of St. Thomas's ordinary procedure, which concludes to the need of a maximum only by passing through efficient causality first. The second procedure is valid; the first (a current Neoplatonic formulation taken over by Thomas) is not. The fifth, from final causality, concludes to the need of an intelligent cause of the universe and is fine as far as it goes. But it needs completion to reach a single infinite Intelligent Cause of all beings, as also do the first and second ways.

All these arguments, except the third, can be reworked or expanded to speak more directly to us today, I believe. I have tried to work out my own version in chapter 8 of this collection. But the most profound and metaphysically effective proofs for God already extant in Thomas's texts are to be found elsewhere, imbedded in his participation metaphysics, as I note in my book *The Philosophical Approach to God*, chapter 2. They are not used in the beginning of the *Summa Theologiae* because they do not start directly from sensible data, as St. Thomas is committed to doing here, it seems, but from his own metaphysical theory of participation. I throw out these all-too-brief remarks on St. Thomas's argument for God only as a challenge and invitation to Thomistic thinkers, for fuller development elsewhere.

NOTES

1. Etienne Gilson, *The Christian Philosophy of St. Thomas Aquinas* (New York: Random House, 1956; rpt. Notre Dame, Ind.: Univ. of Notre Dame Press, 1994), ch. I: "Existence and Reality." For a history of the rise of this "existential Thomism," see Helen James John, "The Emergence of the Act of Existing in Recent Thomism," *International Philosophical Quarterly*, 2 (1962), 600–625.

2. *De Veritate*, q. 1, art. 1, ad 3; *Expositio in Libros Metaphysicorum*, IV, lect. 2, n. 6.

3. *De Potentia*, q. 2, art. 1: "It is in the nature of every actuality to communicate itself as far as it is possible." Cf. *Summa contra Gentes*, II, ch. 6–8, and the rich textual study on this point, Joseph de Finance, *Etre et agir* (2nd ed.; Rome: Università Pontifica Gregoriana, 1961). For my own fuller development, see chapter 3 of this collection: "Action as the Self-Revelation of Being: A Central Theme in the Thought of St. Thomas."

4. *Summa contra Gentes* II, ch. 94, and II, ch. 79: "The operation of a thing shows forth both its existence and its nature."

5. See chapter 2 of this collection: "The 'We Are' of Interpersonal Dialogue as the Starting Point of Metaphysics," and John Knasas, *The Preface to Metaphysics: A Contribution to the Neothomist Debate over the Start of Metaphysics* (New York: Peter Lang, 1990).

6. Cf. the classic treatments of participation: L. B. Geiger, *La participation dans la philosophie de S. Thomas d'Aquin* (Paris, 1942); Cornelio Fabro, *La nozione metafisica di partecipazione secondo S. Tomasso d'Aquino* (2nd ed.; Turin, 1950), together with his synthesis of his years of research on participation, "The Intensive Hermeneutics of Thomistic Philosophy: The Notion of Participation," *Review of Metaphysics*, 27 (1973–74), 449–90; L. De Raeymaeker, *La philosophie de l'être* (Paris: Vrin, 1947)—Eng. trans. *The Philosophy of Being* (St. Louis: Herder, 1954); and my own articles, "The Limitation of

Act by Potency: Aristotelianism or Neoplatonism?" *New Scholasticism*, 26 (1952), 157–94; "The Meaning of Participation in St. Thomas," *Proceedings of the American Catholic Philosophical Association*, 26 (1952), 147–57; and "What Cannot Be Said in St. Thomas' Essence-Existence Doctrine," *New Scholasticism*, 48 (1974), 19–39.

Since the appearance of this article we now have the fine scholarly study of John Wippel, "Thomas Aquinas and Participation," in *Studies in Medieval Philosophy* (Washington, D.C.: Catholic Univ. of America Press, 1987), pp. 117–58.

7. See my article "What Cannot Be Said in St. Thomas' Essence-Existence Doctrine" (note 6 above); "The Role of Essence in St. Thomas' Essence-Existence Doctrine," *Atti del Congresso Internazionale di San Tomasso, 1974* (Naples: Edizioni Domenicane, 1981), V, 9–15; William Carlo, *The Ultimate Reducibility of Essence to Existence in Thomistic Metaphysics* (The Hague: Nijhoff, 1966), with my preface. The position of Carlo, which I lean toward with some adaptation, has been strongly criticized by Fabro, in note 115 of his article cited in note 6 above, and by not a few other Thomists, including Joseph Owens. I have had to tone down my support of Carlo due to their criticisms.

8. Johannes Metz, *Christliche Anthropozentrik* (Munich: Kosel, 1962).

9. Cf. Karl Rahner, *Spirit in the World*, trans. W. Dych (New York: Herder & Herder, 1968), pp. 68–71: "The Original Unity of Being and Knowledge as Being-Present-to-Itself"; see also J. de Finance, "Being and Subjectivity," *Cross Currents*, 6 (1956), 153–78.

10. *Summa Theologiae*, I, q. 29, art. 3.

11. For a fuller development of this point, see my article, "The Self as Source of Meaning in Metaphysics," *Review of Metaphysics*, 21 (1967–68), 587–614, and my book, *Person and Being* (Milwaukee: Marquette Univ. Press, 1993).

12. *Summa Theologiae*, I, q. 105, art. 5: "Every substance exists for the sake of its operations"; *Summa contra Gentes*, III, ch. 113: "Each and every thing shows forth that it exists for the sake of its operation; indeed, operation is the ultimate perfection of each thing." See also de Finance, *Etre et agir* (note 3 above).

13. For a fuller development of this point, see chapter 6 of this collection: "To Be Is to Be Substance-in-Relation."

14. *On Spiritual Creatures*, art. 3; *Summa contra Gentes*, I, ch. 18.

15. "We must find another way to state how the elements are, on the one hand, genuinely united and, on the other, are not entirely deprived of their nature but remain in the mixture after a special manner. It is the active forces emanating from the substantial forms of the elementary bodies which are conserved in the mixed bodies. Consequently, the substantial forms of the elements exist in the mixture not with respect to their actuality (*non quidem actu*) but with respect to their active power (*sed virtute*)." *De Mixtu Elementorum* (*Opera Philosophica*, ed. Marietti, Rome, 1954, p. 155); trans. with notes by V. Larkin, "On the Combining of the Elements," *Isis*, 51 (1960), 67–72.

16. Cf. my essay, "Causality and Time," in *Experience, Existence and the Good: Essays in Honor of Paul Weiss*, ed. I. C. Lieb (Carbondale: Southern Illinois Univ. Press, 1961), pp. 143–57.

17. Cf. My essay discussing this whole question, proposing a "creative completion," or perhaps "revision," of St. Thomas, "A New Look at the Immutability of God," in chapter 9 of this collection; also my later book, *The Philosophical Approach to God* (Winston-Salem: Wake Forest Univ. Press, 1979).

18. E.g., *De Potentia*, q. 3, art. 5–6; *Summa Theologiae*, I, q. 44, art. 1; q. 65, art. 1; q. 93, art. 6; *De Veritate*, q. 2, art. 14; *Summa contra Gentes*, II, ch. 15.

2

The "We Are" of Interpersonal Dialogue as the Starting Point of Metaphysics

In this paper I am speaking explicitly from within the tradition of Thomistic realist epistemology and metaphysics, though the point may well apply to other approaches. I am not saying this is the only, or the one necessary, starting point for Thomistic metaphysics. But I believe it is a significantly, perhaps uniquely, fruitful one for our time, with definite advantages over other past and current ways of entering into the subject. Let me explain.

Any authentic Thomistic metaphysics, it is commonly agreed, will embody a realistic epistemology. The human intellect, in fact any intellect, is made for being, has a natural affinity for being, of which the prime analogate is always actually existing being, being in act. And the root of intelligibility in any being is always the act of existing (*esse*) in some way or another. "That which first falls under the apprehension (of the human intellect) is being, the understanding of which is included in anything whatever that one grasps intellectually."[1] And the proportionate or connatural object of human knowing in particular, within the wider horizon of being itself, is the nature of material beings, that is, form-in-matter. All this is commonly accepted by Thomists, although how they work out in detail the systematic justification of this realism will depend on the different traditions of Thomism.

But exactly how in the concrete we make contact with real being in the instantiations accessible to us, and which, if any, of these are more or less privileged or fruitful for further philosophical development, are for the most part passed over by the various Thomistic schools. Transcendental Thomists insist—rightly, I think—on starting with judgments containing the copula "is," though some of them (e.g., Bernard Lonergan) remain ambiguous on whether they are dealing with an affirmation of real existence or only a truth that could be verified in merely mental being (logic, mathematics, etc.).[2] Gilson and his school insist on the "immediate realism"[3] of sense knowledge and are unwilling to get involved in any modern type of "critical realism" that attempts to work out a critical justification of epistemological realism that would take seriously the bridge problem between mind and reality, as did the Louvain school. Other disputes on the proper starting point of metaphysics concern whether, with the traditional Dominican school, metaphysics can be reached only by passing through an Aristotelian type of philosophy of nature that would establish the existence of immaterial being (God as Prime Mover) and thus enable the analogy of being to get going; or whether, with John Wippel, Joseph Owens, John Knasas, etc.—rightly, I think—an existential Thomism is not bound by these Aristotelian restrictions and can start immediately from the range of our ordinary experience of being.[4]

But even if these intra-Thomistic disputes were solved, this would still not get us down to the nitty-gritty problem of which, if any, case of real sensible being is more fruitful to start with, both from the point of view of a secure realism and of fecundity for further metaphysical development. My point in writing this article is to suggest that there is indeed a privileged starting point within real sensible being which at once establishes both a secure realism and a peculiarly fruitful vantage point for further metaphysical development. Although I appreciate Gilson's insistence on a direct realism of knowledge and the futility of trying to deduce in some way the reality of the world outside the subject from anything like a Cartesian *cogito*, still we cannot just ignore the great epistemological struggles of modern philosophy over realism as though they never happened and left no mark on the Western philosophical consciousness.

This is especially true of the great Immanuel Kant, whose brooding figure stands like a Colossus blocking the road to realism for later thinkers and intimidates so many contemporary philosophers. Though few if any contemporaries now hold onto his universal, timeless, a priori categories of human thought, nonetheless his basic thesis that the human mind projects its own forms onto reality rather than receiving them from reality still echoes as a dominant chord in many contemporary positions, such as the linguistic and cultural a priori's of Nelson Goodman (man as "worldmaker" through language), Hilary Putnam (in his various anti-realist phases, though he now seems to have swung back to more of a realism), etc. Although these contemporary a priori's are no longer universal for all human minds but relative to a given culture and are no longer unchanging but evolving through time, the essence of the Copernican

The "We Are" of Interpersonal Dialogue

revolution remains intact, namely, that it is our thinking that gives form to the world rather than the world that gives form to our thought.

But there is one privileged type of experience that is central to all human living, one that must be experienced by any philosopher who actually does philosophy in discourse and writing—an experience that stares us in the face every day (unless we are alone on a desert island)—and yet cannot be accounted for by any anti-realist epistemology, in particular the Kantian variety. It is astounding to me how this experience has remained a blind spot in all the classical modern epistemologies from Descartes on, until the twentieth-century interpersonalist phenomenologies, and how even the various Thomistic realistic schools have for the most part not thematized it explicitly. This is the experience, without which none of us could be truly human, of knowing other human beings as equally real with ourselves, as like us (sharing the same nature or powers of action, in particular the power of speech), and able to engage in meaningful dialogue with each other. This experience can be condensed as follows: "I know that *we are*, that *we are like each other*, that *we can engage in meaningful communication with each other*." The evidence? We actually do so, basically successfully, many times; in fact, any successful use of a common language, which we clearly did not make up and teach ourselves or each other, already bears witness to this. The privileged "place" where all this is most vividly revealed is the *interpersonal dialogue*.[5]

To perceive the revelatory power of this experience, one must actually enter into it, *live* it existentially first, then reflect on it. One cannot deduce it a priori from any *cogito* or purely solitary experience. It must happen to us; and unless it does, it will be impossible for us even to raise the question of realism or any other epistemological position, which is always an affirmation *to* someone, an affirmation we are prepared to explain and defend.

Let us unpack the implicit content in the experience of carrying on a sincere *dialogue* with a respondent, where one exchanges meaningful messages (*information*) with the other, sincerely asking questions the answer to which one does not know on one's own, and listening to the answers which make sense and lead to successful practical action in the real world, e.g., "Where did you put the beer?" "Would you like a drink before dinner?" "Will you marry me?" "Do you know what I heard about my boss today?" "Do you believe in God?" etc., etc. What is implicitly being affirmed here?

Epistemological Implications

1) *I am real* (actually, actively present), because I am aware of myself as actively thinking, communicating, and receiving (being acted upon).

2) I am in touch with, present to, *another real being*, on whom I act and who acts in return on me by exchanging information. I cannot seriously believe that my dialogue partner is not real or that I am projecting, inventing him or her; I have to wait for answers to my questions, listen to incoming information that I do not yet know myself. In a word, I am conscious of being acted on, receiving messages from the real beyond my consciousness. The very fact of sharing a common language, which neither of us made up, bears witness to the same fact. In a word, we are both real, *actively present* to each other. I cannot sincerely believe I am projecting the real presence of the other; for then the other, having the same experience, would have to be simultaneously projecting my real presence, and the two rival projections would cancel each other out.

3) This real other is truly *like me*, because it *acts* like me, by talking, communicating in a way I can understand, through words, gestures, writing, etc. I cannot seriously believe I am simply projecting, structuring the action of this respondent out of my own initiative; I truly await expectantly its responses, which I cannot make up—and believe—on my own ("Where is the beer?" "Will you marry me ... go with me to the Grand Canyon?" etc.). This other, therefore, is a talking, thinking, being, using a bodily medium of communication, plus a shared language, just like me.

4) I can—because I do—*receive a pre-structured, pre-formed message from without*, an intelligible message which I understand and can act on to confirm. I cannot sincerely believe that I have simply made up, imposed the basic formal structure on, this message from the other, on my own independent initiative, which would mean I already possessed within me the *information* I am projecting and yet obviously receiving as something new, not previously known by me. It is true that I can add on to a message received from without various further interpretations, implications, etc. Thus if someone tells me "There is a fire in your cellar," if I am a professional firefighter I will add on certain implications of causes and effects; if I am a poet I may add on certain imaginative and emotional overtones, if I am a mother, another set, etc. But no one can seriously believe that what has been said is, "Scotch and soda are being served in the living room." The basic message gets through, not wiped out by the aura of individual inter-

pretation added on in each case. Otherwise meaningful dialogue and communication would be impossible. But it does in fact take place, innumerable times, in our experience. It follows, therefore, that our cognitive equipment is able, and naturally disposed to, taking in already *formed* messages, formed by another real knowing subject outside of or distinct from me, through the pathways of my senses (hearing and seeing), and that reciprocally I can send similar messages of my own to the other. It is not the case, therefore, that my cognitive ability is limited to imposing a priori forms of my own on a raw sense manifold without intelligible forms of its own, as Kant maintains.

5) The I-Thou of interpersonal dialogue, now become a "We," can then turn to explore, share, and discuss the messages coming in to both from a non-human world beyond, and outside the controlling power of, the dialoguers, the common world that may be called "It," or the non-personal real. This will be carried out by the ongoing dialectic of "like me, like us" in this particular way, "unlike us" in this other distinctive way. The "like us" will always be the prime analogate of understanding, but this will shade off by progressive negations as we descend further into the non-human world below us and intensify by progressive additions as we mount higher than ourselves in the world of reality manifested to us—or implied indirectly by what is manifest.

The implications of this primary or central contact with the real, with being, through interpersonal dialogue are powerful and far-reaching. Let us turn back for a moment to Immanuel Kant. Ever since I was initiated to this vantage point of dialogue, it has been a source of wonder to me to observe that Kant quite obviously and without question takes for granted the existence of other persons like himself and just as real as himself, because they are autonomous centers of dialogue who are capable of dialoguing with him, i.e., who understand the German language, taught to both from without, and can receive and send, basically intact, intelligible messages from and to each other. In fact, he became quite indignant when other philosophers did not get his message straight but misinterpreted it as, for example, either idealism or realism.

Yet nowhere in his works does he ever discuss how it is possible to know other human beings as real, as objectively like himself in cognitive ability, and as able to receive from each other intelligible messages, basically intact, originating from outside the receiver and given prior intelligible form by an independent sender, in a word, how *information* can be successfully communicated at all—despite some accidental "noise" added as the time and distance of the means of communication increase. In a word, there is not a word in Kant as to how interpersonal dialogue is possible at all; it is simply taken for granted as the implicit framework of all his writing, including his correspondence with others over the meaning of his message. Nor is any such explanation of justification of interpersonal knowledge and meaningful dialogue found in any of the classical Western epistemologists up to the twentieth century, until the phenomenologists in fact. Even there it is well known what difficulty Husserl, with the Kantian hangovers in his thought, found in trying to fit in and justify knowledge of other egos.

Furthermore, not only does Kant in fact not attempt to justify his presumed knowledge of other human persons as equally real with himself, like himself, and able to carry on meaningful dialogue with him. It would be *impossible* for him to do so without abandoning several central claims of his own epistemology (at least as laid forth in the *Critique of Pure Reason*). Thus (1) Kant insists that we cannot know any thing-in-itself as real outside of the field of our own subjective experience—certainly not its nature, but in fact not even its real existence as in any way determinate. For then our knowledge would be firmly anchored in something objectively real in the thing-in-itself outside of us; and furthermore, "existence" or "being" for Kant *means*—and can consistently mean—nothing more than the positing by the mind of a synthesis between its own a priori subjective forms of the mind (categories) and the by-itself not intelligible manifold of sense data, always within the subjective field of the knower's consciousness only.[6] Just how far Kant is willing to admit that he knows the reality of his own self as subject is not clear; but it seems that he finally is forced to admit that he knows his own self as really present and the source of his own cognitive actions, though the further nature of this self remains unknown. But in the experience of an authentic successful interpersonal dialogue, it is impossible for him or anyone else to believe sincerely that the other is not equally as real as his own self and equally interacting with him, to believe that he is somehow positing the other's reality and action from within himself. For if this analysis were accurate, then the other would have to be equally positing Kant himself as real—which does not make sense. The two cannot be at the same time reciprocally positing each other in existence. Either both are known and implicitly affirmed as real (actively present) or neither.

(2) Secondly, Kant insists—as the core of his Copernican revolution—that the outside world does not *inform* our minds, but the reverse: our minds impose their own a priori forms of sense and

understanding on the raw sense manifold coming from without; we inform the world, rather than the world informing us. It is therefore impossible in his system for our minds to receive any prestructured intelligible forms from without. The matter of our knowledge comes from without, the form from within. But in a meaningful dialogue the whole point is that we do in fact succeed in taking in meaningful, intelligible forms (a message, some *information*) from without, preformed, prestructured by an active source other than ourselves. Otherwise we have not yet understood the other, gotten his message straight. And Kant himself was indignant when others did not, he thought, get his message straight but significantly *mis*interpreted it, either carelessly or culpably.

But if we can in this instance, endlessly repeated, take in with basic accuracy intelligible forms prestructured by another, independent of ourselves, through the medium of our senses (so that the form is carried somehow basically intact through the senses themselves), then the basic Kantian contention is broken through decisively. Surely it would make no sense for Kant to try to claim that in fact he is actively structuring the very formal message coming from the other person. For then the other person would have to be doing the same to Kant's own message, and as a result neither would be able to understand the message of the *other*, nor *mis*understand it, let alone protest righteously that the other has not been sufficiently *attentive* to—receptive of—the message one has communicated to him in their commonly understood language.

Once this ban on receiving formal messages from the outside world has been lifted, a whole new perspective on our cognitive relationship with the world opens up. If it is possible to receive preformed messages from without in an interpersonal dialogue, mediated through the senses, why should it not be possible to receive preformed messages from other non-human dialogue partners in the world, communicating with us through the medium of our senses, but in non-linguistic ways? If we can receive one sort of preformed message through our senses, why not many others? Thus we are led into a Thomistic vision of the universe as a vast system of interactive communicating centers, with ourselves as privileged self-conscious centers in the midst of it all. Action is the self-revelation of being; every being, insofar as it is in act, is self-communicative, as St. Thomas never tires of repeating.

To sum up, then, reflection on the lived experience of sincere interpersonal dialogue reveals with an evidence not open to prudent, realistic doubt that (1) I am in touch with *another being as real as myself,* i.e., an actively present, actively self-communicating subject; (2) I know the *nature* or whatness of this other real being as *like me*, sharing similar cognitive and communicative abilities, hence as a thinking, talking being, i.e., an embodied mind; (3) I can therefore *take in information*, intelligibly structured messages from the outside world through my sense receiving set, with significant (not necessarily perfect or complete) accuracy, and communicate the same to others in a common world.

Note that the mode of argumentation, or better, explication at work here is not that of a logically necessary deduction from the data of an experience but a progressive unfolding or unpacking of implications perceived by reflective insight as flowing out of the data. The necessity is not logical but under the pressure of "retorsion": i.e., if one does not accept the conclusion, there emerges a "lived" contradiction between the explicit content of the position one is affirming and what is being implicitly affirmed by one's action—here the performance of carrying on the dialogue—not a logical but a "lived" contradiction. In other words, at the same time that one is denying that he is dealing with another real being like himself, or that he is really taking in a prestructured formal message from outside, he is also in fact acting—and cannot help doing so as long as the dialogue continues—as though his dialogue partner is equally real with himself and each one is receiving a meaningful message from the real other, a message not constructed by his own mind but by the other. When a philosopher's explanatory theory thus contradicts or is irreconcilably at odds with his lived experience, it is clearly the theory that must yield, especially since in this case he cannot go on acting like a philosopher, that is, explaining and defending his position to others, without engaging in meaningful dialogue with them, with all the implications of the latter. Thus a basic philosophical method for all areas of thought is at the same time uncovered.

What is the significant difference between the encounter with real being in the experience of interpersonal dialogue and the encounter with it in some subhuman, say inanimate form, e.g., a tree, or rock, or river? One can certainly, I believe, achieve the justified recognition of being in touch with a real being distinct from oneself in such an experience. One can even work out carefully, by trial and error experimentation, some reliable knowledge of its nature, by its mode of action on us. I am not denying this at all. But the difficulty is that when we are dealing with the subhuman, especially the subanimal and inanimate world today, the tendency for a modern thinker is to slip quickly into the attitude of the scientist, bringing his own creatively constructed hypothesis to the experience to query nature according to it. This method is indeed appropriate in view of the obscurity of the deep nature of matter to us, due to its inaccessibility to our direct sense experience. Thus it is all too easy for us to imagine that it is we who are imposing our own mentally constructed forms on the world rather than receiving them from it. The key factor is really that the subhuman, especially the inanimate, world cannot talk back to us and correct us at once if we are misinterpreting it.

The dialogue experience is quite different in this respect. Our partner in the dialogue can immediately respond to us, showing he has understood our message but is correcting it in some way as involving a misinterpretation of his own message. And by the very fact of so doing, this other being immediately reveals not only that it is real, but that it has a *nature like us*, i.e., is an intelligent, talking being using a body to communicate. In no other experience of knowing does the known so quickly and decisively reveal its essential nature by its mode of action. And this remains true even if the content of the message communicated is so complex or ambiguous that it needs a lot of further, perhaps problematic, interpretation. The very fact of a meaningful, recognizable dialogue at all immediately reveals to us not only that we are in touch with another real being but that we know an essential aspect of its nature, enough to distinguish it from plants, animals, etc. Hence the privileged character of the experience of interpersonal dialogue as the starting point not only for epistemology, as we have just seen, but also for metaphysics, as we shall presently see.

There is one last advantage of the dialogue starting point that deserves to be mentioned before we go on to its metaphysical implications. It quietly cuts through, or perhaps steps out of, the whole discussion over *foundationalism* and *anti-foundationalism* that has been raging so intensely in contemporary epistemological circles. The foundationalists, in order to insure the certitude of ongoing a posteriori or empirical knowledge, believed they had to discover certain basic items of knowledge that by themselves were incontrovertible and self-sufficient, on which further knowledge, interpretations, etc., could then be safely built. They tended to seek these in basic sense data. The anti-foundationalists, on the other hand, tried to show that no such self-sufficient foundational items could be found. Each one always revealed assumptions and relations to further frameworks, etc. The search for incontrovertible foundations of knowledge was illusory. Though the foundationalists retorted that without foundations the whole subsequent structure of knowledge became shaky and subject to arbitrary overturning and reconstruction, it seems they are in retreat at present. Few contemporary thinkers are willing any more to defend any strong version of foundationalism, in view of the difficulties so effectively pressed home by their opponents.

A Thomistic epistemological approach, especially one grounded in interpersonal dialogue, does indeed uncover a secure foundational *experience*. But it is not one based on any atomic bit of sense knowledge considered as self-sufficient or incontrovertible by itself alone. The "foundation," if one wishes to call it such, is a rich wholistic matrix, assimilated by a synthesis of sense data, intellectual insight, and prudent judgment which requires the personal responsible involvement of the knowing person as a whole. The sensory input is indeed an indispensable part of the evidence, but it is never the whole picture. There is no knowledge of the real outside world attainable by some purely automatic impersonal logical machinery, bypassing the role of personal responsible judgment by the knower, who must size up prudently the situation as a whole. What St. Thomas offers us in epistemology is, as Lonergan has aptly put it, "reasonable affirmation," not Cartesian apodictic certitude, so incontrovertible that the opposite is *logically* contradictory. Such a position bypasses the intransigent extremes of both foundationalism and anti-foundationalism.

IMPLICATIONS FOR THE DEVELOPMENT OF METAPHYSICS

1) The encounter with real or existential being is clear and powerful. Real being is revealed as *active presence*, as self-communicating active presence, which distinguishes it decisively from merely mental being, i.e., the presence of an idea merely as thought about in the mind, e.g., mathematical and logical entities, possibles, hypotheses, imaginative constructions, etc., all of which are unable to initiate activity on their own.[7]

2) The intellectual awareness of *We are* immediately reveals to us real (i.e., actually existing) being, not as a solitary ego or object, but as a *field of interaction* which is at once *one yet many*. The I and Thou of the dialogue are *both real*, actually existing, therefore sharing in the common attribute of existence (*esse* for St. Thomas): "We *are*." Yet the I and the Thou are each irreducibly distinct beings, because distinct centers of sending out communications and receiving them: "*We* are"; the I is *not* the Thou; they are *two*, irreducibly distinct from each other while at the same time joined in interactive communication with each other—distinct yet related. Each of the beings also reveals itself as endowed with a distinctive nature or essence: that of an intelligibly talking, hence thinking, being, communicating by means of a material

body endowed with sensory modes of communicating with similarly endowed beings; i.e., each is an embodied mind.

The state is now set for the whole dialectical analysis of being as a *participation system*, each being participating in the all-embracing actuality of existence by its own act of existence, that makes it to be an active presence in the world, and yet restricted by its own particular limiting essence to be *this* being and not *that* one. The fundamental essence/existence structure of reality, the centerpiece of Thomistic metaphysics, is now ready to be worked out.

3) The participation of two distinct real beings in the same essential mode or species of being is also revealed, because the I and Thou reveal themselves as *like each other*, as similar in nature, both embodied minds, a "We" different from all the other non-human real beings we encounter together in our common world. This sets the stage for the metaphysical analysis of the one and the many in the order of essence, ending up in the structure of shared form and individuating matter.

4) From the start the basic dyadic complementarity within each being is made manifest: its substantiality and its relationality. Each being exists *in itself* (not as a part of any other being), as an originating center of action; yet it is also *related* to others. To be real is to be substance-in-relation.[8]

5) Another advantage follows from taking the dialoguing "I" as the primary analogate or instance of real being. This reveals that being (at least from a certain level upwards) is not merely an object, "out there" before a mind, capable of being comprehended adequately by abstract conceptual analysis, but has an *inner subjective dimension*, as a unique, self-aware subject or "I," that transcends all conceptual analysis and can only be grasped intuitively by immediate lived awareness from within or recognized by connatural affinity in another subject, a "Thou," distinct from oneself. Thus Thomism, beginning with the person as subject and ending with Transcendent Person Being as the supreme level of being, can truly be called a personalist philosophy. This counters the criticism—not entirely unfounded, as Joseph de Finance pointed out some time ago—of contemporary personalist thinkers that Thomistic metaphysics tends to treat all being, including the human, as an object for impersonal objective analysis, with biological organisms as the primary model of being, following the approach of Aristotle, and thus fails to recognize the ineffable subjective depth of being as found in persons.[9]

6) At the same time the *interpersonal context of truth* emerges for further development later. Truth possessed within tends naturally to

embody itself in language and to take the form of affirmation *to* another person in a common community-owned language, to become implicitly therefore an affirmation before and to the whole community, and to seek concurrence from the dialogue partner and implicitly from the whole community. Each person must indeed verify a truth individually for himself or herself, but feedback from the others, the community, is an important confirmatory factor in the security of one's conviction. A shared truth always carries more weight than a solitary one.[10]

All of the above points are, of course, just seminally present in the initial experience of interpersonal dialogue and need further conceptual unpacking as the metaphysics systematically unfolds. But they are present there more powerfully and luminously, I believe, than in any other non-personal encounter with being. Note too that this interpersonal starting point can be used equally by any one of the various Thomistic schools, and does not—or does not have to—prejudice any further distinctive method of developing the basic realistic encounter with real being. It is just the most powerful and luminous instance of such an encounter, and the one most richly pregnant with further implications.

Conclusion

To sum up, I am suggesting that the most fruitful starting point of Thomistic metaphysics—in the sense only of the initial paradigm encounter with real being (actually existing being), from which the richest notion of being can be brought to reflective awareness—is neither the "I am" of Descartes, nor the experience of the real but non-personal sensible world, nor the neutral "S is P" of any affirmative true judgment (because embracing indeterminately both real and mental being). It is rather the "We are" of interpersonal dialogue. In a word, the full dimensions of what it means "to be" can be found only in *personal being*, in its *interpersonal manifestation*. Why not start there from the beginning?

Notes

1. *Summa Theologiae*, I–II, q. 94, art. 2. On the grounding of intelligibility in existential being (*esse*), see *Summa contra Gentes*, I, ch. 71: "Anything whatsoever has just as much of knowability as it has of *esse*"; *Sum. Theol.*, I, q. 87, art. 1: "Anything whatever is knowable according as it is in act and not according as it is in potency, as is said in *Met. IX*. So something is being and true (intelligible), as falling under knowledge, according as it is in act." Ob-

jects, therefore, which do not themselves exist in actuality are knowable through some connection with something existing, as possibles in their causes, abstractions, hypotheses, etc., in the real act of the mind which thinks them up and sustains them in thought.

2. In his earlier writings, such as *Insight*, Bernard Lonergan systematically defines the real as that which is affirmed by a well-made (virtually unconditioned) affirmation, without distinguishing explicitly between real and mental being, and gives no further criteria for distinguishing real (actually existing) being from mental being, which exists as an idea (or combination of ideas) in the mind. But the difficulty is that logical and mathematical propositions can also be affirmed as true without affirming real being of them. Finally, in "Insight Revisited" and more explicitly in *Method in Theology*, due partly to his own new insights and partly, I think, to the pressure of existential Thomists, including myself, he came around to admit that one must distinguish explicitly real and mental being. This removes the previous ambiguity and in fact is easily integrated into his basic epistemological doctrine of the invariant structure of knowing: data, insight, judgment. But it is now no longer possible to derive real being and metaphysics purely as the objective correlate of the structure of knowing, i.e., merely from the *kind* of act of knowing; it must be also from the content or kind of *evidence* grounding an affirmation, that must come from the object itself. Thus the recognition of action (or some connection with it) is the necessary condition for any affirmation of real existence; metaphysics and epistemology are mutually interwoven from the start. No absolutely "pure" epistemology, prior to and independent of an implicit metaphysics, is really possible, it seems to me, as Lonergan seems to have hoped.

3. Cf. Etienne Gilson, *Réalisme thomiste et critique de la connaissance* (Paris: Vrin, 1939).

4. Cf. John Knasas, "*Ad Mentem Thomae*: Does Natural Philosophy Prove God?" *Proc. Amer. Cath. Phil. Assoc.*, 61 (1987), 209–20.

5. My initial introduction to the notion of language and dialogue as a foundation for philosophical inquiry came from the seminal suggestions of August Brunner, S.J., one of the pioneers of the Catholic personalists in Germany and my professor for a year in my early philosophical training in France. See *La personne incarnée* (Paris, 1947) and *Fundamental Questions of Philosophy* (St. Louis: Herder, 1937). But I did not fully realize the implications for epistemology and metaphysics until I came in contact with the personalist phenomenological movements ten years later while doing my Ph.D. in Louvain. I have worked out the epistemological implications in my essay, "Interpersonal Dialogue: Key to Realism," in Robert Roth, ed., *Person and Community* (New York: Fordham Univ. Press, 1975), pp. 141–53. But the fruitfulness of the *We are* discovered in dialogue as the most pregnant encounter with real being to start metaphysics on its way did not become fully clear to me till recent years. Since Father Gerald McCool in his very generous and insightful article "An Alert and Independent Thomist William Norris Clarke, S.J.," *International Philosophical Quarterly*, 26 (1986), 3–22, remarked

that the personalist encounter with being was one of the distinguishing marks of my brand of Thomistic metaphysics, I thought it was finally time to lay claim formally to this approach to metaphysics.

6. See Martin Heidegger's insightful analysis of the texts, *Kants These über das Sein* (Frankfurt: Klosterman, 1962).

7. Cf. my article, "Action as the Self-Revelation of Being: A Central Theme in the Thought of St. Thomas," *History of Philosophy in the Making: Essays in Honor of James Collins* (Washington, Univ. of America Press, 1982), 63–80.

8. I develop this notion of the dyadic structure of all real being as both substantial and relational in an article, "To Be Is to Be Substance-in-Relation," in *Metaphysics as Foundation: Essays in Honor of Ivor Leclerc*, ed. P. Bogaard and G. Treash (Albany: SUNY Press, 1993), 164–83, now chapter 6 in this collection.

9. This notion is beautifully developed as a corrective to too objectivist a Thomism by Joseph de Finance, "Being and Subjectivity," *Cross Currents*, 6 (1956), 163–78.

10. For this notion of community as the implicit horizon of all truth, see Robert Harvanek, "The Community of Truth," *Intern. Phil. Quart.*, 7 (1967), 68–85.

3

Action as the Self-Revelation of Being: A Central Theme in the Thought of St. Thomas

It is a strange fact, well enough known to Thomistic scholars familiar with the whole of St. Thomas's thought, that the great underlying themes, the central structural principles organizing his philosophical worldview, are not ordinarily highlighted explicitly in their own right, as a modern philosopher would tend to do. The explicit focus of his writing, following the medieval scholastic custom in university teaching, is directed toward the solving of an integrated series of key problems in a given area—for example, "Whether the Soul is the Form of the Body," etc. The central governing principles are *used* constantly, and indeed quite explicitly, to solve these problems, but St. Thomas does not ordinarily thematize them directly in a full-fledged exposition of them in their own right as universal principles. Thus one does not find articles entitled: "Whether Act and Potency (or the Theory of Participation) Are Universal Principles for Understanding All Things." Yet one has not really understood the Thomistic system in its holistic unity and depth until one has thematized explicitly for himself these great underlying principles precisely as universal explanatory principles.

One of these great central organizing themes in St. Thomas's thought, too often left in the shadow, yet running through not only his whole philosophy but also his theology, is the principle that *action is the self-revelation of being*.[1] By this is meant that action, activity, not only follows naturally from being, but is also a natural self-communication and self-revelation of the being that acts, "pointing out," as St. Thomas graphically puts it, both its existence and its essence, both *that* it is and *what* it is.[2] The centrality of such a principle is particularly evident throughout the whole of metaphysics and epistemology. For without it no universe, properly speaking, could exist, that is, the multiplicity of beings would not be "turned toward each other to form a unity" (*universum*), i.e., a real order or system unified by existential bonds between beings. Nor would knowledge be possible of anything real beyond the knower. For unless a being manifested or revealed its presence and nature by some action, it would be impossible to know that it was present at all, let alone its nature (unless, of course, the knower had directly caused its whole being, which would involve action at least on the part of the knower). A being that did not manifest its existence and essence to others by some form of self-revealing action would make no difference at all to the other beings in the universe, and hence might just as well not be at all. A totally unmanifest existence, unreachable even potentially by any kind of action, would be to all intents and purposes equivalent to non-existence, if it could indeed be conceptualized at all.

As a result, I am willing to venture the following risky, but I think well defensible, statement, that the whole of Thomistic epistemology, in its large lines, can be summed up as follows: all human knowledge of the real is an interpretation of action. Yet it is hard to find this basic principle thematized explicitly for itself, in St. Thomas, abstracted from its particular applications. This is what I would like to do in large lines in this essay. The fruit of such an exploration will be, I hope, to highlight not only the unity but the profoundly dynamic character of the entire worldview of St. Thomas, together with its ability to shed light on certain troublesome "bridge" problems that have plagued modern Western epistemology since its new start with Descartes.

I. ACTION AS THE NATURAL OVERFLOW OF BEING

It is impossible to read St. Thomas at any length and not come across the oft-repeated refrain: *agere sequitur esse* (to act follows upon to be). Here are some characteristic texts:

> Every agent acts according as it is in actuality.[3] From the very fact that something exists in act, it is active.[4] Active power follows upon being in act; for anything acts in consequence of its being in act.[5]

Thus it is proper to every being, insofar as it is in act, to overflow into action, to act according to its nature, whether such action be free or necessitated in its modality. The act of existence of any being (its "to be" or *esse*) is its "first act," its abiding inner act, which tends naturally, by the very innate dynamism of the act of existence itself, to overflow into a "second act," which is called action or activity. Every second act of a being points back toward its first act as to its ground and source, and every first act, in turn, points forward to its natural self-expression in a second act. This action may be an *immanent action*, which terminates within the agent itself, as in the case of knowledge or love, or a *transient action*, which terminates outside the agent by exercising some influence on another, as cause on effect, thus manifesting itself to another than itself.[6] In what follows we are thinking more particularly, though not exclusively, of this second kind of action, without which no non-creative being could know any other being in the universe distinct from it.

It might be asked how St. Thomas establishes the natural connection between being and its overflow into action. There is no logical or other way of *deducing* this property of being from anything else more fundamental. It can only be reached by a reflective insight arising from an inductive examination which observes it constantly at work in all the cases and at all the levels of being we know, until we are finally brought to the level of a "metaphysical insight" that this property somehow belongs to the very nature of existential being as such and could not be intelligibly otherwise, in that any being without it would remain beyond the pale of intelligibility, inaccessible to the rest of the real universe in the darkness of its total isolation from all others. To be, in the strong sense of to be real or actually existing, is seen to be ambiguous, incomplete, empty of evidential grounding, unless it includes, as natural corollary, *active presence*, that which *presents* itself positively to others through some mode of action. To be is to be actively co-present to the community of existents, of other active presences. Presence that is not presence in some way *to* the community of other existents slips into the unreachable darkness of the totally unmanifest, the totally concealed (unrevealed), indistinguishable from nothingness to all other beings (one might perhaps argue, even to itself, though we will not venture into these particularly deep waters right now).

II. Action as the Self-Communication of Being

Let us now unpack further the implications of action as the natural overflow of existential being. This is where the full significance of the link between being and action begins to emerge, as St. Thomas sees it. Every being, he says, insofar as it *is* in act, tends naturally to overflow into action, and this action is a *self-communication*, a self-giving in some way. This theme recurs over and over again, in many contexts. Here are a few characteristic texts:

> It is in the nature of every actuality to communicate itself insofar as it is possible. Hence every agent acts according as it exists in actuality.[7]

> To bring forth an actuality is, of itself, proper to a being in act: for every agent acts according as it is in act. Therefore every being in act is by its nature apt to bring forth something in act. But God is a being in act. . . . Therefore it is proper to Him to bring forth some being in act, to which He is the cause of being.[8]
>
> It follows upon the superabundance proper to perfection as such that the perfection which something has it can communicate to another.[9]
>
> Communication follows upon the very intelligibility (*ratio*) of actuality. Hence every form is of itself communicable.[10]
>
> For natural things have a natural inclination not only toward their own proper good, to acquire it, if not possessed, and, if possessed, to rest therein; but also to diffuse their own goodness among others as far as possible. Hence we see that every agent, insofar as it exists in act and possesses some perfection, produces something similar to itself. It pertains, therefore, to the nature of the will to communicate to others as far as possible the good possessed; and especially does this pertain to the divine will, from which all perfection is derived in some kind of likeness. Hence if natural things, insofar as they are perfect, communicate their goodness to others, much more does it pertain to the divine will to communicate by likeness its own goodness to others as far as possible.[11]

Here we touch on the most fundamental dynamism of being itself for St. Thomas. Not only does every being tend, by the inner dynamism of its act of existence, to overflow into action, but this action is both a self-manifestation and a self-communication, a self-sharing, of the being's own inner ontological perfection, with others. This natural tendency to self-giving is a revelation of the natural fecundity or "generosity" rooted in the very nature of being itself. We are immediately reminded of the ancient Platonic tradition—well known to St. Thomas—of the "self-diffusiveness of the Good" (*bonum est diffusivum sui*, as the Latins put it). What St. Thomas has done is to incorporate this whole rich tradition of the fecundity of the Good into his own philosophy of being, turning this self-diffusiveness, which the Platonic tradition identified as proper to what they considered the ultimate ground of reality, the Good, into a *property of being* itself, of which the good now becomes one inseparable aspect (or transcendental property).[12] Whereas in Platonism, and especially Neoplatonism, being itself is only a lesser dimension, on the finite level, of the primal self-diffusiveness or self-communication of the Good, for St. Thomas the good is a derivative property of existential being itself, expressing more explicitly the primal dynamism of self-expansiveness and self-giving inherent in the very nature of being as act of existence. The primacy always lies with existence for St. Thomas. Nothing can be good unless it first actually is; and from the very fact that it is, it naturally follows that it is good, since the act of existence is the root of all perfection in any domain, "the actuality of all acts, and the perfection of all perfections."[13]

We have here penetrated to the very roots of being itself, to the primal spring of its activity without which there would be no universe. There is something mysterious, ultimate, and undeducible about this inherent self-diffusive dynamism of all being, as about all primary things. It cannot be deduced from anything more ultimate but is reached by insight through induction when we finally see that not only is it a fact about all the beings we know, but that it must be so if there is to be a universe, an intercommunicating community of co-existents, at all. It is the dynamo that makes the whole world go round. In its highest form as self-communicative altruistic love, it is the ultimate reason why the Many emerges from the One at all, without which sheerly gratuitous emanation there would be no Many, hence no universe at all.

It is true, of course, that in St. Thomas's participation universe, as in the Neoplatonic one, the self-diffusiveness of all finite participated beings can be traced back to its primal source, the infinite essential goodness of God himself, who, as pure Subsistent Act of Existence (*ipsum esse Subsistens*), is also Love itself. And Revelation here gives us a marvelous further insight, inaccessible to strictly philosophical penetration, into the interior depths of the divine self-communicativeness within its own being, manifesting to us that it is of the very nature of the divine being to pour over into two supreme eternal acts of self-communication of the perfection of its nature, first from the Father to the Son, then from the Father and Son together to the Holy Spirit: the procession of the Son or Logos according to self-knowledge, and the procession of the Holy Spirit according to self-love. The rest of the universe dimly imitates, each thing in its own way, this infinite fullness of self-giving. But it still remains that this mysterious inner process of thoughtful, loving self-communication is not a free decision but belongs to the very nature of the Supreme Being as pure Subsistent Act of Existence. If we try to pursue this trail further and ask why this should be so, why Being itself should *be* self-expansive Love, all trails end in the silence of *the* Mystery. The Ultimate Fact that Being is identically Love precludes all further explanatory moves and serves itself as the ultimate explanatory reason for the entire dynamic nature of the universe.

The principal difference, of course, between St. Thomas and the Neoplatonic tradition of the self-diffusiveness of the Good, to which he clearly owes so much, is that for the latter the self-communication of the supreme source, the One or the Good, is presented as a *necessary* process of emanation, at all levels, including the highest. St. Thomas, both as a Christian *and* as a philosopher, holds firmly to the divine freedom in creation, that God is free to create or not to create finite beings. Because he fears that the "self-diffusiveness of the good" doctrine, if taken too strictly in the order of efficient casuality, might compromise this freedom of creation, he tones down the meaning of the adage, *bonum est diffusivum sui*, to mean the self-diffusiveness of the good in the order of final casuality, the order of the good as attractive goal, not as causal source. In the order of efficient causality, he is willing to concede only that every being is *capable* of active self-communication, has a natural aptitude for it, but does not necessarily have to actualize this aptitude. This is clearly not the original Neoplatonic meaning of the principle, which insists on the active overflow as a kind of natural law, an exigency of the very nature of the good. St. Thomas is also being considerably more cautious here than St. Bonaventure and other Christian Neoplatonists who remain closer to the stronger Neoplatonic doctrine while not denying the freedom of creation by appealing to a kind of spiritual exigency of love by which it would be somehow "out of character" for a loving person, above all God, not to share freely his goodness with others.

It seems to me that St. Thomas is indeed somewhat overcautious here. His own strong statements, quoted above, that it is proper to every being in act to be self-communicative through action, do not easily fit together with his restriction of the law of the self-diffusiveness of the good to the order of final causality. It seems to me he could have kept the stronger meaning of the principle and taken care of the freedom of creation by several other qualifications: (1) he could have appealed to the revealed doctrine of the Three Persons in the Trinity, to show that the necessary law of the self-communication of the good has already been fulfilled in an infinitely perfect way in the inner procession of the Son and the Holy Spirit, which is not free but of the very nature of divine being; then the further pouring over into finite creation no longer becomes necessary but is free; (2) he could have held, as some Christian philosophers have, that while on the one hand it is impossible to deduce from the existence of an infinite Source the necessity of any *one* finite universe flowing from it—since an infinite number of other finite universes is always possible, and the choice must pass through the filters of intelligence and freedom—still one might say that there is a kind of moral exigency of perfect love that it share itself in *some* way, that it would be "out of character," hence not fully intelligible, for it not to. But his caution may have been the better part of prudence, especially in his own day, when the Christian world was facing the strong intellectual threat of the great Arabic necessary-emanation theories of the universe, which clearly left too little place for the divine freedom in creation.

At any rate, once the universe is launched into existence by the loving self-communication of God as First Cause, all finite beings, which are imperfect images of the Source, bear within their very natures this same divinely originated dynamism of active self-communication to others. Thus the many existential bonds of the finite universe come into being. But because *finite* beings are both rich and poor, these bonds go both ways: every finite being insofar as it is in act, is rich, pours over to share its perfection with others; but insofar as it is poor, deficient in the full plenitude of being, it reaches out to receive enrichments of being from others, sharing their riches.[14] Thus the universe becomes a vast interconnected web of interacting beings, reciprocally acting on and being acted on by others, giving and receiving. *To be finite* is *to share*, in all the active and passive meanings of that term.

To sum up this whole section, action, as the natural overflow and self-communicative dynamism of existential being, is the indispensable shuttle on which is woven the web of this, and any other, universe.

III. ACTION AS THE SELF-REVELATION OF BEING

The implications of the above doctrine of action as the self-communication of being are profound and rich, lending themselves to the deepest metaphysical, artistic, and religious meditation, opening out easily into mysticism. We shall now turn our attention to one of the richest philosophical implications or corollaries of the doctrine, namely, that this self-communication of being is also necessarily a *self-revelation* or *self-manifestation* of being. This is where the role of action as the ground of a realistic epistemology emerges more explicitly.

But first let us take a quick look at one of the interesting ontological implications of being as self-communicative. For St. Thomas, as for Aristotle and Neoplatonism, every being, by the very fact that it communicates itself through action, also produces in the recipients of this communication an ontological *self-expression*, a likeness or image of itself. The reason for this flows from the nature of the cause-effect relationship: every effect must in some way resemble its cause, and vice versa. Since the effect proceeds from the cause, receives its being or mode of being, insofar as it is an effect, from its cause, and since a cause cannot give what it does not possess, at least in some equivalent higher way, there must be a relation of at least analogous similitude between effect and cause. Hence every self-communication of one being to another through action of one on the other necessarily brings forth a self-imaging, a self-expression, one might say a self-symbolization, of the cause in the effect. If every being, then, turns out to include a natural dynamism toward self-communication through action, we can say truly, in more than a metaphorical sense, that every being is naturally a *self-symbolizer*, an icon or image-maker, in some analogous way like an artist, expressing itself symbolically, whether consciously or unconsciously.[15] No wonder that the human being has an innate drive toward imagemaking, if *all* beings do, from the very fact that they are beings in act. The difference between humans and lower beings, why we call one an artist and not the others, is that those below us are limited to an endlessly repetitive self-imaging according to their already determined nature, whereas we have the freedom to make images not only of ourselves but of the whole universe in relation to us in endlessly creative new perspectives and angles of insight.

We might add that this notion of every being as innately ordered toward self-symbolization opens up a profoundly illuminating harmony between philosophy and theology, reason and faith, in St. Thomas's worldview: the self-symbolizing tendency in all the finite beings we know turns out to be an imperfect participation or imitation of the inner being of God himself, revealed to be supremely and perfectly self-symbolizing in its eternal interior procession of the Son from the Father and the Holy Spirit from both. But again why the divine being should be this way, why it is the "nature" of Being itself to be this way, leads our minds to the end of explanation in the unsoundable depths of the Ultimate Mystery, expressed impersonally as the fecundity of being as the good, personally as the identity of Being and Love.

IV. ACTION AS THE KEY TO A REALISTIC EPISTEMOLOGY

The key problem in any realistic epistemology is how finite non-creative knowers like us can know a world of real beings "outside of" or distinct from our own consciousness, so that our immanent knowledge or conscious representation of these beings *corresponds* authentically to the reality of this world as it is in itself, in a word, so that our knowledge of it is *true*. The basic type of Platonic solution to the problem, echoed creatively but always recognizably through the Augustinian and other later derivatives of the Platonic tradition, is that the knower is illuminated from within himself and from above, by a direct intuitive insight, however dimmed it may be for various historical contingent reasons, into the ideal forms or pure intelligible patterns that are constitutive of the intelligible core of these things; but the locus of these intelligible forms, from which they are received by the knower, is not the imperfect individually existing instances of these forms found around us in our horizontal world of change and action, but the separate, pre-existent ideal world of these forms in their pure intelligible state, either as found in the apparently self-subsisting Platonic World of Ideas, or in the Divine Ideas of Neoplatonism and St. Augustine, eternally existing in the Divine Mind itself (i.e., the secondary level of the Divine *Nous* for Plotinus; the Divine Logos, co-equal with the Father, for Augustine and all orthodox Christian Platonists). We must turn within and be illumined from above, not directly from individually existing things themselves, if we are to know their true being.

The fundamental criticism of this theory of direct intuitive knowing of the essence of other beings, advanced by the whole Aristotelian-Thomistic tradition, is that it does not do justice to, or cannot be squared with, our actual experience of human knowing: its dependence on sense knowledge, its slowly growing character through trial and error and interactive feedback with the real through experiential contact with it, its always incomplete perspectival character, its non-intuitive character, for which the intentionality of judgment is a substitute, etc. We need not elaborate on this here, well known as it is to most of our readers. For St. Thomas, then, although we do have a general divine illumination in the form of a created participation in the divine light by our own individual agent intellect, all knowledge of particular real beings or kinds of being must come through the illumination or self-revelation of things themselves in direct contact with us. Since we have no direct intuition into the substantial forms of things immanent within them—not only of beings distinct from us but even of our own being—there must be some mediating bridge by which real beings distinct from us enter into the interiority of our consciousness in some way and manifest themselves trustworthily to us.

The only bridge is the mediation of action, if understood in its full ontological depth as the self-revelation of the being of the agent that is its source. Since all beings are constantly in some way (though perhaps intermittently) flowing over from their inner act of being into self-communicative, self-revealing action on the beings within their range of action, any being capable of receiving these influences immediately becomes a receiving center for the surrounding world, a kind of crossroads information-receiving center for the universe as it impinges on that particular location. All that a being has to do is to become conscious, to become aware of itself *as* a receiving set, as the recipient of self-revealing action from the surrounding world, and it is now enabled to interpret the messages, the *information*, contained within this incoming action, *as* messages from these surrounding beings, *as* the self-revelation of these beings to it through the mediation of their structured action upon it. A human being is precisely such a self-conscious receiving set, a *Dasein*, as Heidegger beautifully puts it, a *There*-Being, placed in the midst of the material cosmos with the ability to receive the self-imaging messages of all the material beings around it, insofar as they can act upon its body with a high enough energy input to be able to be brought up beyond the minimum threshold of sense perception, and then interpreted by intelligence. It is our destiny, written into us by the very structure of our nature, to be the ones to *listen* to being, as it reveals itself to us through the mute message of its action, interpret its significance, gather into unity its multifarious voices, speak out the *logos* of Being (as mediated by the many beings which are its bearers), and respond accordingly by our own action.

Action as the self-revelation of being is thus the key for St. Thomas to all knowledge of all beings other than itself by a knower that must be receptive and not creative of its objects. Since the action that flows out from a being is not simply an indeterminate surge of raw energy, but pours out from, and is self-expressive of, the whole unified inner being of the thing, both its act of existence and its essence, its action cannot help but be *essence-structured action* revealing or manifesting to any potential receiver both the actual existence and the essence of the being from which the action originates. As St. Thomas puts it, with his typical condensed brevity:

> The operation of a thing manifests both its substance [essence] and its existence.[16]
>
> The operation of a thing shows forth its power, which in turn points to [or points out: *indicat*] its essence.[17]

The action of a being upon us as a conscious receiving set reveals to us first, therefore, the actual existence of the being in ques-

Action as the Self-Revelation of Being

tion, *that* it is, is really present, in the world of actual existents. Action, by the very fact that we do not originate or control it, but receive it to some degree passively, "suffer" its influence, and are controlled or determined by it willy-nilly, is the natural sign of the real presence of another-than-self. It then at the same time, because it is structured action, reveals to us the essence or nature of the agent precisely as *this kind of actor on me* (and subsequently on others, as our observation widens). This is precisely what our knowledge of the essences of real beings comes down to: we know them as such and such *kinds of actors*, distinguished from others by such and such a set of *characteristic actions*. Such knowledge is genuinely revelatory of the essence, for it enables us to know that the being truly has within itself such a nature, possessing such a degree of perfection and power, that it can originate such a self-communicating, self-expressing, self-imaging action.

But notice immediately the built-in limitations of such a mode of knowing through the interpretation of action. We cannot "zap in" by direct unmediated intuition to "see" intellectually the inner act of existence and especially the nature of the agent as it abides in itself behind the actions, *apart from and independently of these actions*. We have no such intuitive knowledge of essences—including our own—for St. Thomas. We can know real beings—including ourselves in fact—only to the extent that they actually reveal their natures by their actions. But no single action of a finite being can ever reveal totally, in a single exhaustive flash, the entire essence of that being. Every action of a finite being (or even the action of an Infinite Being as received in a finite being) is always at once revealing and concealing, to use Heidegger's marvelously apt language. It does reveal something of the inner nature; otherwise it would not be action at all. But it also leaves unrevealed further depths or aspects of the reservoir of active potency within it; and though finite in itself, the latter is still inexhaustible to our knowledge because of its hidden ontological connections with every other being in the universe and especially with its Infinite Source, God himself. To know even the least finite thing fully as it is, with all its relations, we would have to know it precisely as an image of God, and how it proceeds from and expresses its original, which is hidden from us in the depths of the Infinite.[18]

It is not generally recognized how modest St. Thomas is in his claims for our knowledge of the essences of real things.[19] Yet he says with all the explicitness desirable that we human knowers cannot know the inner essential forms of things directly as they are in themselves:

> The substantial forms of things, which, according as they are in themselves, are unknown to us, shine forth to us (*innotescunt*) through their accidental properties.[20]
>
> Sometimes a created intellect does not arrive at the essence of what it knows directly through itself (as do the angels), but only through the mediation of what surrounds the essence, as though through doors placed around it; and this is the mode of apprehending in man, who proceeds to the knowledge of the essence of a thing from its effects and properties. Hence in this knowledge there must be certain discursive character.[21]

As a result St. Thomas does not hesitate to maintain that no human knower can ever come to know perfectly the essence of anything, even a fly:

> Our knowledge is so weak that no philosopher was ever able to investigate perfectly the nature of a single fly. Hence we read that one philosopher passed thirty years in solitude in order that he might know the nature of the bee.[22]

Thus the abstraction of form from matter in St. Thomas's theory of knowledge cannot be equated with the popular misapprehension that the whole essential form of material beings somehow pops out automatically whole and entire under the X-rays of the agent intellect, somewhat as a sausage pops out of a sausage machine. The abstraction of form does indeed give us an authentic *sighting* on the form, but always incompletely, according to the perspective of our horizon of inquiry and the aspects of the form which are revealed by the particular action received.[23]

In the light of this doctrine of knowledge through action as the partial self-revelation of a being to a given knower, the necessary incompleteness of all human knowledge of essences turns out to be derived from two complementary sources. On the other hand, there is the limitation on the side of the self-revealing action, which, as we have seen above, can never totally reveal in a single act or series of them the full essence of a finite being in all its natural depths of potentiality and act. The second source of limitation comes from the side of the knower himself. As St. Thomas never tires of repeating in its application to knowledge, "Whatever is received is received according to the mode of the receiver."[24] Hence, whatever the knower receives from the self-communication of the known to it through action will always be measured by the receptive capacities of the knower, especially evident in the thresholds and channels of receptivity at the primary level

Action as the Self-Revelation of Being   57

of data input, our sense receiving sets. Thus we can perceive light rays only within a limited section of its total spectrum of wavelengths; we can only see a body from one visual perspective at a time, etc. Here the whole contemporary insistence on the perspectival character of all human knowing can be assimilated easily enough into Thomistic epistemology, even including the partially active a priori contributions and transformations brought to the knowledge relation by the knower, though St. Thomas himself has only laid down the basic principles of receptivity through action and has not worked out all the far-reaching philosophical and theological consequences.

We could also express the above doctrine of action as the bridge between knower and known in the language of *intentionality*, as St. Thomas himself regularly does. Intentionality in general is that property of something by which it tends dynamically and relationally toward something else (*intendere*). This can either be in the ontological order by active tendency, or in the cognitive order in the form of a natural sign or image which points back to the source which it manifests and represents. Intentionality understood in its full richness as including both of the above is indeed the key to knowledge for St. Thomas. It includes a double movement of intentionality, only one aspect of which has been recovered by Brentano, Husserl, and contemporary phenomenology. There is first the incoming *ontological intentionality of action* itself into the knower, which tends naturally to produce a self-expression, a similitude, of itself in an apt receiver. This similitude, which is a self-expression of the agent projected through its form, leaving the being's matter and actual existence behind, is not the physical or natural being (*esse naturale*) of the agent, which remains within itself, but a projected similitude, (an *esse intentionale*) received in the knower according to the mode of the knower, and, when recognized *as a natural similitude, image, or sign* of its source, points back by the whole dynamism of its relational being to the source from which it came and of which it is the projected self-image. The second, complementary movement of *cognitive intentionality* now occurs when the consciousness of the knower, fecundated or informed by the image brought into it by the incoming intentionality of action, recognizes it explicitly *as a sign* or message from another and reaches out dynamically in the cognitive order, through the mediation of the sign, to *refer it by an intending relation* back to the thing itself from which it came. Thus, it retraces the incoming path of ontological intentionality by its own cognitive movement within consciousness, pointing back to the thing through the referential act of judgment. St. Thomas even sums up the whole activity of the universe in a dazzling synthetic vision under the image of the great circle of intentionality, which proceeds from God to the universe, through the universe's action into man as knower, and from man back again to God its source. God by his creative action first projects his own divine ideas by ontological intentionality into created things, where they become the substantial forms of active natures; then the latter project themselves by self-communicative, self-imaging action into apt conscious receivers such as ourselves, again by ontological intentionality; we, then, recognizing the projected intentional similitudes within our consciousness *as* signs and intentional similitudes, retrace by cognitive intentionality the incoming ontological intentionality of things back to their original sources in the active natures of the beings themselves, and then further trace these by causal inference back to their own original Creative Source, recognizing and paying homage to it as such. Thus, the great circle of intentionality begins from God, passes through the created universe to us, then through us as knowers and lovers back to its Source again. Such is the dynamism of action, as it originates in the order of consciousness, passes into the ontological order, then transforms itself again into the order of consciousness, thus synthesizing being and consciousness into a single unified cosmic process of self-manifestation. To be, once again, is to be self-communicative.[25]

V. Application to Kantian Agnosticism

It seems to me that here lies the only satisfactory response to the challenge of Immanuel Kant that the human mind is incapable of transcending its own consciousness to know things-in-themselves, that it is not informed by the real world from without but projects its own a priori forms to inform the raw material of sensation from within. We notice first that Kant himself admits the necessary role of action in our knowledge. He insists that the human knower is not creative of its objects, as in idealism, but must wait for the world to act upon it. On the other hand, he insists that we cannot reach outside the immanent circle of our own consciousness to know the thing-in-itself, as it is in itself, but only as we structure the incoming raw material of sense by our own innate a priori forms. What this comes down to is that Kant on the one hand admits the necessity of the action of the thing-in-itself on us, but on the other hand denies that such action is in any way *revelatory* of the being from which it proceeds. Action is not in any way a self-communication, an information-bearing message from its source, but merely the delivery of amorphous material with no intelligible structure of its own, waiting to be intelligibly structured by us. The intelligible message is ours, not the thing's itself.

But Kant cannot have it both ways. He cannot hold *both* that the things in themselves truly act upon us, penetrate our consciousness, and at the same time that this action is non-informative, non-communicative of anything in the nature of these agents, in a word, that action is completely non-revelatory of nature. For such a notion of non-communicative action cannot be thought through coherently; it is an emasculated mental construct or abstraction, leaving out an integral part of what it abstracts, as though the conceptual abstraction of action from form and structure allowed an actual separation in reality. Real action of its very nature proceeds from the total being of the agent that is its source, according to its nature, and thus cannot help but be essence-structured action that is a self-manifestation precisely of that nature as actually existing. To be consistent Kant should either deny the role of action entirely, and thus move over to idealism—which he vehemently rejects—or accept the role of action and then admit that it is *to some degree* revelatory of its source.[26]

We might speculate that one consideration that blocks Kant's acceptance of action as an information-bearing medium, revelatory of the thing-in-itself, is an impossibly high ideal, inspired by the rationalists before him, of what such objective knowledge would have to be. He seems to be convinced that if we do not know the thing-in-itself directly and intuitively, without mediation of any kind, precisely as it is in itself apart from, prior to, and independently of any action emerging from it, then we do not know it at all. There is no middle ground, i.e., the knowledge of a thing through the mediation of a self-manifesting action received in another, which action as a natural sign or icon of the agent *points back* to what the agent *must* be in itself in order to originate such an action. Knowledge of a nature as *this kind of actor* is for Kant no knowledge of the nature at all, which presumably would have to be in purely formal static terms, like the objects of geometry. Action is not a *natural sign* of anything. But it is precisely this middle ground of moderate "relational realism" that St. Thomas occupies—the only kind of epistemological realism, it seems to me, that fits our human condition. And after all, what is it that is most significant and crucial for us to know about the real world around us: the static inner essences of things as they abide in themselves alone in splendid isolation, or as they actually relate to us existentially and *make a difference* to us by their self-communicative action? The notion of a real being totally prescinding from all self-communication is probably not intelligible at all. If to be self-communicative belongs to the very inner nature of being in act, as St. Thomas invites us to recognize, then to form a notion of real being that abstracts from this is to leave behind the living core and abstract only an empty formal shell.

Thus Kant, demanding a utopian ideal of objectivity for realistic knowledge, which he rightly saw was unattainable, abandons realism entirely, throwing the baby out with the bath. On the other hand, the more modest action-mediated realism of St. Thomas we have outlined above does indeed provide adequate support for a carefully qualified *correspondence theory* of truth. Such a correspondence, however, can only be a dynamic correspondence or correlation between knowledge and known, not at all a naive picture theory representation purporting to mirror the object statically exactly as it "looks" if seen in itself apart from all action. What action as a natural sign reveals of its agent-source is not a mirror image or picture copy, but the presence in the thing of a set of *dispositional properties* (active potencies, in Thomistic terms) *for action* that characterize this being as distinct from others. It is quite possible for us through the mediation of action to recognize, classify, and draw out the implications of such active potentialities. But it is impossible in principle to draw exact pictures or copies of them. No active potentiality as such can be seen, touched, heard, felt, etc. (which is one reason empiricists must banish them like poison from their universe). Yet the knowledge of the dispositional properties of things is the most important and consequence-laden thing we need to know about them. It is just what Kant rejects as not up to his standards for objective knowing that is what we most want and need to know about things in order to live with them safely and fruitfully.

One of the surprising results of taking over this action-mediated realism as the basis for one's epistemology is to discover how aptly it fits the needs of contemporary physicists as they advance into the increasingly strange world of subatomic quantum physics. Physicists have now, they tell me, had to give up any attempt to describe subatomic matter in the old mechanistic terms of fully determinate measurable states of particles as they are in themselves independently of any interaction with the physical observer and his instruments. They have had to settle for a description of the subatomic world in terms of dispositional properties to react within such and such a limited range of ways to the active intervention of an observer using such and such instruments as intermediaries. Subatomic particles are known as *potential actors* on the stage with so and so, as potential "dance partners" with so and so. Surprising as it may seem to some, I am convinced that St. Thomas himself would be (or should be, if he understood the data and remained consistent with his own principles) quite at home

Action as the Self-Revelation of Being 61

with such a knowledge of the real world as true (humanly accessible) knowledge of the real world *the way it really is*, as the kind of world it really is.

We are now in a position to sum up our whole analysis of Thomistic epistemological realism as follows: action as the self-communication and self-revelation of being is the key to the whole of Thomistic epistemology: all knowledge of the real, for St. Thomas, is an interpretation of action. But accepting action as the medium of knowledge of the real also commits us to accepting the limitations built into its revelatory power both on the part of the finite communicator and the finite receiver: all action is both revealing *and* concealing. The self-revelation of being to the human observer is necessarily a *chiaroscuro* of light and darkness.

VI. ACTION AS THE SELF-FULFILLMENT OF BEING

We have seen above how for St. Thomas all being naturally tends to overflow into action, and how such action is the natural self-communication and self-revelation of being, thus becoming the key to a realistic knowledge of being. Let us return now very briefly to a last crowning piece in St. Thomas's metaphysics of action. It is that action is not only the natural self-communication and self-manifestation of being, but also the final perfection of its *self-realization* or *self-fulfillment*. He is quite explicit on this point, as a few texts will suffice to show:

> The proper operation of each thing is . . . its end [or goal].[27]
> Every substance exists for the sake of its operation.[28]
> Each and every thing shows forth that it exists for the sake of its operation; indeed operation[activity] is the ultimate perfection of each thing.[29]
> All things exist for the sake of their operations.[30]

The reason is that operation or activity is the passing into actuality of the active potencies of a being, and actuality is always better than potency, as the natural self-realization or self-fulfillment of its corresponding potency. Action is thus the final natural fruition or self-expression of any real nature, which *is* a unified center of natural potencies or dispositional properties for action. It follows that the final fruition of any being, its peak of self-realization, is reached only in its *self-communication to others*, its self-sharing with others. The final perfection of the whole of being, therefore, is to form a community of reciprocally self-communicating actors, which, on the level of self-conscious beings, is but another name for love. We leave the reader to meditate on his own on the mind- (and heart-) expanding implications of such a metaphysics of being and action.

Let us pause, before concluding, only to note how radically different is this notion of substance, as abiding center of activity, naturally oriented towards self-fulfillment through activity, from the so-called "classical" notion of substance attacked and rejected by so many, if not most, modern philosophers after Descartes and Locke. For Descartes, substance is defined as a self-enclosed essence which needs nothing, save God, to exist. For Locke, substance seems to be an inert, static, unknowable, underlying something whose sole role is to support accidents, somewhat like a pincushion in which pins are stuck. Bergson, process philosophers like Whitehead, and many others have justifiably criticized this static, self-enclosed notion of substance; but thinking this is *the* or the only classical notion of substance, they have gone on to reject the notion of substance entirely. How far removed both from this notion of substance and its criticisms is the authentic Thomistic conception! With its roots sunk deep in the metaphysics of action, it defines substance as an abiding center of activity, subsisting in itself as an autonomous center, but totally oriented toward self-communication through action as the supreme fulfillment of its being, a fulfillment which necessarily draws it into the vast web of interacting co-existents which make up the community of real beings. It would be a shame if contemporary philosophy, with its sensitivity to process and dynamism, were to let slip away from it unrecognized the rich resources of this highly dynamic notion of substance, just because modern philosophy has lost the secret of it from Descartes on, just because its Heideggerian "forgetfulness of being" has included the forgetfulness of being as active.[31]

Conclusion

To sum up in a nutshell all that I have tried to unfold in the above paper: (1) Action, for St. Thomas, is the *natural overflow of being in act*. (2) This overflow of action becomes the self-communication of being, thus drawing together the multiplicity of real beings into a true *universe*, a community of interacting members turned toward each other to form a dynamic unity of order among themselves through the bonds of action. (3) As the *self-revelation* of being, action lights up beings for each other, making mutual knowledge of each other possible, thus drawing the universe together in an *intentional* unity through knowledge and love, where the whole is recreated consciously in every personal member. To be is to self-communicate; to know is to pick up within oneself the self-communication of being. For "the actuality of each thing," St. Thomas tells us, in an extraordinarily pregnant phrase that integrates into his own system the whole Neoplatonic metaphysics of light—and also quite a bit of Heidegger— "is like an inner light, proper to that being,"[32] which shines forth through action to light up other beings. To know is to be "lit up" within oneself by the self-illumination of active being. And finally, (4) this process of self-communication and self-revelation manifests itself as the *supreme perfection* and *self-realization* of every being, the final *raison d'être*, of being itself.

NOTES

1. Perhaps the finest study developing this whole theme on action and being is the still unsurpassed work of Joseph de Finance, *Etre et agir dans la philosophie de S. Thomas* (2nd ed., Rome: Università Gregoriana, 1960).
2. *Summa contra Gentes*, II, ch. 79. All translations will be my own.
3. *De Potentia*, q. 2, art. 1.
4. *Sum. c. Gentes*, I, ch. 43.
5. *Ibid.*, II, ch. 7.
6. De Finance, *Etre et agir*, ch. VII, sec. 3: "L'acte second."
7. *De Potentia*, q. 2, art. 1.
8. *Sum. c. Gentes*, II, ch. 6.
9. *Ibid.*, III, ch. 69.
10. *Expositio in Libros Sententiarum*, I, dist. 4, q. 1, art 1.
11. *Sum. Theol.*, I, q. 19, art. 2.
12. On this whole question, cf. J. Péghaire, "L'axiome *bonum est diffusivum sui* dans le néoplatonisme et le thomisme," *Revue de l'Université d'Ottawa*, 2 (1932), 5–32; M. J. Nicolas, "Bonum est diffusivum sui," *Revue thomiste*, 55 (1955), 363–76; de Finance, *Etre et agir*, ch. II: "Le dynamisme de l'acte."
13. *De Potentia*, q. 7, art. 2, ad 9.
14. See text at note 11.
15. Cf. *Sum. Theol.*, I, q. 19, art. 2; *Sum. c. Gentes*, I, ch. 19; II, ch. 16, 23, 43, etc., and de Finance, *Etre et agir*, p. 71. This is also a favorite theme of the philosopher-theologian, Karl Rahner. See his "Theology of the Symbol," in *Theological Investigations*, IV (London: Darton, Longmans, Todd, 1966), especially section 1: "The Ontology of Symbolic Reality in General," p. 224: "Our first statement, which we put forward as the basic principle of an ontology of symbolism, is as follows: all beings are by their very nature symbolic, because they necessarily 'express' themselves in order to attain their own nature." And again, p. 228: "Being as such, and hence as one, for the fulfillment of its being and its unity, emerges into a plurality—of which the supreme mode is the Trinity." Even within a finite being this takes place first

within the being itself, in that the finite substance expresses itself in emanating first its faculties, then its accidental operations, from within itself, which then return, so to speak, through their fruition in operation, to fulfill the substance itself, completing the cycle of self-realization through self-expression.

16. *Sum. c. Gentes*, II, ch. 79.

17. *Ibid.*, II, ch. 94.

18. See the profound treatment of this in Josef Pieper, *The Silence of St. Thomas* (New York: Pantheon, 1957), ch. II: "The Negative Element in St. Thomas."

19. Two fine treatments of this much-neglected point can be found in G. B. Arbuckle, "St. Thomas and the Doctrine of Essence," in J. K. Ryan, ed., *Studies in Philosophy and the History of Philosophy* (Washington, D.C.: Catholic Univ. of America Press, 1963), II, 104–36; Ralph Gehring, "The Knowledge of Material Essences according to St. Thomas," *Modern Schoolman*, 33 (1955–56), 153–81.

20. *Sum. Theol.*, I, q. 77, art. 1, ad 7.

21. *Expositio in Libros Sentent.*, III, d. 35, q. 2, art. 2, sol. 1.

22. *Expositio in Symbolum Apostolorum*.

23. Cf. esp. the article of Arbuckle cited in note 19.

24. *Sum. c. Gentes*, II, ch. 74, etc.

25. On the great circle of intentionality, see *Sum. Theol.*, I, q. 105, art. 3; I, q. 56, art. 2; *De Anima*, art. 20; *Expositio in Libros Sentent.*, II, d. 12, q. 1, art. 3, ad 5; and the fine article of André Hayen, "L'intentionalité de l'être et métaphysique de la participation," *Revue néoscolastique* 42 (1939), 385–410, clearer on this point than his book, *L'intentionnel selon S. Thomas* (2nd ed., Paris: Desclée de Brouwer, 1954).

26. See the critique of Kant in my essay, "Interpersonal Dialogue as the Key to Realism," in Robert Roth, ed., *Person and Community* (New York: Fordham Univ. Press, 1975), pp. 141–75.

27. *Sum. c. Gentes*, III, ch. 26.

28. *Ibid.*, I, ch. 45.

29. *Ibid.*, III, ch. 113.

30. *Sum. Theol.*, I, q. 105, art. 5.

31. See chapter 6 of this collection, "To Be Is to Be Substance-in-Relation."

32. *Expositio in Librum de Causis*, cap. 1, lect. 6.

4

The Limitation of Act by Potency in St. Thomas: Aristotelianism or Neoplatonism?

In a challenging paper which Dr. Charles A. Hart presented for discussion at a regional meeting of the American Catholic Philosophical Association, entitled "Footnotes to the Five Thomistic Ways," he prefaced his exposé with the following remarks:

> Perhaps the most important change in the understanding of the fundamental structure of Thomistic metaphysics in recent times is the recognition of the primacy of the decidedly Neoplatonic influence in the formation of that fundamental structure as opposed to the traditional view that Aristotelian influences were the most important. I refer, of course, to the Neoplatonic doctrine of participation.... This view of Thomism with participation as the center doctrine would make that system primarily radically revised Platonism expressed in Aristotelian notions of potency and act with an extension of the meaning of these latter notions which is not found in Aristotle but is original with St. Thomas. In this light we would consider the metaphysics of St. Thomas to be a highly original synthesis with Platonic influence superseding that of Aristotle in view of the central character of the doctrine of participation for St. Thomas.[1]

Although the present writer, in evaluating the results of the above-mentioned movement, would prefer to elevate the influence of Aristotle nearer to equality with that of Neoplatonism, Dr. Hart's statement as a whole is an admirably clear and succinct résumé of an important recent trend among Thomistic scholars in the interpretation of the genuine historical filiation and inner intelligibility of the metaphysical system of St. Thomas. The best-known names of scholars associated with this movement have thus far been in France, Belgium, and Italy.[2] But after this article was almost completed my attention was called to work of an Irish Thomist which has just come out and which pushes even more strongly in the same direction. It is significant to note that his research was carried out independently of the continental writers and almost finished before he became acquainted with their published works, with which he agrees on most substantial points. His study, however, limits itself to the analysis of the role of participation within the system of St. Thomas himself and touches only incidentally on the historical roots of the doctrine.[3]

Thus far there has appeared in English no detailed summary of the historical evidence upon which this new trend of interpretation is founded. The purpose of the present article is to fill this lacuna. Our method will be to select as focal point of investigation what is generally conceded to be the keystone of the Thomistic metaphysical system, the well-known principle of the limitation of act by potency. Our aim will be to discover precisely what elements go to make up this theory, what are their historical roots, and in the light of these sources to discern the full meaning of this extremely rich and pregnant principle.

The peculiar interest of selecting the doctrine of act and potency as center of attention lies in the fact that it constitutes one of the most obvious and apparently exclusively Aristotelian elements in the Thomistic synthesis. If, then, it develops from our investigation that even such a principle cannot be fully understood and justified in terms of purely Aristotelian metaphysics but requires the introduction of the Neoplatonic theory of participation, the reader will have before him at once an interesting test case and a summary of the general position that the doctrine of participation plays a central role in the metaphysics of St. Thomas.

Such a study, too, may add an at least partly original contribution to the investigations already made in this direction. For it is a surprising fact that, although the historical sources of several of the main applications of the act-potency principle, such as the compositions of essence and existence and matter and form, have been the subject of much able scholarly research for many years, there exists nowhere as yet any detailed analysis along similar lines of the act and potency principle itself. This paper, therefore, will attempt to sketch the outline of this fascinating and as yet unwritten history.

THE PROBLEM

Perhaps the best way to open our study is to point out the main problem which forces one into historical investigation in order to find its solution. The problem is this. It is commonly admitted by both defenders and opponents of Thomism that the keystone of the

The Limitation of Act by Potency

Thomistic metaphysical system is the celebrated and much fought over principle, "Actus non limitatur nisi per potentiam," i.e., no act or perfection can be found in a limited degree in any being unless it is conjoined with a really distinct limiting principle whose nature is to be a potency for that act.[4] Now what has up till recently been the traditional and almost unchallenged interpretation of this principle is the following. The doctrine in all its essentials was already contained in Aristotle. St. Thomas took it over directly from him, but in so doing developed it and extended it so as to include in its applications the essence and existence composition which was his own original contribution. The extension introduced by him, however, was only an explicit unfolding of what was already implicit in the original Aristotelian insight, all the implications of which Aristotle himself was not yet able to discern clearly. Thus the principle even in its Thomistic form, according to this interpretation, remains essentially Aristotelian in origin and inspiration.

This position is reaffirmed unhesitatingly by one of the most distinguished and widely recognized leaders of modern Thomism, Father Garrigou-Lagrange, O.P., in one of his latest books translated into English under the title *Reality: A Synthesis of Thomistic Thought*. He writes as follows of the principle of the limitation of act by potency:

> Aristotle already taught this doctrine. In the first two books of his *Physica* he shows with admirable clearness the truth, at least in the sense world, of this principle. Act, he says, is limited and multiplied by potency. Act determines potency, actualizes potency, but is limited by that same potency.... Aristotle studied this principle in the sense world. St. Thomas extends the principle, elevates it, sees its consequences, not only in the sense world, but universally, in all orders of being, spiritual as well as corporeal, even in the infinity of God.[5]

On the other side of the picture, however, are a number of facts calculated to arouse suspicions as to the accuracy of the above interpretation. First, it is noteworthy that, despite the categorical assertion of Father Garrigou-Lagrange in the above quotation, neither here nor anywhere else in his numerous writings on this doctrine does he ever quote or refer to any precise text where Aristotle himself affirms the limiting role of potency with regard to act. What is more disconcerting, a careful examination of the entire first two books of the *Physics*, referred to as teaching the doctrine clearly, reveals that nowhere in them does there occur any mention of the word or the idea of limit in connection with potency. Nor have I been able to find in any other

Thomistic author a precise reference to any text of Aristotle which would bear out the above position.

These puzzling facts led the present writer to undertake a direct examination of all the passages in Aristotle which deal with either act and potency or its applications. The results were entirely negative. Nowhere could we discover any text from which one could conclude, in accord with the accepted norms of objective historical interpretation, that Aristotle himself ever held the doctrine that potency plays the role of limiting principle with respect to act, which if unmixed with potency would be unlimited.

This textual analysis receives strong confirmation from the fact that if we turn to the modern scholarly studies of Aristotle as well as to his ancient commentators we find that not one of them so much as mentions the principle of the limitation of act by potency as forming part of the Aristotelian teaching on act and potency.[6] What is even more decisive, to my mind—and surprising, though I have never seen it reported anywhere—is the fact that throughout the entire extent of St. Thomas's own commentaries on Aristotle, not excepting that on Book IX of the *Metaphysics*, which deals exclusively with act and potency, there is not a single mention of potency as limiting act nor is there any occurrence of the classic formulas expressing the limitation principle which abound in his independent works.[7]

Such a consistent silence in the commentaries of St. Thomas regarding one of his central metaphysical principles, supposed to have been drawn directly from Aristotle, surely cannot be the result of mere accidental omission. The fact that St. Thomas is here in agreement with all the other scholarly commentators on Aristotle, both ancient and modern, in not attributing this doctrine to his master cannot but lead us to suspect that the inspiration of the act-potency limitation principle is perhaps not so obviously and exclusively Aristotelian as many modern Thomists seem to have taken for granted, and that the Angelic Doctor is perhaps a more accurate historian of the source of his own doctrine than certain of his disciples today.

It seems undeniable, therefore, that we are in the presence of a genuine and intriguing historical problem. Just what is the authentic historical parentage of the Thomistic limitation principle and what light does this shed on the inner character of the Thomistic synthesis itself? In the limited space which follows we can do no more than present a schematic outline of this long and interesting history.[8]

The first requisite for unravelling the complex threads which interweave to make up the Thomistic act and potency doctrine is to recognize that it contains two distinct elements. The first is a compo-

The Limitation of Act by Potency

sition of two correlative metaphysical principles called act and potency, first introduced by Aristotle to explain the process of change. The second is the relating of these two principles to each other in terms of a theory of infinity and limitation, which, it must be admitted by all, cannot be found explicitly in Aristotle. The historian of St. Thomas must trace the origins of both these elements and not take it for granted that because the two are inseparably united in Thomistic metaphysics they must also have been so joined from their first appearance in the history of thought.

FINITE AND INFINITE IN THE PRE-SOCRATICS

The first of the two above-mentioned elements to emerge in the history of Western thought was the theory of infinity and limitation.[9] The term infinite (*apeiron*) first appears in Greek philosophy with the Pre-Socratic Anaximander, who identified it with the primal principle of all things:

> 1. The Non-Limited is the original material of existing things; further, the source from which existing things derive their existence is also that to which they return at their destruction, according to necessity....
> 3. This [the Non-Limited] is immortal and indestructible.[10]

The concept at first remains vague and unanalyzed. Its function is to express the hypothesis of an inexhaustible womb of nature from which proceeds the endless sequence of generations of new beings but which itself can be no particular one of the elements and qualities which successively inform it. Anaximander himself seems to manifest a certain awe and reverence before this mysterious, quasi-divine first principle. The Greek mind at this initial stage seems to be hesitating, not yet committing itself as to whether the infinite should be identified with the supremely perfect or with the supremely imperfect.

But the inability of the early Greek thinkers to transcend material categories or to distinguish between philosophy and natural science, their growing preoccupation with astronomical problems, and the very manner in which they framed their fundamental problem, "What is the first principle *out of which* all things are formed?" gradually led them—if not Anaximander, at least his successors—to identify the infinite with the indeterminate, formless substratum or raw material of the universe, the primeval chaos of matter in itself, as yet unperfected by the limit of form. Emerging out of it and opposed to it was the finished or perfect cosmos, formed, limited and intelligible.

The Pythagoreans gave a further impetus to the same orientation of thought by their doctrine that all things are composed of two sets of opposing principles: a principle of limit or perfection, identified with the odd numbers, the good, the male, light, etc., and a principle of illimitation or imperfection, identified with the even numbers, the evil, the female, darkness, etc. The finished cosmos is formed by a process in which the primal Monad, or One, the principle of limit, progressively extends its ordering and limiting activity outward from the center on the formless infinity of the surrounding nebula or space.

The same conception reappears as fundamental also in the thought of the first metaphysician, Parmenides. The great sphere of the totality of Being, he tells us, must be limited all around precisely because it is complete and perfect; for if it were unlimited it would necessarily be unfinished and imperfect.[11] A similar association of limit with perfection and of infinity with imperfection could be traced through most of the other Pre-Socratics, as, for example, in the Heraclitean notion of the fundamental principle, fire, which is kindled and extinguished according to measure and limit, or in the infinite space of the Atomists, identified with non-being and opposed to the being of the solid, limited atoms.[12]

Thus, after a first moment of hesitation, the Greek mind set firmly in a conception of the finite and the infinite which was to dominate the entire current of classical thought up to Neoplatonism in the second century A.D. According to this conception the infinite is identified with the formless, the indeterminate, the unintelligible—in a word, with matter and multiplicity, the principles of imperfection—whereas the finite or limited is identified with the fully formed, the determinate, and therefore the intelligible—in a word, with number, form, and idea, the principles of perfection. It is evident that within such a framework of thought the notion of a principle of perfection as of itself unlimited and receiving limitation from a principle of imperfection would be quite meaningless. The relations are just the reverse.

PLATO

Plato, following closely in the footsteps of the Pythagoreans, takes up the same basic doctrine and makes it one of the central pieces in his metaphysical blueprint of the universe. He calls it:

> the parent of all the discoveries in the arts . . . a gift of heaven, which, as I conceive, the gods tossed among men by the hands of a new Prometheus, and therewith a blaze of light; and the ancients, who were our betters and nearer the gods than we, handed down

The Limitation of Act by Potency

the tradition, that all things of which we say "they are" draw their existence from the one and the many, and have the finite and infinite implanted in them.[13]

According to the Platonic metaphysics, all realities below the supreme idea of the Good (or the One) are a "mixture" of two opposing principles, the limit and the unlimited, which reappear with analogical similarity on all the levels of reality from the world of ideas to the half-real world of sensible things. The principle of limitation is consistently identified with number, form, idea, and being, as the source of intelligibility and perfection. The principle of illimitation, on the other hand, is identified with the formlessness and indeterminacy of pure matter and multiplicity as such, and therefore with "otherness" or non-being, as the source of unintelligibility and imperfection. Thus at all levels it is the principle of limit or measure which, imposed on the wilderness and chaos of the infinite, i.e., on the indeterminate substratum of matter, multiplicity, and non-being, delimits, determines, and defines it, thus conferring upon it form, intelligibility, and being.[14]

We see here emerging in sharp relief the irresistible tendency of the classical Greek mind (and one of its great weaknesses)—reflected in its art and in a thousand different cultural manifestations—to identify perfection with clear-cut limited form, to identify intelligibility as such with the human mode of intelligibility, i.e., with definition by distinct, clearly delimited concepts. In such a perspective, where finite essence is taken as the type of perfect being, it is clear that the relations between being and non-being will be quite different from those between *esse* and essence in the Thomistic outlook. In the Platonic framework it is participation in the idea of being which makes a particular idea to be precisely *what* it is, i.e., this particular well-defined essence. It is participation in non-being or otherness which, by negating the indeterminate or infinite multitude of all other ideas, preserves this particular essence distinct from all the others and prevents it from melting into them in a blur of unintelligible confusion. Thus, disconcerting as it may appear to a Thomistically trained mind, and difficult to think through for anyone, Plato clearly situates the limit on the side of being and infinity on the side of non-being: "In every idea there is a definite amount of being and an infinity of non-being."[15]

What has happened seems to be this. Although Plato had the genius to discover the doctrine of participation in general and the necessity of some principle of negation or imperfection in reality, his equally deep-rooted conception of perfection as distinct form, and hence of finite and infinite as correlatives of perfect and imperfect, prevented him from carrying through his analysis of participation to its more natural consequence, i.e., to expression in terms of a limitation of the higher by the lower. It is essential to remember this if we wish to avoid the overzealous attempts of certain modern Thomists to find in Plato's doctrine of being an anticipation, defective principally in terminology, of the Thomistic limitation of *esse* by essence.[16] The spirit of the two doctrines is profoundly different, and is rooted in far more than mere terminology.

But, it may be objected, what of the supreme idea of the Good or the One in Plato? Is it not above being and essence, as he says in the *Republic*,[17] and hence infinite? It is certainly not a mixture of limit and infinity, like the other ideas, since it is absolutely one and simple. But the fact is that Plato never calls it infinite. Indeed, in view of his habitual notion of the infinite as correlated with indeterminacy and imperfection this would surely have seemed to him a kind of blasphemy. On the other hand, neither does he call it explicitly finite. Perhaps the most accurate answer is to say that he was groping for a new category to express the absolute and the transcendent and that the inadequacy of his metaphysical terminology, chiefly his concept of infinity, did not allow him to formulate satisfactorily what he dimly intuited. But if we must choose, it seems more probable, arguing from the rest of his doctrine on the correlation of idea with number as principle of limit and intelligiblity, to conclude that the supreme One was somehow linked in his mind with the notion of supreme Measure or Limit as such, source of all other limitation and hence of intelligibility and perfection.[18]

We are still far, however, from any positive conception of infinity as linked with perfection as such.

Aristotle

We come now to Aristotle. In the light of the deeply-rooted Greek tradition before him, it should come as no surprise to discover that his own theory of infinity remains dominated by the same inspiration. In fact, he is obviously proud of the fact that he is the first to follow the latter out to its rigorous logical conclusions in what is undoubtedly the most complete analysis of the notion of infinity in ancient thought.[19] The result of this analysis is that the essential nature of the infinite is to be that which is of itself the incomplete, the indefinite, or the indeterminate, and hence the imperfect. It is an attribute of time, as without end, of the series of numbers, as capable of in-

The Limitation of Act by Potency

definite augmentation, and of matter, as being formless and indeterminate in itself, considered apart from form. Its proper definition is that which always has some part of itself outside of itself.

No complete substance, therefore, can exist as actually infinite.[20] The terms are mutually exclusive. For the perfect, which is but a synonym for the complete or finished, is precisely that which has an end, and the end, he says, is a limit.[21] The very words in Greek derive from the same root (*telos*: end, and *teleios*: complete or perfect) and betray the close affinity between the two concepts. This allows Aristotle to make a rich play on words in a sentence which sums up admirably the classical Greek notion of infinity: "Nature flees from the infinite, for the infinite is unending or imperfect, and nature ever seeks an end."[22]

Let us apply this theory now to the doctrine of act and potency. In the light of what has gone before we should expect, a priori, if Aristotle is to be consistent with himself and with the almost unanimous Greek tradition before him, to find the principle of limit identified with perfection or act and illimitation with imperfection or potency. We are not disappointed. In what is the type par excellence of act and potency for Aristotle, namely, the composition of form and matter, he tells us explicitly that the role of form or act is to impose a limit on the formless infinity of matter in itself and thus confer upon it determination and intelligibility:

> It [the infinite] is unknowable *qua* infinite; for the matter has no form. (Hence it is plain that the infinite stands in the relation of part rather than of whole . . .). . . . But it is absurd and impossible to suppose that the unknowable and indeterminate should contain and determine. . . . For the matter and the infinite are contained inside what contains them, while it is the form which contains.[23]

We recognize here immediately the classic Platonic notion of form conceived as principle of limit and hence of intelligibility.

St. Thomas takes over intact this perspective into his own system. But he adds to it another dimension, so to speak, in which the relations are reversed and matter also appears as limiting form.[24] This new dimension, however, can have meaning only within the framework of some kind of participation doctrine, where form itself would be conceived either *modo Platonico*, as subsisting separately in its own right as a perfect plenitude or, for St. Thomas, a pre-existent idea in the mind of a Creator.

There is no room for such a perspective in the universe of Aristotle. He has closed the door to it by his explicit rejection of all ontological participation or transcendence of material forms.[25] It is quite true that he does teach explicitly that forms of themselves are unique and can be multiplied only by reception in matter.[26] But nowhere does he say or imply that such multiplication involves a process of limitation by matter of a form which by itself could be called infinite. On the contrary, he insists against Plato that every specific form is received whole, entire, and equally in every individual of the species.[27]

The guiding image here is clearly not that of matter or potency as a container which contracts the plenitude of form or act; it is rather that of form as a stamp or die, fully determined in itself, which is stamped successively on various portions of an amorphous raw material such as wax or clay. Such a multiplication can appear rather as an expansion than as a limitation of the form. The two perspectives are quite different, though, as St. Thomas has shown, by no means mutually exclusive. It is poor history, therefore, to argue from St. Thomas's much richer analysis of multiplication of form in terms of participation and limitation to the conclusion that Aristotle also must have understood his own theory of multiplication in the same way. The fact is that there is no trace of such an interpretation in the commentaries on Aristotle until the advent of Neoplatonism.

What, then, is the genuine meaning and purpose of the act and potency composition in Aristotle? There is only one: as function of the problem of change. Whatever is capable of change of any kind—and only that—must have within it in addition to its present act a principle of potency, or capacity to receive a further act. It is this potency which enables a being to be inserted in the endless cosmic cycle of change; it is therefore essentially forward-looking and involves as one of its constituent notes the property of remaining always "in potency," that is, capable of becoming what it is not as yet. Act, on the other hand, is always identified with the fully complete, the actually present. Pure act, therefore, is simply a correlative of the immutable, i.e., of pure actualized form, complete in all that is proper to it and incorruptible. It is this immutability, self-sufficiency, and incorruptibility which for Aristotle is the primary characteristic of the "divine" and the perfect.[28]

In the notion of act so conceived there is no necessary implication of infinity, at least in the substantial order.[29] In fact, Aristotle has no difficulty in admitting some fifty-five of his prime movers, each one pure act or pure form but in virtue of its form distinct from all the others.[30] Substantial infinity would simply have no meaning in this Aristotelian universe; there is no ultimate common perfection deeper than form, such as existence for St. Thomas, in which the hierarchy of

The Limitation of Act by Potency

forms could participate according to different degrees or limits. Each form is an ultimate and an absolute in its own right. Correspondingly potency can have no connotation of limiting a plenitude which would be found elsewhere in a higher degree.[31]

The accuracy of the above interpretation of Aristotelian act and potency can be strikingly verified by examining a test case where the conditions for Thomistic potency are fulfilled but not the Aristotelian. If it is true that potency for Aristotle signifies always and only the capacity of a being for future change in a given order, it should follow that where there is a being with no possibility of change in a particular order there can be no potency in it in that order, even though the being in question is clearly what a Thomist would call limited in perfection in the static hierarchy of essences. Such a test case is found made to order in the Aristotelian heavenly bodies. According to his cosmology these were subject to change only in the accidental order of local motion, but were immutable and incorruptible in their essences. Aristotle does not hesitate to draw the rigorous consequence, disconcerting and embarrassing though it may be to a Thomist. It follows, he says, that there is no potency in them in the substantial or essential order but only an accidental potency to local motion, even though their essences are evidently of the corporeal order and less perfect than the immaterial intelligences which move them.[32]

It seems undeniable, therefore, that the notion of a potency which would be a purely static receiving and limiting principle, excluding all possibility of change in the same order—such as is the essence of pure spirits in the Thomistic system—would have no place whatever in the Aristotelian plan of the universe and would probably have appeared quite unintelligible to him, if not an open contradiction in terms: a non-potential potency! A moment's analysis, in fact, of such a principle will reveal that it would be quite meaningless and superfluous unless it played the role of limiting subject in a participation framework; and with this, of course, Aristotle would have nothing to do.

PLOTINUS AND NEOPLATONISM

The search for such a framework forces us now to leap five centuries down to Plotinus and Neoplatonism. It was in this profoundly different intellectual and spiritual atmosphere that there appeared for the first time in Western thought a doctrine of participation linked with a wholly new concept of infinite and finite, correlated now with the perfect and the imperfect respectively in a complete reversal of the age-old classical Greek tradition.[33]

The emergence of the new notion of infinity seems to have been provoked not by any internal progress of philosophical speculation by itself but by the impact of the mystery religions of the East, now infiltrating the Roman Empire on all sides. The latter brought with them a new notion of the divinity, a divinity of power and mystery, master of the limitless spaces of the heavens discovered by the new Syrian astronomy, above all rational human concepts, but with whom the believer could enter into salvific personal union by mystical or other non-rational means.[34] The center of the new thought was Alexandria, melting pot of east and west. The influence of Judaism, too, was not inconsiderable, chiefly through Philo, who appears to have been the first recorded thinker in the west to apply to God a synonym for infinite: uncircumscribed (*aperigraphos*).[35]

Contrary to what we might expect, Christianity itself seems to have had little traceable influence on the development of the concept. Christian thinkers followed rather than led the movement. The first Christian texts calling God infinite do not appear till the fourth century, and precisely in those circles which are known to have been influenced by Neoplatonism.[36] In fact, the first school of Christian philosophers, that of Clement and Origen in Alexandria just prior to Plotinus, well into the third century, were still following the old Platonic notion of infinity and holding that God's will and power should not be called infinite because they would then be unintelligible even to Himself.[37]

Plotinus deliberately set out to meet the challenge of his day: to integrate the essence of the new religious intuitions from the east with the old rational Platonic metaphysics, and thus to stem the invading tide of irrational superstition threatening to inundate the Roman Empire through the Oriental cults and sweep away the values of the old Hellenic civilization. The result was a powerful and original synthesis which was to exert an immense influence on Western thought ever since. It was in this context that appeared the new emanationist metaphysics of infinity and limitation correlated with participation.[38]

In this view of the universe, the old Platonic order of limited, intelligible essences, composed of form as perfecting limit imposed on the infinity of sensible or "intelligible" matter, is still preserved. But their relation to the supreme One by emanation introduces a new dimension or function of the limiting principle, that of limiting what is above it as well as what is below it. In this perspective all the intelligible essences below the One now appear as limited and hence imperfect participations of this supremely perfect and absolutely simple first principle, which somehow embraces within itself the perfection of all the

The Limitation of Act by Potency

lower determinate essences but is none of them in particular. The One, therefore, must be above all particular intelligible determination or essence, and can be described only as a supreme indetermination or infinity, not of defect but of excess. Forced to invent a new terminology, Plotinus for the first time in western thought uses the old Greek word for the infinite, *apeiron*, to express this radically new content of indetermination as identified with the plenitude of perfection of an unparticipated source compared to the limited participations below it.[39]

Many of the Plotinian texts on the infinity of the One carry an astonishingly familiar ring to Thomistic ears. Even the central intuition of the Thomistic limitation principle, namely, that a perfection cannot be limited except by something else, is formulated explicitly with all the clarity and vigor desirable. For example:

> It [the One] is not limited: by what indeed would it be limited? It possesses infinity because it is not multiple and because there is nothing to limit it. . . . It has therefore no limit either in itself or in something else; otherwise it would be at least double. (V, 5, 10–11)
> We must examine whence come these ideas and their beauty. Their source cannot be one among them. . . . It must be above all powers and all forms. The first principle is that which is without form, not that it is lacking form, but that all intelligible forms come from it. That which is produced by that very fact becomes a particular thing and possesses a form proper to it. But who could produce the unproduced? . . . It is infinite. . . . How could anything else measure it? (VI, 7, 32)
> It would be ridiculous to try to circumscribe such an immensity as belongs to the One. It is necessary, therefore, that the One be without form. And being without form, it is not essence; for an essence must be an individual, hence a determined being. (V, 5, 6)
> All [the ideas] come from the same principle . . . and the same gift imparted to a multitude of beings becomes different in each one that receives it. (VI, 7, 18)

There are, of course, many profound differences between the Plotinian and the Thomistic metaphysics of being. One of the most serious is that Plotinus, still following Plato on this point, identifies being with limited essence and hence is forced to place the One above being and intelligibility and to identify the ultimate perfection of the universe as unity rather than existence.[40] But on the basic problem of the metaphysical significance of finitude and its relation to perfection we cannot but agree with Joseph de Finance when he says:

In asking the question, What could limit the One?, Plotinus is implicitly affirming that limitation needs to be justified, and that it can only be so by a degradation of being. The problem of the finite is posed and virtually resolved in the same way as in St. Thomas.[41]

This basic Plotinian intuition of participation in terms of an infinite source and a limiting participating subject is organized into a rigid systematization by Proclus, the "Scholastic" of Neoplatonism, in his famous textbook of Neoplatonic participation metaphysics, entitled *The Elements of Theology*.[42] This handy compilation in thesis form exercised a powerful influence on subsequent medieval thought. It reached the thirteenth-century Scholastics chiefly through the work of the Pseudo-Dionysius, a thinly veiled Christian adaptation of it, and the celebrated *Liber de Causis*, accepted through most of the thirteenth century as a bona fide work of Aristotle until St. Thomas himself discovered from the first Latin translation of Proclus in 1268 by his friend William of Moerbeke that the *Liber de Causis* was only a compilation from *The Elements of Theology*.[43]

Despite the often corrupt and obscure text available to the thirteenth century, this little book presents clearly enough the central participation framework of Neoplatonism in terms of infinite source and limited receiving subject:

> The first Goodness pours down goodness over all things by a single influx. But each thing receives of this influx according to the measure of its own power and its own being. The goodness and gifts of the first cause are diversified by virtue of the recipient . . . some receive more, others less.
>
> The power of the first caused being is infinite only with respect to what is below it, not to what is above it; for it is not the pure power [i.e., absolutely unparticipated] of the first cause, which is limited neither from below nor from above.[44]

St. Thomas appeals explicitly to the second text above as authority for his own doctrine of the relative infinity of pure spirits, each in its own species.[45]

The implicit supposition, too, behind the whole doctrine of Boethius's influential little treatise on participation, the so-called *De Hebdomadibus*, is nothing else but the same fundamental Neoplatonic participation-limitation theory, which can be summed up in this widely repeated formula: Every pure (i.e., unparticipated) form is infinite. Therefore every finite creature must be a composite of form and receiving, limiting subject.[46] This basic principle, interpreted strictly,

The Limitation of Act by Potency 79

results in the Franciscan doctrine of the universal composition of form and matter in all creatures. The identical principle is taken over by St. Thomas but transposed in a highly original stroke of genius, so that the ultimate perfection now becomes the "quasi-form" of *esse*, the act of existence, instead of form-essence, and the latter becomes itself the limiting, participating principle.

The point we wish to make here is that the general structure of the limitation principle (1) is by no means original with St. Thomas; (2) is clearly Neoplatonic in origin and is so recognized by St. Thomas himself; (3) was a widely accepted commonplace both before St. Thomas and by his contemporaries. The latter point is strikingly illustrated by a text from St. Bonaventure which sounds as though it were a quotation from Thomas himself:

> Every creature has finite and limited being . . . but wherever there is limited being, there is something which contracts and something which is contracted, and in every such there is composition and difference: therefore every creature is composite: therefore none is simple.[47]

St. Thomas

In the light of the foregoing history, the elements involved in the Thomistic act-potency limitation principle now fall quickly into place. On the one hand was the central piece of Aristotelian metaphysics, the doctrine of act and potency. Its weakness was that it was geared exclusively thus far to the context of a change process. Its strength was that it was admirably adapted to express a structure of metaphysical composition within a being, while at the same time safeguarding the intrinsic unity of the composite resulting from the union of two incomplete, correlative principles. On the other hand was the central piece of the Neoplatonic metaphysical tradition, the participation-limitation framework. Its strength lay in its ability to express satisfactorily the fundamental genetic and hierarchic structure of the universe, that is, the relation of creatures to a first Source conceived at once as exemplary, efficient, and final cause of all. Its weakness lay in the fact that it habitually left vague, unexplained, and dangerously ambiguous the unity of the composite resulting from the superposition of participated on participant, whether of form on matter or of higher form on lower form.

The achievement of St. Thomas was to recognize that the strength of each doctrine remedied precisely the weakness of the other and to fuse them into a single highly original synthesis, condensed in the apparently simple yet extremely rich and complex formula: Act is not limited except by reception in a distinct potency.[48] In order to effect this synthesis, however, he had to subject both doctrines to profound modifications. First, he had to empty the participation-limitation structure of its original Neoplatonic content, that is, of the vast hierarchic procession of reified universal concepts—the Porphyrian tree transplanted into reality—so characteristic of the whole Platonic tradition (at least in its Aristotelian interpretation), dominated by the primacy of form and the ultra-realism of ideas. In its place he substituted as the fundamental ontological perfection of the universe the supra-formal act of existence, participated first directly by essential form, as limited potency in pure spirits, then dispersed, so to speak, in material beings, by being communicated through specific forms to their multiple participations in matter.

Secondly, he had to disengage the Aristotelian act and potency theory from its hitherto exclusive attachment to a change context, and to add to the already existing dynamic "horizontal" function of potency a new dimension, the static "vertical" function of receiving subject limiting a higher plenitude in a participation framework. Furthermore—and this was the most violent wrench to the old Aristotelian concept—this new second function could now be found in some cases entirely separated from and even exclusive of the first, as in the case of potency as essence of the essentially incorruptible, immutable pure spirits.

What to my mind is most revealing, and what convinces me that St. Thomas was quite conscious of the sources of his doctrine and what he was doing with them, is the fact that the study of his works in chronological order enables us to observe the synthesis actually being put together, block by block. For the suprising fact—which I have never seen mentioned anywhere before—is that throughout the early works of St. Thomas, up to and exclusive of the *Contra Gentiles*, the limitation principle is never found expressed in terms of act and potency but exclusively in its traditional Neoplatonic form or a close paraphrase, e.g., "Every abstract or separated form is infinite."[49] The standard practice is then to deduce the real distinction of essence and existence from this principle in terms of participant and participated. Only at this last stage does he say that wherever there is a relation of received and recipient there must be a composition of act and potency. Thus act and potency take on the aspect of limitation only as a kind of *post factum* consequence, so to speak, not as a first principle.[50] As a sample, let us quote one text that is a gem for clarity and preci-

The Limitation of Act by Potency

sion in illustrating the two-step development of the synthesis: first participation, then act and potency:

> Every created substance is composed of potency and act. For it is manifest that only God is his own act of existence, as though essentially existing, insofar, that is, as his act of existence (*suum esse*) is his substance. And this can be said of no other being: subsistent existence can be only one. It is therefore necessary that any other thing be a being by participation, such that in it the substance participating existence is other than the existence itself that is participated. But every participant is related to what it participates as potency to act. So, therefore, every created substance is composed of potency and act, that is, of that which is and its act of existence, as Boethius says in his *De Hebdomadibus*.[51]

It is only from the *Summa contra Gentes* on that he appears to realize the possibility of fusing both the limitation principle and act and potency into a single synthetic principle. Now for the first time we find appearing the well-known formulas quoted so often in Thomistic textbooks, such as, "No act is found limited except by potency," "An act existing in no subject is limited by nothing", etc.[52] Here too for the first time we find explicitly stated the reason for the transposition of the compositions resulting from participation into act and potency: because only in terms of act and potency can the intrinsic unity of any composite being be maintained. Over and over again St. Thomas now tells us: from two entities in act it is impossible to make an *unum per se* (an intrinsic unity). Wherever there is an intrinsic unity, one component must function as act, the other as potency.[53]

Conclusion

The final result of the fusion of the two theories into a single coherent synthesis can thus properly be called neither Aristotelianism nor Neoplatonism. It is something decisively new, which can only be styled "Thomism." It may appear, indeed, to modern Thomists that the union of the limitation principle with Aristotelian act and potency is an obvious, almost self-evident step. The fact is, however, that for some fifteen centuries the two doctrines flowed along side by side in separate streams—frequently in the same thinker, since most of the Neoplatonists from Plotinus on also used Aristotelian act and potency to explain change in the lower world of matter—without its ever occurring to anyone, it seems, to join one to the other. We believe it adds considerably to our appreciation, not only of the full extent of the genius of Thomas but of the full meaning and rich complexity of the act and potency principle, to realize that he was the first thinker in Western philosophy to be able to effectuate a successful synthesis of the two basic insights of the Aristotelian and Neoplatonic traditions and thus to fuse into one the best elements of the two main streams of western philosophical thought.[54]

If the foregoing analysis is correct, we find ourselves forced to the conclusion that it is no longer possible without the most serious qualifications to evaluate the philosophical contribution of St. Thomas—as some of the most distinguished modern historians of Thomism have done—as a decisive option for Aristotle against Platonism.[55] On the contrary, we feel with an increasing number of contemporary Thomists that, at least in metaphysics, St. Thomas has taken Plato—or, more accurately, Plato transformed by Plotinus—into so intimate a partnership with Aristotle that the metaphysical system of the Angelic Doctor can legitimately be described, in the words of a recent historian of participation in St. Thomas, either as an Aristotelianism specified by Neoplatonism, or as a Neoplatonism specified by Aristotelianism. The Italian Thomist, Fabro, opts for the latter. One could have justification for doing so, but I now think it more accurate, in view of St. Thomas's own intentions, to opt for the former.[56]

NOTES

1. This paper was first delivered at the Dec. 1, 1950, meeting of the local chapter of the American Catholic Philosophical Association, held at Georgetown University, and its contents summarized by Charles Hart, "Twenty-five Years of Thomism," *New Scholasticism*, 25 (1951), 3–45.

2. To mention only a few of the best known: L.-B. Geiger, O.P., *La participation dans la philosophie de S. Thomas d'Aquin* (Paris, 1942); Joseph de Finance, S.J., *Etre et agir dans la philosophie de Saint Thomas* (Paris, 1945); Louis de Raeymaeker, *Philosophie de l'être* (2nd ed., Louvain, 1947); André Hayen, S.J., *L'Intentionnel dans la philosophie de S. Thomas* (Brussels, 1942); Cornelio Fabro, *La nozione metafisica di partecipazione secondo S. Tomasso d'Aquino* (2nd ed., Turin, 1950).

3. Arthur Little, S.J., *The Platonic Heritage of Thomism* (Dublin, 1949).

4. E.g., I. Gredt, O.S.B., "Doctrina thomistica de actu et potentia contra recentes impugnationes vindicatur," *Acta Pontificiae Academiae Romanae S. Thomae Aquinatis*, 1 (1934), 35: "Haec propositio constituit fundamentum philosophiae aristotelico-thomisticae." This is also freely admitted by one of the most searching Suarezian critics of the Thomistic system, L. Fuetscher, *Akt und Potenz* (Innsbruck, 1933), 68.

5. R. Garrigou-Lagrange, *Reality: A Synthesis of Thomistic Thought* (St. Louis: Herder, 1950), pp. 43–44. Similar affirmations can be found also

in Paulo Dezza, S.J., *Metaphysica Generalis* (Rome, 1945), p. 124; and in Carlo Giacon, *Atto e potenza* (Brescia, 1947), p. 46.

6. This is true even of the few direct and detailed studies of the Aristotelian doctrine done by Thomists, e.g., A. Baudin, "L'Acte et la puissance dans Aristote," *Revue thomiste*, 7 (1899), 39–62, 153–72, 274–96, 584–608.

7. There is one text linking essence and existence with act and potency in terms of a participation argument: *In VII Phys.*, c. 10, lect. 21, nn. 12–13 (ed. Leonina). But here St. Thomas is meeting a difficulty brought up by Averroës much later and develops his answer far beyond the text of Aristotle; he is also careful not to attribute his own answer directly to Aristotle.

8. A more detailed articulation of the whole participation doctrine in St. Thomas, of which the limitation of act by potency is an integral part, can be found in my article, "The Meaning of Participation in St. Thomas," reprinted as chapter 5 of the present collection.

9. Strange to say, there is but scanty detailed and reliable work on the history of these notions. The following are the most useful, though not always well documented and reliable: J. Cohn, *Geschichte des Unendlichkeitsproblem im abendländischen Denken bis Kant* (Leipzig, 1896); R. Mondolfo, *L'infinito nel pensiero dei Greci* (Florence, 1934); H. Guyot, *L'Infinité divine depuis Philon le Juif jusqu'à Plotin*, avec une introduction sur le même sujet dans la philosophie grecque avant Philon (Paris, 1906); C. Huit, "Un chapitre de l'histoire de la métaphysique," *Revue de philosophie*, 4 (1904), 738–57; 5 (1905), 44–66; P. Descoqs, *Praelectiones Theodiceae Naturalis* (Paris, 1935), II, 600–22: "Notes sur l'histoire des notions d'infini et de parfait"; R. Eisler, *Wörterbuch der philosophischen Begriffen* (4 Aufl., Berlin, 1930), III, 306–20.

Since the original publication of this article the long-awaited scholarly research of Leo Sweeney, S.J., has happily become available: *Infinity in the Presocratics* (The Hague: Nijhoff, 1972); and *Divine Infinity in Greek and Medieval Thought* (New York: Peter Lang, 1992). We still disagree, however, as to whether Plotinus held an infinity in the intrinsic being of the One (which I defend) or only an infinity of power to produce an endless number of effects across infinite time, which Aristotle also held. See my article, "Infinity in Plotinus," cited in note 39.

10. Fragments 1–3 in H. Diels, *Fragmente der Vorsokratiker* (5 Aufl., ed. W. Kranz, Berlin, 1934), I, 89; K. Freeman, *Ancilla to the Pre-Socratics* (Cambridge, Mass., 1948), p. 19.

11. Frag. 8 (Diels), trans. J. Burnet, *Early Greek Philosophy* (4th ed., London, 1930), p. 176: ". . . hard necessity keeps it within the bonds of the limit that holds it fast on every side. Wherefore it is not permitted to *what is* to be infinite; for it is in need of nothing; while if it were infinite it would stand in need of everything."

12. For the doctrine on the finite and the infinite in the Pre-Socratics, see the works mentioned in note 10, the standard general studies of the Pre-Socratics, such as J. Burnet, *Early Greek Philosophy*, and for one of the most succinct and objective summaries of all the ancient testimony available, Kathleen Freeman, *The Pre-Socratic Philosophers: A Companion to Diels, Fragmente*

der Vorsokratiker (2nd ed., Oxford, 1949). See also the valuable work of Leo Sweeney mentioned in note 9.

13. *Philebus*, 16c (trans. B. Jowett, *Dialogues of Plato*, 3rd ed., London, 1892).

14. We have summarized Plato's own synthesis of the theory of ideas and the theory of finite and infinite. The sources for the former doctrine are well known and can be found in any standard study in the broad lines which interest us here. The main sources for the latter, which are not so well known, are the following: *Philebus*, 16–18; 23c–30; 61–67; *Statesman*, 283b–285a; *Laws*, IV, 716c. The integration of the two theories into a synthesis is already indicated clearly in the *Sophist*, 256e, but was not worked out fully, it seems, until the later oral teaching as reported by Aristotle, e.g., in *Metaph.*, I, ch. 6 and 9; XIII, ch. 4, 5, 8. One of the most illuminating presentations of this synthesis can be found in L. Robin, *Platon* (Paris, 1934), ch. IV.

15. *Sophist*, 256e. Cf. A. Dies, *La définition de l'être et la nature des idées dans le Sophiste de Platon* (2nd ed., Paris, 1932), p. 127, and the commentary of F. Cornforth, *Plato's Theory of Knowledge* (London, 1935).

16. For example, C. Giacon, *Il divenire in Aristotele* (Padua, 1947), 42–45; P. Dezza, note 5 above; P. Geny, "Le problème métaphysique de la limitation de l'acte," *Revue de philosophie*, 19 (1919), 138.

17. *Republic*, VI, 509b.

18. See the penetrating remarks along this line by J. de Finance, *Etre et agir*, p. 48. Robin, however, tries to argue that the Good must be above the Limit (*Platon*, pp. 156, 169).

19. Principally in *Physics*, III, ch. 4–8; *Metaph.*, XI, ch. 10.

20. *Physics*, III, ch. 5; *Metaph.*, XI, ch. 10.

21. *Physics*, III, ch. 6, 207 a 14.

22. *De Generatione Animalium*, I, ch. 1, 715 b 14 (*Basic Works of Aristotle*, ed. R. McKeon, New York, 1941, p. 666).

23. *Physics*, III ch. 6, 207 a 30–37 (*Basic Works*, p. 267).

24. Cf. *Sum. Theol.*, I, q. 7, aa. 1–2; III, q. 10, a. 3 ad 1; *Quodlibet*. III, q. 2, a. 3: "Just as matter without form has the note of infinity, so too form without matter."

25. *Metaph.*, I, ch. 6 and 9.

26. *Metaph.*, XII, ch. 8, 1074 a 33; VII, ch. 8, 1034 a 5–8.

27. *Categories*, ch. 5, 3 b–4 a.

28. The doctrine of act and potency is developed principally in *Physics*, I–II, esp. I, ch. 6–9; *De Generatione et Corruptione*, esp. I, ch. 3–4; *Metaph.*, IX. The best collection of texts is in E. Zeller, *Die Philosophie der Griechen* (4 Aufl., Leipzig, 1921), II–2, Kap. 6–7. Cf. also, in addition to the works mentioned in note 6, W. Ross, *Aristotle* (2nd ed., London, 1930); O. Hamelin, *Le système d'Aristote* (Paris, 1920); A. Rivaud, *Le problème du devenir et la notion de la matière dans la philosophie grecque depuis les origines jusqu'à Théophraste* (Paris, 1906); A. Mansion, *Introduction à la physique aristotélicienne* (2nd ed., Louvain, 1945); and the penetrating study of J. LeBlond, *Logique et méthode chez Aristote* (Paris, 1939), 306–431.

The Limitation of Act by Potency 85

29. Aristotle does argue that the Prime Mover must have an infinite power of moving, in *Metaph.*, XII, ch. 7, 1073 a 5, and in detail in *Physics*, VIII, ch. 10. Though an important affirmation for the history of thought and later developments, in Aristotle himself it is geared to a purely physical problem, deduced by purely physical and dubiously valid arguments (a limited force cannot move through infinite time) and has no echoes in the rest of his system. In fact, since the Prime Mover moves only as final cause, without consciousness of efficient activity on its part, it is hard to see what literal positive meaning the term "power" could have here.

30. Cf. P. Merlan, "Aristotle's Unmoved Movers," *Traditio*, 4 (1936), 1–30.

31. After this article was completed my attention was called to the important work published by Joseph Owens, *The Doctrine of Being in the Aristotelian Metaphysics* (Toronto: Pontifical Institute of Mediaeval Studies, 1951), one of the first really scholarly studies of Aristotle by a Thomist, which confirms my own interpretation of Aristotle's conception of being and perfection as radically "finitist." See p. 305, n. 19, and p. 297: "Perfection is equated with finitude and coincides with form. This philosophy of act does not lead in the direction of the omnipotent Christian God."

32. *Metaph.*, IX, ch. 8, 1050 b 6–34; VIII, ch. 5, 1044 b 27. See St. Thomas's solution of the difficulty by his own doctrine of the distinction between essence and existence, *In VIII Phys.*, c. 10, lect. 21, nn. 12–13.

33. For the history of this remarkable revolution in thought, see the works cited in note 9. As Léon Brunschvicq aptly sums it up: "Enfin le cours de l'histoire se transforme lorsque, dès les premiers siècles du Christianisme, l'infini cesse décidément d'être l'imparfait et l'inachevé, principe de désordre et de mal qu'il faut dompter et limiter pour le soumettre à la loi de la mesure et de l'harmonie. Le Divin change de camp: il passe du fini à l'infini" (*Le rôle du Pythagorisme dans l'évolution des idées*, Paris, 1937, p. 23).

34. The new notion of the divinity as infinite is attributed to the Syrian religions by the celebrated expert on oriental religions, Franz Cumont, *Les religions orientales dans le paganisme romain* (4th ed., Paris, 1929), 117–19.

35. *De Opificio Mundi*, VI, 23 (Loeb ed. by F. Colson and G. Whitaker, New York, 1929, I, 19); *De Sacrificiis Abelis et Caini*, XV, 59, (Loeb ed., II, 139).

36. E.g.: St. Hilary of Poitiers, *De Trinitate*, I, 5–7 (Migne, *PL*, X, 28), in the West, who began this work in 356 during his exile in the East, and in the East St. Gregory of Nyssa, *Contra Eunomium*, I (Migne, *PG*, XLV, 340D), written in 381. On the latter's doctrine of infinity and its relation to Neoplatonism, see H. Urs von Balthasar, *Présence et pensée: Essai sur la philosophie religieuse de Grégoire de Nysse* (Paris, 1942). The earliest Christian text I have thus far been able to discover is in a papyrus fragment of a Preface from the early Egyptian liturgy (c. 300) in the *Florilegium Patristicum*, VII, 1, *Monumenta Eucharistica et Liturgica Vetustissima* (ed. J. Quasten, Bonn, 1935), p. 38: ". . . Lord of all power . . . who alone without limit puts limits to all. . . ." The term occurs nowhere explicitly in Scripture itself.

37. Cf. the extremely interesting text of Origen (just before Plotinus), *De Principiis*, II, 9 (Migne, *PG*, XI, 225–26), where he maintains the divine will cannot be infinite, for then God could not know himself, since the infinite is unknowable. Rufinus, his disciple, later toned down this text in his own edition, as noted by Migne, in order to defend his master's orthodoxy, then under attack.

38. For the general doctrine of Plotinus, see the standard works, esp. John Rist, *Plotinus: The Road to Reality* (Cambridge Univ. Press, 1967); Emile Bréhier, *The Philosophy of Plotinus* (Univ. of Chicago Press, 1958); A. H. Armstrong, *The Architecture of the Intelligible Universe* (Cambridge Univ. Press, 1940), and the excellent brief treatment in his *Introduction to Ancient Philosophy* (Westminster, Md.: Newman, 1940), esp. p. 187.

39. The best texts are: *Enneads*, IV, 3, 8; V, 5, 4–6 and 9–11; VI, 5, 11–12; 6, 2; 7, 17, and 32–42; 8, 9 to end; 9 entire (ed. E. Bréhier, *Plotin: Ennéades*, Paris, 1924–38). The following texts are the author's own translation, based on the French of Bréhier, since the MacKenna translation is very free. See also my article, written after this one, "Infinity in Plotinus," *Gregorianum* 40 (1969), 75–98.

40. *Enneads*, V, 5, 6; VI, 2, 1. Cf. St. Thomas's elegant solution to the problem of the "Platonici" by showing how the First Cause can be said to be above *ens*, i.e., *ens participatum* (being as paricipated) but not above *esse* (the act of existence itself): *In Librum de Causis*, lect. 6.

41. *Etre et agir*, p. 50.

42. Cf. the excellent text, with introduction, translation, and commentary by E. Dodds, *Proclus: The Elements of Theology* (Oxford, 1933).

43. On its influence, see the works mentioned in note 2, esp. that of Fabro.

44. I have translated from the Latin text used by St. Thomas in his commentary, *Expositio supra Librum de Causis* (ed. Mandonnet, *Opuscula Omnia*, Paris, 1927, I, 193ff.). The texts used are from Prop. 20 and 16.

45. *De Ente et Essentia*, ch. 5; ed. Roland-Gosselin (Paris, 1926), p. 39.

46. Text and translation can be found in the Loeb edition, *The Theological Treatises*, ed. H. Stewart and E. Rand (London, 1926), under its proper title, *Quomodo substantiae*.... See also Thomas's commentary on it, *Expositio supra Librum Boethii de Hebdomadibus* (ed. Mandonnet, *Opuscula*, I, 102ff.), and, for its influence, the works of Fabro and Geiger mentioned in note 2, and H. Brosch, *Der Seinsbegriff bei Boethius* (Innsbruck, 1931).

47. *In I Sent.*, d. 8, p. 2, q. 2, f. 2 (ed. Quaracchi, *Opera Omnia*, 1882–1902, I, 167 A).

48. In an article of summary like this it is obviously impossible to give a full textual exposition of the Thomistic synthesis of participation with act and potency. The following, however, are some of the most characteristic texts, in chronological order, where the two elements may be seen working together: *Sum. c. Gentes*, I, ch. 43; II, ch. 52–54; *De Potentia*, q. 1, a. 2; q. 7, a. 2 ad 9; *Sum. Theol.*, I, q. 7, aa. 1–2; q. 50, a. 2 ad 4; q. 75, a. 5 ad 1 and 4; *De Spiritualibus Creaturis*, a. 1; *De Substantiis Separatis*, ch. 3 (a remarkable *tour de*

force attempting to reconcile directly Plato and Aristotle, but where the Aristotelian text is stretched beyond recognition), and ch. 6 (ed. Mandonnet); *Quodlibet.*, III, q. 8, a. 20; *Compendium Theologiae*, ch. 18–21; *In VIII Phys.*, c. 10, lect. 21; *In Librum Dionysii de Divinis Nominibus*, c. 5, lect. 1. For further development see my article, "The Meaning of Participation in St. Thomas," now chapter 5 of this collection, and the fine study, that appeared long after this article was written, by John Wippel, "St. Thomas and Participation," in *Studies in Medieval Philosophy*, ed. John Wippel (Washington, D.C.: Catholic Univ. of America Press, 1987), pp. 117–58.

49. E.g.: *In I Sent.*, d. 42, q. 1, a. 1, sol.; d. 8, q. 1, a. 2, Contra et sol.; d. 8, q. 2, aa. 1–2, sol.; d. 8, q. 5, a. 1, Contra 2; d. 48, q. 1, a. 1, sol.; *In III Sent.*, d. 13, q. 1, a. 2, sol.; *De Ente*, ch. 4–5; *De Veritate*, q. 2, a. 9; q. 27, a. 1 ad 8; *Quodlibet.* VII, q. 1, a. 1 ad 1; *In Boeth. de Hebdom.*, lect. 2.

50. E.g.: *De Ente*, ch. 4; cf. the classification of arguments in Fabro, *La nozione metafisica di partecipazione*, pp. 212ff.

51. *Quodlibet.*, III, q. 8, a. 20.

52. *Compend. Theol.*, ch. 18; *Sum. c. Gentes*, I, ch. 43; and the other texts cited in note 48.

53. Cf. *Sum. C. Gent.*, I, ch. 18, init.: "In every composite there must be act and potency. For it is impossible for many components to become unqualifiedly one (*simpliciter unum*) unless there is something in this unity which is act and something which is potency. For things that exist in act are not unified except as though bound together or gathered together (*colligata vel congregata*), and these are not unqualifiedly one." Cf. *Sum. C. Gent.*, II, ch. 53 entire; *De Spir. Creat.*, a. 3; *De Potentia*, q. 7, a. 1; *In VII Met.*, lect. 13, n. 1588.

54. Cf. the rich concluding chapter of Fabro, *La nozione metafisica di partecipazione*, p. 338: "Platonismo ed Aristotelismo: Originalità della Sintesi Tomista."

55. E.g.: E. Gilson, "Pourquoi saint Thomas a critiqué saint Augustin," *Archives d'histoire doctrinale et littéraire du moyen âge*, I, (1926), 126. The same position has been taken uncompromisingly by one of Gilson's ablest collaborators on this side of the water, Anton Pegis, in the Introduction to his excellent edition of the *Basic Writings of St. Thomas Aquinas* (New York: Random House, 1945). We note that this point has been one of the few to elicit expressions of disapproval from reviewers.

56. Fabro, op. cit., p. 354. I feel obliged here to take note of a work of fine scholarship that appeared after the publication of this article: Robert Henle, S.J., *St. Thomas and Platonism: A Study of the* Plato *and* Platonici *Texts in the Writings of St. Thomas* (The Hague: Nijhoff, 1956), from which the author and others in the Gilson school seem to have drawn conclusions at variance with those we have reached in this article, namely, that because in almost all the texts in his entire work where St. Thomas mentions Plato or the Platonists he criticizes the Platonist position and opts for an Aristotelian one, *therefore* he has made a decisive option for Aristotle against Platonism. But notice the limitations of the research method itself. *Only* those texts are considered in which St. Thomas *explicitly* mentions *Plato* or *Platonici*. The fact

of the matter is, however, that there is a large series of texts, which we have used in this article, where St. Thomas freely uses Neoplatonic themes, in particular participation, but without ever mentioning any source, at least any obviously Neoplatonic one. He simply appropriates for himself and uses both the themes and the language. All these texts slip through the sieve of Henle's research without his appearing to notice it and the severe restrictions this puts on any conclusions drawn from it. The premise is true, but the wider conclusions do not follow from it. Why does St. Thomas thus seem to conceal his Neoplatonic indebtedness? Perhaps because he wanted to detach himself firmly from the realism of ideas always attached to Platonism; also, I think, because he wanted to present his primary project as the assimilation of Aristotle into Christian thought. Whatever the reason, it should be clear that one cannot legitimately conclude from the fact that he does not ordinarily mention his Neoplatonic sources that he is not taking over for himself both their themes and their language.

5

The Meaning of Participation in St. Thomas

During the last fifteen years the notion of participation has become more and more the focus of attention on the part of Thomistic historians and metaphysicians. As a result of an important series of studies by European scholars, such as those of Fabro, Geiger, de Finance, De Raeymaeker, the very recent work of Arthur Little, the Irish Jesuit, and not a few others, the doctrine of participation has now emerged as one of the central structural pieces of the whole philosophical system of St. Thomas. The same studies also bring out the unmistakable indebtedness of the Angelic Doctor to the Neoplatonic tradition for the main lines of this theory.[1]

The consequence has been to force us to revise considerably our estimate of just what constitutes the characteristic "personality," so to speak, of the Thomistic system, both as regards its inner structural unity and its authentic historical relations with its predecessors. When the modern Thomistic revival began under Leo XIII in the latter part of the preceding century, it was the Aristotelian facet of St. Thomas's philosophy which was the first to emerge into the limelight and to occupy the attention of Thomistic historians.[2] It soon became apparent, however, as independent historical study of both Aristotle and St. Thomas progressed, that the originality of the latter and his independence of Aristotle were considerably greater than had been suspected. The fundamental point of difference was accurately analyzed as lying at the very heart of the metaphysics of being, namely, in the radical shift of equilibrium operated by St. Thomas from form and essence to the act of existence or *esse* as the metaphysical core of every being and the basic unifying perfection of the universe. Perhaps the single figure to whom we owe most both for the scientific justification and the successful propagandizing of this interpretation is Professor Gilson.[3]

But Professor Gilson and his numerous competent disciples continued—and still continue, it appears, with almost the same vigor today—to insist that one of the essential keys for understanding the historical significance of St. Thomas is to recognize his philosophy as a decisive option for Aristotle and against Platonism.[4] If, however, the conclusions of the recent movement of studies highlighting the importance of participation and its Neoplatonic affiliations are correct, as we believe they are in the main, then it would appear that the peculiar genius and historical significance of the Thomistic system lie not in that it was an option for Aristotle as against Platonism but rather in that it was a deliberately wrought and highly original synthesis between *both* of these great main streams of Western thought. It is in the light of this challenging difference of perspective in the interpretation of Thomism as a whole that the study of the meaning of participation in St. Thomas takes on its special interest and significance at the present time.

Participation before St. Thomas

In order to evaluate more accurately both the indebtedness of St. Thomas to the tradition before him and the originality of his own contribution, we shall begin by sketching in a few brief strokes the key stages in the development of the doctrine of participation up to his time.[5]

The technical theory of participation was first launched into the stream of Western philosophy by Plato. It consisted essentially in the affirmation that wherever there is a many there must be a one, i.e., wherever there is a multiplicity of members all of which possess some common attribute there must also be some one superior source possessing the same attribute in unmixed purity and perfection, from which each of the inferior recipients derives its own diminished and imperfect participation.[6] The exact nature of this participation or imitation is left vague and obscure by Plato himself and has been the subject of endless controversy ever since.[7]

In addition to the obvious defect in the Platonic theory of its confusion between the logical and the ontological orders, we would like to call attention to another deficiency too frequently overlooked. This is the fact that Plato was unable to express the participation structure in terms of the limited reception by the participants of a perfection that exists in its source in a state of illimitation or infinity. This is the position that St. Thomas, following the whole Neoplatonic tradition, was to hold.

This path was closed to him because he had taken over from the Pythagoreans and Parmenides the classical Greek theory of the finite and the infinite, according to which the infinite was identified with the indefinite formless unintelligibility of matter, multiplicity, and non-being as such, whereas the finite—or better, the limit—was equated with number, form, and idea as the principle of perfection. Thus, although he admitted a mixture of limit and infinity in all orders of participation, it was always the higher principle which limited and perfected the lower, and not vice versa.[8]

This deficiency was remedied in large part by Plotinus. By his theory of the emanation of the ideas themselves from a supreme supraformal source, he introduced a whole new dimension of the infinite as a plenitude of positive perfection, indetermination by excess instead of by defect. Thus for the first time was introduced the principle of the illimitation of an unparticipated perfection and its limitation by reception in a participant.[9] Form, too, as limit now took on a double role, not only of perfecting that which was below it but also of contracting a plenitude above it.

This Plotinian intuition of participation in terms of infinity and limitation was reduced to rigid technical formulation by Proclus, the Scholastic of Neoplatonism. He laid down with new explicitness the necessity of composition or distinction between the participating subject and the participated perfection as an essential condition of every participation.[10]

This basic Neoplatonic structure of participation was passed down to the medieval Christian thinkers, in varying stages of explicitness, clarity, and adaptation to the Christian view of the universe, through the mediation of such influential sources as Pseudo-Dionysius the Areopagite, St. Augustine, Boethius, the Arabs, and the famous *Liber de Causis*. The latter, which was actually a garbled compilation from Proclus, allowed a large dose of pure Neoplatonism to be introduced under the name of Aristotle, since it was believed up until 1268 to be a genuine Aristotelian work. The essence of the doctrine was summed up and transmitted under the handy formula, "Omnis forma pura est infinita" (ever pure or unparticipated form is infinite), and appears to have been accepted in some form or other as a fundamental category of thought by most of St. Thomas's predecessors and contemporaries.[11] The most serious defects of the theory, which still clung to it from its Neoplatonic origins were: (1) its lack of clear distinction between genuine ontological participations and mere logical subordination of abstract concepts; (2) its tendency to superimpose layer after layer of participated forms upon the receiving subject with no intrinsic unifying principle to knit together the composite into a genuine per se unit; (3) the tendency in its non-Christian forms to make the entity of the participating subject as recipient independent of the higher source of the perfection participated.

General Meaning of Participation in St. Thomas

In the light of this brief historical survey we shall be better able to appreciate what St. Thomas did with the materials he had to work with. To begin with, the general meaning and purpose of the doctrine of participation in St. Thomas is the same as in all the systems which had used it before him. It is a theory for rendering intelligible a "many" in any order in terms of a higher one, in other words, for explaining the common possession in many subjects of a given attribute, whether in the logical or the ontological order, by reference to a higher source from which all receive or participate in some way the perfection they possess in common. Thus we find it used to explain the sharing of all the members of a species in the same specific form, the sharing of many specific forms in the same genus, and the sharing of all beings in the same transcendental perfection of existence received from the one supreme Source, God. But it is important to note from the start one of the most essential characteristics of St. Thomas's way of handling this schema, namely, the extreme analogical flexibility with which he adapts it to its applications in these different orders. Though the basic relational structure remains always similar and clearly recognizable, the mode in which the different elements are verified varies widely in each application. Hence it is never possible to argue from the particular aspects proper to one case to the presence of the same aspects in any other case.

Let us now examine more in detail precisely what the term participation means. There is an occasional "weak" use of the word in a very general sense as a mere synonym for having or possessing something in any way at all. But the more common use is in the "strong" or technical sense, and it is in this that we are interested here.[12] In his earliest works, such as the *De ente et essentia* and the *Commentary on the Sentences*, St. Thomas frequently uses the term and the theory, but without any detailed explanation of just what he means by it.[13] It is not until we come to the *Commentary on the De Hebdomadibus of Boethius*, where for the first time he was forced to handle the problem of participation explicitly, that we find a formal definition and analysis. There he tells us: "To participate is to receive as it were a part; and therefore when anything receives in a particular manner that which belongs to another in a universal [or total] manner, it is said to participate it; as man is said to participate animal, because he does not possess the intelligible notes (*ratio*) of animal according to the latter's total 'community' [i.e., universality]; and for the same reason Socrates participates man; in like manner also a subject participates an accident, and matter form, because the substantial or accidental form, which of itself as such is common [or unparticularized], is determined to this or that subject; and similarly an effect is said to participate its cause, and especially when it does not equal the power of its cause, as, for example, if we say that air participates the light of the sun because it does not receive it with the same brightness that it has in the sun."[14] St. Thomas does not mention here among his examples the participation of *esse* by essences because that is the very subject he is trying to illustrate.

This description give us clearly enough the essential structure of relationship involved in participation and its analogical character, though it by no means expresses all the conditions required. Nowhere else do we find so complete an analysis, but it is possible to check its adequacy and fill it out with further precisions and details from numerous other parenthetical explanations. Thus one finds other briefer quasi-definitions substantially the same as the above, e.g.: "For to participate is nothing else than to receive partially from another";[15] "Whatever is participated is determined to the measure of the participant, and thus is possessed partially and not according to every mode of its perfection";[16] "A subject is finite with reference to that which it participates, because that which is participated is received in the participant not according to its total infinity but in a particular manner."[17]

The essential elements of any participation structure according to the above texts are therefore three: (1) a source which possesses the perfection in question in a total and unrestricted manner; (2) a participant subject which possesses the same perfection in some partial or restricted way; and (3) which has received this perfection in some way from, or in dependence on, the higher source. Mere similarity between two terms is not enough. There must be some link of dependence of one on the other as well as partial possession in one and total in the others.[18] The totality and dependence involved may be either in the purely logical order of subordination of concepts by extension, or in the purely formal order of similarity and dependence resulting from exemplarity, or implying even efficient causality whenever the participation touches the order of existence as such.

The term, participation, therefore, is a condensed technical way of expressing the complexus of relations involved in any structure of dependence of a lower multiplicity on a higher source for similarity of nature. It will thus be St. Thomas's chosen tool for expressing the fundamental relations of dependence of creatures on God both for their origin and their analogical imitation of His divine essence,[19] provided, of course, he can find some one basic perfection which is shared by both God and creatures and is the core of all perfections. The latter condition is precisely what is provided by his own largely original doctrine of the act of existence.

Let us examine now in more detail each of the elements in the participation structure. First, the source. Since the source is by definition that which is the ultimate font of the perfection in question, it cannot receive the latter from somewhere else but must possess it by essence, that is, in virtue of its own essence. Its essence, therefore, must be simply identical with this perfection, it must not merely *have* the latter as part of its essence but must *be* it totally, in perfect purity and simplicity. For if its essence were composed, it would necessarily have to be caused and therefore receive or participate the perfection in question from another instead of being its source.

St. Thomas frequently posits and even analyzes in some detail this basic opposition between the two modes of possession of a perfection, namely, by essence and by participation, e.g.: "Something is predicated of a subject in two ways: in one way by essence, in the other by participation; for light is predicated of an illuminated body by participation, but if there existed some separated [i.e, pure or unmixed] light it would be predicated of it by essence."[20] The mutual exclusiveness of these two modes of possession enables him to use them to construct another definition of participation: "That which is totally something does not participate it but is by essence identified with it. What, however, is not totally identified with something but has something else joined with it is properly said to participate."[21]

Two other properties follow immediately from the fact of the source's possessing its perfection by essence and hence without composition. First, the source must be unique. For if there were two sources, both possessing the same perfection by essence in perfect simplicity, there would be no way of distinguishing between them.[22] Moreover, diversity as such can never be the ultimate sufficient reason for similarity.[23] Secondly, the perfection must be present in the source in a state of infinity or unrestricted plenitude, though the source itself may still be limited in another higher order. The reason is the same as that for unicity: since the perfection is present in perfect simplicity, there is nothing else to limit it. Besides, it is evident that since it is the unique source none of its participations could be more perfect or complete than itself. The source must always by nature be a plenitude.[24]

St. Thomas develops both of these points on many different occasions throughout his works. They are the keys to his explanation both of the relative infinity and unicity of each angelic form within its species and of the absolute infinity and unicity of God in the ultimate order of being. In every participation structure, therefore, the source will possess its perfection by identity of essence and hence be simple, unique and infinite. In the order of abstract concepts, however, this infinity will be nothing more than the negative infinity of an as yet unparticularized universal.[25]

Let us now turn to the participant subject. Since it does not possess its perfection by essence but as received from another and contracted in some way, it cannot be simple but must be composed of the perfection received and the subject or capacity receiving and limiting it: "Whenever anything is predicated of another by participation, it is necessary that there be present there something other than what is participated; and therefore in every creature which has existence the creature itself which has *esse* is 'other' than the *esse* which it has."[26] This distinction between the component principles will be either rational or real according as the participation itself takes place in the logical or ontological order.

Every participant subject, therefore, must be composed and limited in order to be distinguished from its source. This law gives us the key to the fundamental metaphysical structure of all finite beings in the system of St. Thomas, whether in the order of matter and form or of essence and existence.

SYNTHESIS WITH ARISTOTELIAN ACT AND POTENCY

What we have seen so far has been at bottom only a reworking of the basic framework of participation as handed down to St. Thomas by the Neoplatonic tradition. His originality has consisted in the skill with which, guided by his keen sense of analogy and of the difference between the ontological and the conceptual orders (always so blurred in the Neoplatonists), he has adapted this framework to a realistic metaphysics of existence and an epistemology of abstraction. The next and last step in the analysis, however, represents a peculiarly original stroke of genius on his part. This is the transposition of the whole structure of participation, especially of the metaphysical structure within the participant subject, into the technical Aristotelian framework of metaphysical composition in terms of act and potency. "Every subject," he tells us, "which participates something is compared to that which it participates as potency to act: for by that which it participates it becomes in act such a participant. . . . Therefore every created substance is compared to its act of existence as potency to act."[27]

What is the reason for operating this transposition? St. Thomas tell us again with all the desired explicitness: "In every composite there must be act and potency. For a plurality (*plura*) cannot become simply one unless there be there something which is act and something else which is potency."[28] In other words, what St. Thomas has done is to put his finger on what was perhaps the greatest single weakness of the Neoplatonic doctrine throughout its whole tradition, namely, the lack of any adequate metaphysical explanation to safeguard the intrinsic unity of the compositions resulting from participation. He has remedied this by transposing the whole framework into the only adequate theory of unity in metaphysical composition so far developed, the Aristotelian doctrine of act and potency as correlative, incomplete metaphysical principles, intrinsically ordered one to the other so as to form a *per se* unit.

In so doing, of course, he had to alter radically the old Aristotelian notion of potency from its original exclusive use as function of the cosmic cycle of change, always ordered toward a future different act,[29] and adapt it to a new, primarily static role as limiting, receiving subject in a Neoplatonic participation structure. The resulting highly original synthesis is summed up admirably in the celebrated but not always adequately understood Thomistic principle of the limitation of act by potency: Pure or unreceived act is infinite; act is limited only by reception in a really distinct potency.[30]

It is our contention that it is impossible to understand this principle in terms either of pure Aristotelianism or pure Neoplatonism. It is not pure Aristotelianism, because Aristotle (like Plato), accepted the classical Greek notion of the finite as the perfect and the infinite as the imperfect; hence there is not only no mention but no place in his system for a theory of act as infinite and potency as limit.[31] Nor is it pure Neoplatonism, because no Neoplatonist had ever used Aristotelian act and potency to express participation. This synthesis is peculiarly the work of St. Thomas's own genius, fusing into an organic unity the best of these two main streams of Western philosophy.

The fact that he knew precisely what he was doing and was not under the naive delusion that he was merely developing an implicit Aristotelian doctrine seems indubitable to the present writer for two reasons. First, the fact that in his early works, though he uses constantly the limitation principle correlated with participation, the latter is never once expressed in terms of act and potency. It is only dating from the *Contra Gentes* in 1256 that the classic formulas, "Act is not limited save by potency," etc., begin to appear, together with the explanation that every composition must be in terms of act and potency to ensure its unity. Secondly, nowhere in his commentaries on Aristotle, to the end of his life, does he ever mention, let alone attribute to his master, the principle of the *limitation* of act by potency, though he uses it constantly in his independent works. Such a consistent silence can scarcely have been a mere coincidence.

APPLICATION TO MATTER-FORM AND ESSENCE-EXISTENCE

We have space here for but one last remark. Though the compositions resulting from participation in the orders of matter and form and essence and existence are both ontological, it is only in the order of essence and existence that all the elements in the participation structure take on full ontological value. The only case where the source of a participated perfection enjoys genuine ontological subsistence as a positive, intensive plenitude is in the case of the transcendental analogous perfections, all reducible to *esse*, whose source is God, *Ipsum Esse Subsistens*. By the principle that the one as source of the many may be merely analogous in similarity and need not necessarily be univocal, St. Thomas sweeps away with a single stroke the vast Neoplatonic superstructure of subsistent specific, generic, and accidental forms, reducing them all to dependence on a single ontological source in the order of the one basic ontological perfection of *esse*. This one source is God, sole efficient cause of all being as such, and ultimate exemplary cause of all forms by His divine ideas.[32]

As a result, the thesis of the limitation of form by matter, though it still reproduces analogically the basic participation schema, must be watered down, so to speak, to a more modest, non-qualitative significance. Since every member of a species receives its specific form totally and equally in the qualitative order,[33] limitation here can mean only restriction in the spatial-quantitative order by comparison with a source which can exist only intentionally as an idea in a mind, where it is endowed with an infinity that is only the negative infinity of indetermination of a universal idea as such. The extremely analogical, non-intensive, half-conceptual meaning of limitation here does not always seem to have been sufficiently taken into account by the expositions of this thesis in many Thomistic textbooks.

CONCLUSION

Such, then, as far as we have been able to condense it into so short a space, are the essential characteristics of the Thomistic doctrine of participation: a formal relational framework, clearly recognizable as taken over from the Neoplatonic tradition, transposed—at least in its realistic applications—into the technical Aristotelian terms of act and potency, its ontological content emptied of the original Platonic ultra-realism of forms and replaced with the one basic analogical perfection of *esse*, and the whole applied with a consummate sense of analogy to the different orders both of reality and of ideas—such is the highly original synthesis that is Thomistic participation. In view of the central role of this theory in his philosophical system and of the unmistakable Neoplatonic core within it, we believe, with Professor Fabro in his work on participation, that it is no longer legitimate to characterize accurately Thomistic philosophy as an option for Aristotle against Platonism. Rather has St. Thomas taken both Aristotle and Plato (or more accurately, Plotinus) into so intimate a partnership that one can call his synthesis either an Aristotelianism specified by Platonism or a Platonism specified by Aristotelianism, and in some respects, at least in metaphysics, the latter may be more accurate.[34]

NOTES

1. Cf. Cornelio Fabro, *La nozione metafisica di partecipazione secondo S. Tomaso d'Aquino*, 2nd ed. (Turin, 1950); L. -B. Geiger, *La participation dans la philosophie de S. Thomas d'Aquin* (Paris, 1942); J. de Finance, *Etre et agir dans la philosophie de S. Thomas* (Paris, 1945); L. De Raeymaeker, *Philosophie de l'être* (Louvain, 1947); Arthur Little, S.J., *The Platonic Heritage of Thomism* (Dublin, 1949), a book of uneven worth but with many valuable insights; André Hayen, S.J., *l'Intentionnel dans la philosophie de S. Thomas* (Brussels, 1942), etc. Since this article was first published a fine piece has appeared by John Wippel, "Thomas Aquinas and Participation," in *Studies in Medieval Philosophy*, ed. John Wippel (Washington, D.C.: Catholic Univ. of America Press, 1987), pp. 117–58.

2. Cf. F. Van Steenberghen, "L'interprétation de la pensée médiévale au cours du siècle écoulé," in *Scholastica Ratione Historica-Critica Instauranda: Acta Congressus Scholastici Internationalis*, 1950 (Rome, 1951), p. 33. Characteristic examples of this period are the classic treatises of T. de Régnon, *Métaphysique des causes* (Paris, 1886), and especially A. Farges, *Théorie fondamentale de l'acte et de la puissance, du moteur et du mobile* (Paris, 1886), in which there is not a single mention of the principle of the limitation of act by potency, now recognized as the core of the Thomistic act-potency theory.

3. For example, in his well-known books, *Le Thomisme*, 5th ed. (Paris, 1944), ch. 1: "Existence and Realité"; and *Being and Some Philosophers* (Toronto, 1950).

4. Cf. E. Gilson, "Pourquoi saint Thomas a critiqué saint Augustin," *Archives d'histoire doctrinale et littéraire du moyen âge*, 1 (1926), 126, and the

The Meaning of Participation in St. Thomas 99

uncompromising Introduction of Anton Pegis to his excellent edition of the *Basic Writings of St. Thomas Aquinas* (New York, 1945).

5. For the best treatment available so far, see Part I of Fabro's work on participation mentioned in note 1.

6. Cf. *Republic*, 507 b (trans. Jowett): "There is an absolute beauty and an absolute good, and of other things to which the term 'many' is applied there is an absolute; for they may be brought under a single idea, which is the essence of each."

7. A good treatment of its place in the overall metaphysical synthesis of Plato, gathered from his unwritten works, is that of Léon Robin, *Platon* (Paris, 1934), ch. 4, and the illuminating commentary of William Lynch, *An Approach to the Metaphysics of Plato through the Parmenides* (Washington, D.C.: Georgetown Univ. Press, 1959).

8. For a brief history of the notions of finite and infinite and their connection with participation and Thomistic act and potency, see my article, "The Limitation of Act by Potency: Aristotelianism or Neoplatonism?" *New Scholasticism*, 26 (1952), 167–94, reprinted as chapter 4 of this collection.

9. E.g.: "We must examine whence come these ideas and their beauty. Their source cannot be one among them. . . . It must be above all powers and all forms. The first principle is that which is without form, not that it is lacking form, but that all intelligible forms come from it. . . . It is infinite. . . . How could anything else measure it?" (*Enneads*, VI, 7, 32; text of Bréhier, trans. my own). "All come from the same principle . . . and the same gift imparted to a multitude of beings becomes different in each one that receives it" (*Enneads*, VI, 7, 18). Cf. V, 5, 6 and 10–11.

10. Cf. E. Dodds, *Proclus: The Elements of Theology* (Oxford, 1933), esp. Prop. 2: "All that participates in unity is one and not-one . . . since participation in unity implies a distinct participant."

11. Cf., for example, the discussion on the infinity and simplicity of God in St. Bonaventure, *In I Sent.* d. 8, p. 2, q. 1–2; d. 43, q. 1–3; also Peter John Olivi, *Quaestiones in II Lib. Sent.*, q. 16 (ed. Jansen, Quaracchi, 1922), I, 320: "Every form that is not received and participated in another than itself is most absolute, most simple, most universal, most infinite, and in brief is the supreme being and God himself."

12. Cf. Geiger, *La participation*, p. 11ff.

13. Cf. *De Ente*, ch. 5 (ed. Roland-Gosselin, Paris, 1926, pp. 38–39); *In I Sent.*, d. 8, q. 1, a. 1–2; d. 48, q. 1, a. 1.

14. *In Boeth. de Hebdom.*, lect. 2 (ed. Mandonnet, *Opuscula Omnia*, Paris, 1927, I, 172–73). We are here following Geiger's obviously correct emendation of the text, which puts the comma after "universaliter," and not before it: op. cit., p. 48, n. 2.

15. *In De Caelo et Mundo*, c. 12, lect. 18, n. 8 (ed. Leonina, III).

16. *Summa c. Gent.*, I, ch. 32 (following Geiger's obvious emendation of "participati"—a mere tautology—to "participantis").

17. *In Lib. de Causis*, lect. 4 (ed. Parma, XXI, 725A).

18. "Whatever possesses something by participation is traced back (or

drawn back: *reducitur*) to that which possesses it by essence, as to its principle and cause" (*Compend. Theologiae*, c. 68; ed. Mandonnet, *Opuscula*, II, 37). Cf. also *De Potentia*, q. 6, a. 6; *De Spir. Creat.* a. 10; *Sum. C. Gent.*, III, ch. 69; *In II Met.*, lect. 2 (ed. Cathala, n. 296).

19. Little brings out this point well, showing how it is this doctrine of participation which makes Thomism (and, in its own way, Platonism) a fundamentally religious philosophy, and how the lack of it was the principal metaphysical deficiency of Aristotelianism (*The Platonic Heritage of Thomism*, pp. 272ff.).

20. *Quodl.* II, q. 2, a. 3 (ed. Mandonnet, *Quaestiones Quodlibetales*, Paris, 1926). See also *In Boeth. de Hebdom.*, ch. 2; *In Dionys. de Div. Nom.*, ch. 4, lect. 14; *In Libr. de Causis*, ch. 9; *Sum c. Gent.*, II, ch. 52.

21. *In I Met.*, lect. 10, n. 154.

22. *De Ente*, ch. 4–5; *In I Sent.*, d. 43, q. 1, a. 2; *Sum c. Gent.*, II, ch. 52 and 93; *Sum. Theol.*, I, q. 50, a. 4; *De Spiritualibus Creaturis*, a. 1 and 8; *De Substantiis Separatis*, ch. 6 and 12.

23. *De Veritate*, q. 2, a. 14; *De Pot.*, q. 3, a. 6.

24. E.g.: *Sum c. Gent.*, I, ch. 43: "Then, too, anything which has a certain perfection is the more perfect insofar as it participates that perfection more fully. But there cannot be, or even be conceived of, any mode by which a perfection may be possessed more fully than by that which by its very essence is perfect and whose being is its goodness. In no way, therefore, is it possible to think of anything better or more perfect than God." Cf. also *Sum. c. Gent.*, II, ch. 15; *In Lib. de Causis*, ch. 9 and 16; *De Pot.*, q. 1, a. 2; *Sum. Theol.*, I, q. 7, a. 1–2; I, q. 50, a. 2 ad 4; *Quodl. III*, q. 2, a. 3; *In Dionys. de Div. Nom.*, ch. 5, lect. 1; ch. 13, lect. 1; *Compend. Theol.*, ch. 18–21; *De Ente*, ch. 5; *In I Sent.*, d. 43, q. 1, a. 1.

25. *Quodl.* XI, q. 1, a. 1 ad 2; *Sum. Theol.*, I, q. 7, a. 1; I, q. 16, a. 7 ad 2; I, q. 16, a. 7 ad 2; I, q. 86, a. 2 ad 4.

26. *Quodl.* II, q. 2, a. 3. Cf. also *In I Sent.*, d. 46, q. 1, a. 1; d. 8, q. 5, a. 1, contra 2; *Quodl.* III, q. 8, a. 20; *In Dionys. de Div. Nom.*, ch. 4, lect. 14.

27. *Sum c. Gent.*, II, ch. 53. Cf. also *Quodl.* III, q. 8, a. 20; *De Spir. Creat.*, a. 1; *De Subst. Sep.*, ch. 3, init.; *Sum. Theol.*, I, q. 75, a. 5 ad 1 and 4.

28. *Sum c. Gent.*, I, ch. 18 init.; see also ibid., II, ch. 53; *De Spir. Creat.*, a. 3; *De Pot.*, q. 7, a. 1; *Sum. Theol.*, I, q. 3, a. 7; *De Subst. Sep.*, ch. 5; *In VII Met.*, lect. 13, n. 1588; *De Anima*, a. 12 fin.

29. Cf. the test case of the heavenly bodies, which Aristotle declares have no potency in the order of essence, because they are not mutable and corruptible in their essences, but only in the accidental order of local motion: *Met.*, IX, 8, 1050 b 6–34; VIII, 5, 1044 b. 27.

30. Cf. *Sum. C. Gent.*, I, ch. 43: "An act existing in nothing is limited (*terminatur*) by nothing;" *Compend. Theol.*, ch. 18: "No act is found to be limited except through a potency which is a receptive power (*vis receptiva*)." Cf. *De Pot.*, q. 1, a. 2.

31. Cf. my article, "The Limitation of Act by Potency: Aristotelianism or Neoplatonism?" *New Scholasticism*, 26 (1952), 178. My own position, ar-

rived at independently, is confirmed by Little, *The Platonic Heritage of Thomism*, pp. 185, 188–89, 203: "The centre of Thomas's system is the concept of potency as the principle of limitation. . . . The centre of Aristotle's system is the concept of potency as a principle of change or motion implying in material things a process of evolution or gradual assimilation *towards* the Pure Act (which for Aristotle means the Perfect Action). Thomas admitted Aristotle's doctrine, but as a *secondary* function of potency. The difference of Thomas from Aristotle is toward Plato."

Compare with the above the still widely accepted position among many Thomists, represented by R. Garrigou-Lagrange, O.P., who, in his *Reality: A Synthesis of Thomistic Thought* (St. Louis: Herder, 1950), pp. 43–44, asserts categorically that Aristotle clearly taught the limitation of act by potency. Unfortunately neither he nor any other Thomist provides any texts to back up their contention. This Thomistic doctrine moves already in a different intellectual world from that of Aristotle.

32. *De Subst. Sep.*, ch. 8 and 9; *Sum. Theol.*, I, q. 44, a. 3 ad 2; *Quodl.* III, q. 3, a. 6; *In Lib. de Causis*, lect. 3 and 12; *In Dionys. de Div. Nom.*, ch. 5, lect. 1.

33. Cf. *Sum. Theol.*, I, q. 93, a. 4 ad 3; I–II, q. 52, a. 1; I, q. 76, a. 4 ad 4.

34. Cf. the challenging and insightful concluding chapter of Fabro, *La nozione metafisica di partecipazione* . . . , entitled: "Platonismo ed Aristotelismo: Originalità della Sintesi Tomista," esp. p. 354.

6

To Be Is to Be Substance-in-Relation

The aim of this paper is to operate a double retrieval. It is first to retrieve the classical (pre-Cartesian) notion of substance as dynamic, as an active nature, i.e., an abiding center of acting and being acted upon—one of the richest insights, in my judgment, of ancient and medieval thought; and secondly, to integrate it more closely with the notion of relation as an intrinsic dimension of being—a notion which has become one of the most distinctive and highly developed instruments of later modern and contemporary thought. The two belong together in any adequate metaphysics, I submit, as intrinsically complementary aspects, distinct but inseparable, of what it means to *be*, to be a *real being* in the full and proper sense of the term.

Unfortunately the two notions, originally joined together, have become sundered and more and more opposed to each other as modern philosophy has unfolded since Descartes, partly due to the pressure of modern mathematized science, with its almost exclusive focus on relations as the locus of intelligibility in nature. On the one hand, the classical notion of substance as active nature imbedded in a network of relations resulting from its acting and being acted on has been gradually distorted in successive stages throughout the history of post-Cartesian thought. I like to call this chapter in the history of substance "The Sad Adventures of Substance in Modern Philosophy from Descartes to Whitehead."

The three successive phases of this distortion can be summed up as (1) the Cartesian self-enclosed substance; (2) the Lockean inert substance as unknowable substratum; and (3) the Humean separable substance, rejected as unintelligible—which it indeed is as so understood. All of these have been repudiated—and rightly so—by the majority of late modern and contemporary thinkers. But nothing adequate has replaced them; the authentic classical notion has apparently slowly sunk out of sight (save in the contemporary Aristotelian and Thomistic traditions, which themselves have remained somewhat isolated from the main streams of modern philosophy). As a result, real being tends to be reduced to nothing more than a pattern of re-

To Be Is to Be Substance-in-Relation

lations with no subjects grounding them, or a pattern of events with no agents enacting them. The fundamental polarity within real being between the "in itself" and the "toward others," the self-immanence and the self-transcendence of being, collapses into the one pole of pure relatedness to others.

On the other hand, one can overstress the other side of the polarity, focusing exclusively on the notion of substance as in-itself, unchanging substratum, the ground of all attributes and relations and thus the primary instance of being. Then relations become second-class citizens in the hierarchy of being, not only ontologically posterior to substance in the order of being—which they must be—but also of secondary importance compared to it. This danger is latent from the beginning in the classical notion of substance, especially in its originator, Aristotle, insofar as the substantial forms that were the intelligible core of substances were necessary and eternal, whereas relations to others were (for the most part) contingent and changing. The priority of substance, which Aristotle is so justly proud to have discovered, tends to push too much into the background the complementarity of relations as equally intrinsic to being.

The medievals, especially St. Thomas, restored in principle the complementarity between substance and relation by their doctrine of real being as intrinsically ordered toward action and self-communication; for all action necessarily generates a web of relations between agents and recipients. Christian revelation, through the medium of theological explication, also had a significant philosophical input on the meaning and importance of relations. This came principally through the doctrine of God as Triune, where the personhood of the three Persons, Father, Son, and Holy Spirit, is constituted entirely through relations. The notion of the human being as by nature social, hence as imbedded in a web of relations to others in the social and political community, also clearly implied the key role of relations. This aspect is quite explicit in Aristotle too.

Nonetheless, in fact, when St. Thomas and the other medievals worked out their technical philosophical analysis of what it means to be a person, their principal focus was on identifying precisely the root of the "incommunicability" or uniqueness of the person, human or divine, as distinct from every other. This was important for theological reasons, e.g., for understanding the distinction of the divine Persons within the unity of the divine nature, as well as why the human nature of Christ was complete as a nature but was not a person on its own as distinct from the divine Person who assumed it as its own. As a result, although the aspect of person (and hence of substance) as intrinsically relational was explicitly affirmed in the case of the divine Persons and clearly implied for all persons and substances in terms of the underlying Thomistic metaphysics of being as by nature active and self-communicative, still this relational aspect of all substances as actual existents did not receive the same explicit full-dress philosophical analysis as the *in-itself* aspect of substance, existing as *distinct* from all others. The full implications of his own metaphysics of existence as act had not yet been drawn fully into the light by Thomas himself, nor perhaps fully even by his followers to this day.

Hence what is needed, it seems to me, is first to retrieve the classical notion of substance as *active* and *self-communicative*. This would be a corrective of the principal distortions of substance that have become endemic to modern thinking about it. Secondly, it is necessary to retrieve the full value of the *relational* dimension of being, as intrinsically complementary to substance and of equal importance with it. This dimension, left too much in the shadow in classical thought, has been one of the most brilliant and fruitful contributions of modern thought, but by losing its roots in substance, in the "in-itself" of being, has become overdeveloped in a one-sided way and upset the dyadic balance of being. To sum up the point of this communication in a word, to be real is to be a *dyadic synthesis* of substance and relation; it is to be *substance-in-relation*. This is true both of God and of all other beings, in analogously different ways. It belongs to the very nature of being itself, both in its supreme instance and in all the finite images thereof.

I. Retrieval of the Classical Notion of Substance

The main point here is to retrieve the aspect of substance as active and self-communicative, thus generative of relations. I shall draw principally on the thought of Aquinas because of the richness of his underlying metaphysics,[1] in particular his notion of being as active and self-communicative.

The primary instance of real being is the individual existent as a "nature," i.e., as an abiding center (no matter for how long) of its own characteristic actions and the ultimate subject of which attributes are predicated, but which itself is predicated of no other subject as an attribute or part. This ability to exist *in itself* as an ultimate subject of action and attribution and not as part of any other being is what it means to be called a *substance* (from the Latin *sub-stans*: that which "stands under" all its attributes as their ultimate subject). To stand thus "in itself" does not mean that the entity thus characterized is not *related* to others. As we shall see, the intrinsic orientation toward self-expressive action that is also characteristic of all natures—hence of all substances—implies that all substances will be related at least to some others. But it does mean that no substance, no real being in an unqualified sense, can be nothing but a pure *relation*. A relation in the real order must relate something, making it a relat*ed*, or the relation itself self-destructs. As the Buddhists have long insightfully argued, if all beings are nothing but relations, such that A is nothing but a relation to B, and B is nothing but a relation to A, then neither one has "own being" and both disappear into "emptiness" (*sunyatta*)—a point often naively overlooked, it seems to me, by many modern Western philosophers who cavalierly dismiss substance for relation as the primary mode of being.

Thus wherever there is any real being at all, there must be substance, or being in a substantial mode, either within the being itself or grounding it as its ultimate subject of inherence. The basic classical argument for the necessity of substance wherever there is real being runs as follows: It is impossible that every instance of real being should be a part of, inhering in, some other being, which in turn inheres in some other and so on to infinity. An infinite regress is not possible here, since the necessary fulfilling conditions for any being to exist would be endlessly deferred, never in principle fulfilled. Nothing could ever get going in reality at all. Hence there must always be substance somewhere in being to ground whatever else is there. (In this basic sense, it seems to me, even the Whiteheadian actual entities must be considered as substances, since they exist somehow as subjects in themselves, not merely as parts of others, even though they subsist only for a moment. His own reason for rejecting substance derives, as we shall see, from the Cartesian distortion of substance as self-enclosed.) As Bernard Lonergan sums up aptly the classical doctrine: substance is that which makes a being to be a "unity, identity, whole."

There are four basic points to note about this conception of substance as the primary instance of real being: (1) it has the aptitude to exist *in itself* and not as a part of any other being; (2) it is the unifying center of all the various attributes and properties that belong to it at any one moment; (3) if the being persists as the same individual throughout a process of change, it is the substance which is the abiding, unifying center of the being across time; (4) it has an intrinsic dynamic orientation toward self-expressive action, toward self-communication with others, as the crown of its perfection, as its very *raison d'être*, literally, for St. Thomas. It is this last aspect that we shall give most stress to and develop more fully in this paper, precisely because it is the one that has been most frequently downplayed, ignored, or denied in modern Western philosophy since Descartes. Let us listen to St. Thomas on this intrinsically active aspect of every being, hence of every substance:

> Every substance exists for the sake of its operation.[2]
>
> Each and every thing shows forth that it exists for the sake of its operation. Indeed operation is the ultimate perfection of each thing.[3]

And since all action proceeding from a being is in some way a self-communication of that being, it follows that:

> It is the nature of every actuality to communicate itself insofar as it is possible. Hence every agent acts according as it exists in actuality.[4]
>
> It follows upon the superabundance proper to perfection as such that the perfection which something has it can communicate to another.[5]
>
> Communication follows upon the very intelligibility (*ratio*) of actuality.[6]
>
> For natural things have a natural inclination not only toward their own proper good, to acquire it, if not possessed, and, if possessed, to rest therein; but also to diffuse their own goodness among others as far as possible. . . . Hence if natural things, insofar as they are perfect, communicate their own goodness to others, much more does it pertain to the divine will to communicate by likeness its own goodness to others as far as possible.[7]

This is a far cry from the Lockean and other modern conceptions of substance as inert, static, unknowable substratum. Action is precisely the way an existing substance manifests its inner being, both its existence and its essence. As St. Thomas puts it:

> The operation of a thing manifests both its substance and its existence.[8]
>
> The operation of a thing shows forth its power, which in turn manifests (*indicat*: points out) its essence.[9]
>
> The substantial forms of things, which, according as they are in themselves, are unknown to us, shine forth to us (*innotescunt*) through their accidental properties.[10]

Every real substance, therefore, is highly dynamic. The whole point of its being is to express itself, to fulfill itself, to share its riches, through action appropriate to its mode of being (its essence). The substance of a being, accordingly, is its perduring, autonomous self-identity, as manifested and fulfilled through activity. It is a serious misunderstanding, then, to describe substance, as has so often been done after Locke, not only as inert but as unqualifiedly *unchanging*. It is an essential ingredient of the classical understanding of substance that the *substance itself changes* in every accidental change. Of course it does; otherwise the change would make no difference at all to the being which undergoes the change, which is absurd. The exact technical formula runs as follows: *In every accidental change the substance itself changes, but not substantially, only accidentally*. It does not become another being, essentially different from what it was before. Being substantially *self-identical*, therefore, is not at all equivalent to being *unchanging*. Real self-identity is dynamic and accommodates a wide range of changes within it, but always within limits. If these are broken down by too extreme a change, its essential self-identity can no longer maintain itself and dissolves into something else.[11]

This notion of substance as dynamic self-identity expressing itself in action—and therefore undergoing accidental change in our finite, material world—is rooted, for Aquinas, in his most significant contribution to metaphysics, the notion that the core of every real being is constituted by its (*esse*) or act of existence, conceived not as form or whatness or essence but as active presence—power-filled presence, if you will (*virtus essendi*). This active presence is limited, indeed, in all beings outside the pure unlimited Act of divine existence, by its distinctive limiting essence. But because of this dynamic inner core, every being, by its very nature as existing being, as being in act, tends naturally to flow over into action according to its essence. And since all action is not only self-manifestation but self-communication in some way, every being is by nature self-communicative, oriented toward presenting itself through action to the community of other real existents and reciprocally receiving their self-communications in its own being. Action is thus the dynamic bond between beings, which, without dissolving them into each other, binds them together to make a *universe* (*universum* = turned toward unity). In his doctrine of existence as self-communicative act Aquinas has integrated the whole dynamism of the self-diffusiveness of the Good from the Platonic tradition into his own metaphysics of being, with appropriate modifications.[12]

The immediate corollary of this notion of dynamic substance is that every substance, as active, becomes the center of a web of relations to other active beings around it. For action by its very nature generates relations with those on which it acts and from which it receives action in turn. Action, in fact, is the primary generator of real relations within the community of real beings. An existing substance, therefore, in St. Thomas's universe, as active, self-communicating presence, cannot *be* what it is without *being related* in some way. To be a substance and to be related are distinct but complementary and inseparable aspects of every real being. The structure of every being is indissolubly dyadic: it exists both as *in-itself* and as *toward* others.

Is this true of God also? From the philosophical point of view, St. Thomas, with the other Christian thirteenth-century thinkers, speaks cautiously here, more cautiously than some before him in the twelfth century. He does not want to say that reason alone can deduce that the divine nature is necessarily self-communicative within itself. The fact that this is so can be known only through the free divine revelation of the mystery of God as Triune, three Persons in one nature. Nor does he want to say that God *necessarily* pours over to share his own goodness in a created universe, as did Plotinus and the Neoplatonic schools; the freedom of creation was a central Christian doctrine, which all Christian thinkers were intent to defend against the necessitarian emanationism of the great Arabic metaphysicians of his time. So he argues by analogy that if all the creatures we know in fact manifest this self-communicativeness of their own goodness, it is necessary that the divine nature, the exemplar of all creatures, should have this same *aptitude* in the highest degree and most "fitting" that it should exercise it.

St. Bonaventure, for whom the fecundity of the divine goodness is a central pillar of his whole philosophy, speaks at times a little more daringly, and I think myself that St. Thomas should have too. He could, for example, have moved further in the direction of Hegel by saying that it is according to the divine nature—inevitable, if you will ("necessity" is perhaps too strong a word, with misleading implications of impersonal compulsion)—to communicate its goodness to *some* finite created world, but to *which particular* finite universe would have to be determined by a free choice, since there is no proportion between any finite universe and the infinite perfection of God such that we could deduce the first necessarily from the second. An infinite number of other finite universes always remain possible for the infinite divine power. The determination of *this* one would have to be the result of free choice and not of nature or necessity.[13]

But although philosophical reason by itself cannot determine the actual mode of the divine self-communication, Christian revelation fills in the picture magnificently, thus shedding brilliant new light on the philosophical explanation of the universe itself. For according to this revelation, although the creation of this finite universe is a free act of God, the inner being of God is by the very necessity of its nature *self-communicating love*, which flowers out into the internal procession of the three Persons within the unity of the divine nature. It is constitutive of the very personality of God as Father that he communicates the whole fullness of the divine perfection (or nature) without remainder to the Son, and that both together, in a mutual act of love, communicate the identical fullness of the same divine nature to their love-image, the Holy Spirit. It is thus of the very nature of being at its supreme intensity to pour over into self-communicative relatedness. And since God is the ultimate paradigm of being, of which all creatures in their distinctive ways must somehow be images, it follows that self-communication and relatedness to others must belong to the very nature of all being as such, and especially to persons as such. This does not mean that a person is *nothing but* a relation to others, as seems to be the case in most contemporary phenomenology and personalist existentialisms with their customary denials of person as substance. A relat*ed* is not identical with the relat*ion* which makes it related, but neither is it separable from it. Every person must bear within it the dyadic structure of in-itself interiority and self-transcending relatedness toward others. All the above is contained implicitly in the very structure and dynamism of St. Thomas's metaphysics of being as self-communicating act, although unfortunately, for various accidental historical reasons, I believe, he did not highlight as explicitly as I have the intrinsically relational aspect of being.

II. Distortions of Substance in Modern Philosophy

The Cartesian Self-Enclosed Substance

Descartes is mainly responsible (although there were slippages toward it in the late scholastic thought just before him) for the introduction of a new definition of substance, carrying with it a significant shift in its meaning. Substance for him is "that which exists by itself, that which needs nothing else but itself to exist."[14] When it was pointed out to him that strictly speaking this can apply only to God, he quickly modified it, when applied to creatures, to "that which needs nothing else save God to exist." Arrived at by his experience of himself as nothing but pure thinking substance, substance is here conceived as related vertically to God, but horizontally independent of other creatures, self-contained and self-sufficient. Later, of course, relations did come in to other things, but they remain adventitious. In its core substance is radical autonomy, as self-enclosed monad, unrelated and self-sufficient. Even its clear and distinct knowledge of the rest of the world is ideally to be deduced from its own innate ideas, not received by action from without.

Note the radical shift in meaning introduced by the apparently innocent change of a single word in the definition. The "in-itself" of the classical definition now becomes the "by-itself" of the Cartesian one. "In-itself" by no means denies relatedness to others or dependence on others as causes; it implies only that its subject is not a *part* of any other being but is an original center of action. "By itself" implies more: self-sufficiency, self-enclosure (at least toward other creatures), essential unrelatedness—or at least the assigning of real relations to a distinctly lower, more adventitious level of existence.

Whether Descartes was fully aware of the significant shift in meaning he had introduced and fully intended it is not clear (there are some indications to the contrary, since he occasionally proposes another more traditional definition). But in fact it is this aura of self-enclosure and essential unrelatedness that got attached to the notion of substance from now on in the history of modern philosophy, and is one main reason why so many have later rejected it. Whitehead, for example, bases his whole rejection of substance explicitly on this Cartesian definition. According to Descartes, Whitehead tells us, substance is that which exists by itself, that which needs nothing else save God to exist. For Whitehead himself the opposite is true. "Actuality is through and through togetherness." Every actual entity is related to and influenced by every other actual entity in the world. Hence it cannot be a substance. Such a notion of substance has no relevance in the real world of intrinsically interrelated process.[15]

After rightly rejecting the Cartesian notion of substance as isolated and self-enclosed, however, Whitehead goes on to reject substance entirely, with no further discussion, as though this were the only available meaning of the term. He seems quite unaware of the whole classical notion of substance as intrinsically dynamic, self-communicative to others, and imbedded in a web of relations generated by action and interaction. I do not blame Whitehead that much for this misunderstanding. He knew Plato well but not Aristotle and certainly not Aquinas. But I do object to contemporary Whiteheadians continuing to argue in the same way: first setting forth the Cartesian notion of substance, then demolishing it—correctly—and then concluding that the case in closed against substance. There may have been some excuse for Whitehead's doing this, coming late as he did to metaphysics, but not for perpetuating the same misunderstanding today.

The Inert, Unknowable Substratum of Locke

Another quite different notion of substance comes in with Locke. This is the identification of substance as the inert, unknowable substratum of accidents, which are alone known to us. These accidental properties need substance as an ontological support, but seem too much like pins stuck in a pincushion, which is itself inert, static, without dynamic, self-communicative relationship with them and through them to the outside world. Although Locke speaks somewhat differently of the self and seems to have started out with a more traditional notion of substance as agent, his growing interest in science and Newtonian physics gradually drew him toward assimilating the philosophical notion of substance to the scientific notion of underlying material substratum, on the model of Newton's atoms that were themselves not active but moved from without.[16]

This notion of substance as essentially inert, passive substratum, unchanging in its being, became deeply inbedded in subsequent Western thought and is one of the main reasons why so many later thinkers to this day reject substance as opposed to activity, development, relationship. It is precisely for this reason that Hegel, for example, felt he had to substitute "subject" for "substance" as the primary instance of being, because the aura of inertness, passivity, and other materialistic connotations that had begun to infect the notion of substance through Locke rendered it inapt to express the dynamic activity and creative self-unfolding proper to the life of spirit. There is much to be learned from Hegel's critique, once substance is understood in the Lockean sense. His solution, however, brought with it its own difficulties: the subject takes on an epistemological dimension in which it tends to become totally productive of its own object.[17]

It is for a similar reason that so many phenomenologists—and psychologists, in their philosophical moments—reject substance, on the grounds that what is really significant in the study of human beings is their activity, their behavior, their dynamic development, their relatedness, not their static, unchanging substance or essence. The retriever of classical substance would, of course, answer that substance is precisely the dynamic principle of all such activity and development, expressing its own self through them.

The Separable Substance of Hume

Still a different—and perhaps the most destructive—distortion is brought in by Hume, with strong roots in the nominalist tradition of William of Ockham. Hume, as is well known, rejects outright the notion of an abiding, self-identical substance, as an invention of the metaphysicians with no grounding in reality. The real (at least as regards our knowledge of it) is nothing more than a succession of discrete sense impressions, bound together in bundles. But the important point for our purposes is *what kind* of substance he rejects and why. It is clear from his arguments and those of his empiricist followers, like Bertrand Russell, that substance is something which, if it existed, would have to be found *separate* (or separable) from its accidental properties, existing in a kind of naked, indeterminate state. Since that is obviously impossible, indeed absurd—there can be, for example, no real human nature that exists as neither old nor young, black nor white, fat nor thin, wise nor ignorant, a pure indeterminate blob without attributes—it follows that no such thing as substance exists as really distinct from its accidents or attributes.

The key to Hume's argument is that whatever exists as really *distinct* from something else must also be *separable* from it—at least in our imagination and, as far as we know, in reality. Thus substance is a metaphysical mirage, a linguistic accident based on our Western subject-object languages and illegitimately projected into the real, as Bertrand Russell has put it.[18] This notion of substance as something not only distinct but *separable* from its accidents, that must be discovered *apart* from them, has been deeply imbedded in empiricist thought ever since and is simply taken for granted as the only notion there is. The metaphysical principle upon which it is based, that all real distinction necessarily implies separability, is again simply taken for granted by Hume as obvious, never explicitly justified or argued for.

According to the classical understanding, on the contrary, a substance is indeed really *distinct* from (i.e., objectively irreducible to) its accidental attributes, but never *separable* from the whole body of them. As center of activity and relations, it must always possess some accidents, though particular ones may come and go. It is immanent in each of them, expresses itself through them, but transcends them all; it is never *reducible without remainder* to any or all of them. I must always have some particular height and weight, but I am not stuck permanently in the present ones.

The association of substance with separability from all its accidents, especially from its relations to others, seems to be one of the main reasons why most, if not all, existentialists—with surprising unanimity on this point despite their other differences—and most phenomenologists reject substance as applying to the human person.[19] For them the person is so inseparable from I-Thou relations to others that its very being is constituted by relations; hence, they believe, it cannot be a substance. Thus for Heidegger the human *Dasein* is not to be identified with substance, the reason being that its very being is intrinsically constituted by its relation to Being as the receiver, interpreter, and spokesman of the latter's self-revelation. But with the denial of substance, the "in-itself" dimension of being, the personal subject tends to dissolve into its relations, to become *nothing but* its relations to others. This culminates in the explicit rejection by the Postmoderns and Deconstructionists of all interiority, of all selfhood as nothing but the creation of literary texts.

What thinkers of this persuasion do not seem to be aware of is that by reducing beings to their relations they fall right into the trap of the Buddhists, based on the identical Humean principle that all real distinction necessarily implies separability. But whereas Hume used it to deny the reality of relations, the Buddhists turn it in the opposite direction to show the total reducibility of all beings to pure mutual relations. They then show that in such a system there is no ontological support for anything—nothing has "own-being," as they say—and the whole collapses into "emptiness" (*sunyatta*). Only non-related being can be truly real, and this is beyond access by concepts and language.

III. The Reintegration of Substance and Relation

It seems to me that we are now in a position to retrieve creatively the full richness of what it means to be, drawing on the resources of both classical and modern thought. We do not have to choose between substance and relation, between the in-itselfness of being and its transcendence toward others, as though they were opposed to or excluded each other. The intrinsic structure of all being is irreducibly dyadic: *substance*-in-*relation*. The dichotomizing of being into one or the other is due to one or more of the successive distortions of the original meaning of substance: the self-enclosed substance of Descartes, the inert, unknowable substance of Locke, or the separable substance of Hume—with numerous variations and interweaving of these themes. Once substance has been reconceived as the in-itself dimension of being that is also by its very nature oriented toward self-transcending, self-communicative action reaching out to others and thus necessarily generative of a web of relations all around it, we can also integrate with it all the rich developments of the relational dimension so characteristic of later modern and contemporary thought, deeply influenced as it is by the relational structure of modern scientific thought. By the very nature of being as active presence, substance and relation are intrinsically complementary to each other, distinct but inseparable. *To be* in the world of real existents is to be *substance-in-relation*.

An important qualification must be added. Substance, like all the major metaphysical concepts, must be understood *analogously*. Like being itself as active presence, it is realized in different degrees of intensity and perfection on different levels of being. Thus the human substance stands out from the common matrix of nature with a fairly strong individuality, autonomy, and self-possession. But as one goes down the scale of being, this in-itselfness, which is a function of the immanent energy of existence as active presence, becomes weaker, less intense, more deeply dependent on the environmental matrix around it, less distinguishable from the fields which envelop it. When we reach the level of subatomic particles, they become interwoven so deeply with these enveloping fields that it is hard to identify where their individuality begins or ends. They exist only minimally as substances. There is more "outside" to them than "inside," we might say.

But it remains an open question scientifically—perhaps even metaphysically?—whether this in-itself dimension, this "interiority" aspect of being could ever fade out entirely and become pure relational field with no particles or centers of action at all. Here my reflections come to touch more closely the recent work of Ivor Leclerc, in whose honor these essays have been gathered, whose life's work has been to revitalize the philosophy—or perhaps more precisely, the metaphysics—of nature. On the one hand, contemporary metaphysicians have wisely become more cautious, in the light of the very strange phenomena uncovered at the fringes of nature by quantum physics, about legislating on a priori philosophical grounds what can be real and what not. Metaphysicians in the past have tended to ground their analyses of being a bit too exclusively on the middle levels of reality more immediately accessible to us in our direct human experience, in particular living things and persons. Thus Aristotle's metaphysics of nature, substance, final causality, etc., find their clearest application on the levels of being from living organisms upwards but become fuzzy when applied below this level. Thus it is not clear in him whether the primal elements, earth, air, fire, and water, are to be classified as primary substances or not. The fringe phenomena of the subatomic world are also an authentic revelation of what it means to be, difficult as it may be for us at present to decipher and articulate just what they are revealing.

Despite this methodological caution, it does seem to me, as I think it does to Professor Leclerc, more solidly plausible to hold that pure relational field theories of material reality as more primordial than particles are not adequate, either scientifically or metaphysically. Scientifically it does seem at present that it is not possible to substitute pure fields of energy for particles. Particles are always needed as correlative with fields, if not as primordially generative of fields. (A metaphysician, of course, cannot settle such questions scientifically.) Metaphysically speaking, it does seem to me that particles of some kind, which at least give the appearance of being more centered and unified, are the more plausible candidates for being the primal individual substances or natures which stand "in themselves" as original centers of action that generate relational fields out of their actions. Could it be, though, that energy fields themselves could have their own form and matter and thus somehow have enough of a unified action of their own to qualify as substances or basic entities in their own right? I am not sure whether or how a metaphysician could in principle rule this out. So I had better take the more prudent path of not trying to settle it with our present state of knowledge but leaving it rather as a question mark still enveloped in mystery. If particles, once paired, now seem to be instantaneously present to each other across space, why could there not be some space-and-time-transcending unity enabling a field to have some centered unity of action?[20]

As we go up the scale of being, on the other hand, the inner autonomy of the in-itself aspect of substances would gradually increase, so that they would stand out more and more distinctively and autonomously from their surrounding and supporting environments, finally attaining the level of self-initiating freedom in their actions, such as we observe in human persons, partially limited though this still remains by outside influences. As we ascend still higher, the autonomy and freedom grow stronger, so that finally in the supreme being the in-itselfness becomes total autonomy and self-sufficiency with all relations to the outside purely the result of its own free gratuitous initiatives. But at all levels real being would always remain dyadic, a polarity of active substance and relation, of in-self interiority and self-transcending outreach toward others.

IV. APPLICATION TO THE HUMAN PERSON

It seems to me especially illuminating to apply this basic metaphysics of being to the level of reality closest and most significant to us, that of the human person. Let us begin with the theme of the proportionate correlativity of substance and its field of relations, in St. Thomas. For him, the higher one ascends on the ladder of being and the more immaterial a being becomes, the more its depth of interiority and self-possession increases, while at the same time, in direct proportion, the field of its relations broadens in scope and deepens in intensity and perfection. As St. Thomas puts it in one of his sweeping synoptic statements:

> The higher a power the more comprehensive is the sphere of objects toward which it is ordered. The entire range over which the soul's activity extends can be ordered into three levels. One of the soul's powers concerns only the body to which the soul is joined; this kind of power is called the vegetative faculty, and its activity affects only the body to which this soul is joined. Then there is in the soul another kind of power that relates to a wider sphere, namely, to all material objects accessible through the senses and not just relating to the body to which the soul is joined. And a third kind of power in the soul is directed toward an even more comprehensive sphere of objects: not only toward all material things but toward all that exists.[21]

Josef Pieper, commenting on this text, sums the point up beautifully:

> To sum it up then: to have (or to be) an "intrinsic existence" means "to be able to relate" and "to be the sustaining center of a field of reference." The hierarchy of existing things, being equally a hierarchy of intrinsic existences, corresponds on each level to the intensity and extension of the respective relationship in their power, character, and domain. Consequently, the spirit-based self, the highest form of being and of intrinsic existence as well, must have the most intensive power to relate and the most comprehensive domain of relatedness: the universe of all existing things. These two aspects combined—dwelling most intensively within itself and being *capax universi*, able to grasp the universe—together constitute the essence of the spirit. Any definition of "spirit" will have to contain these two aspects as its core.[22]

St. Thomas develops in detail the intellectual aspect of this comprehensiveness of relations as one of his favorite themes: "It has been said that the soul is in a certain sense all in all; for its nature is directed toward universal knowledge. In this manner it is possible for the perfection of the entire world to be present in one single being."[23] But the same is true of the will, with its corresponding power to relate to and love all beings in the universe as good. Now since, as we have seen earlier, "every substance exists for the sake of its operations," it follows that the authentic life of the soul, the full flowering of perfection of the human person as such, consists of the fullest and broadest possible self-transcendence toward loving relationships to others. To *be* authentically for a human person is to *live in love*, to express itself by loving, in the broadest sense of the term, to make itself the center of the widest possible web of relationships to all things, and especially to all persons, through our two major self-relating and self-transcending powers, knowledge and love. To live as a person is to live in relation.[24]

St. Thomas has laid down clearly the metaphysical underpinnings of this relational dimension of the person as spirit. But the full phenomenological development of the point had to wait for the rich descriptive analyses of the personalist existentialists and phenomenologists of our own day, such as Martin Buber, Gabriel Marcel, etc. St. Thomas would have been delighted with them, I am sure. But despite all their richness, these descriptions tend too often to stress the relational side of the person so exclusively that the correlative pole of in-depth interiority and self-possession, the in-itself dimension of the person, becomes obscured or even wiped out. The extreme of this tendency has revealed itself in the various forms of Postmodernism, with their openly declared "war against interiority."[25] For St. Thomas there is no need to play down the substance pole of a being in order to safeguard the relational: the substance itself is the active source from which flow the relations as its own self-expression. To absorb the person entirely into its relations, into its "toward-others," is to empty it of anything truly belonging to it that is worth expressing to others. There is no merit in giving oneself totally to others unless one has something to give.

In connection with this notion of the person as intrinsically relational, it is interesting to note that Cardinal Josef Ratzinger, in his often remarkably insightful and creative earlier theological writings, makes the point that the Christian theological tradition did not have to wait for contemporary phenomenology to discover the relational dimension of the person. It was already deeply imbedded in its own Gospel revelation and theological explication of the Trinity, though this has never, he feels, been adequately developed and exploited in the Christian philosophical tradition.[26] The very notion of person in the doctrine of God as three Persons in one divine nature is a totally relational one. Each Person is distinguished from the others solely by its relational character, by "the opposition of relations," as it is technically called; all else in the divine nature is held in common. Thus the Father knows himself *as Father* only in communicating the whole "absolute" perfection of his divine nature to the Son, that is, as Giver; whereas the Son knows himself *as Son* only in receiving this same nature from the Father, that is, as Receiver; so too the Holy Spirit is known only as the love image breathed forth by both Father and Son as the expression of their mutual love. The whole personality of Jesus as expressed in the Gospels is also totally relational, dialogical, *toward the Father*: "All that I have I have received from my Father . . . all that my Father has he has given to me . . . my food is to do my Father's will," etc. So we too come to know ourselves, what we are and who we are, only by looking in the eyes of another, through the loving (or hating) look in the eyes of another person, the "I" through the "Thou" and vice versa.

The notion of the self, the person, as primordially an isolated, atomic individual, only accidentally related to others, came in much later, with Descartes and Locke. It is as alien to the classical and medieval Christian tradition, both theological and philosophical, as their notions of substance are to the classical and medieval one of substance as active relation-generating center. The human person, in fact, comes into existence enveloped in a web of relations of dependence on others even before it can begin to generate its own relations actively: dependence on God as the ultimate source of its being, on its parents for the gift of its nature, on the surrounding environment for the necessary conditions for its survival and growth (air, temperature, food, etc.). And its whole development will consist in relating itself appropriately, both actively and responsively, to the world around it and especially to other persons, both human and divine. The Christian *philosophical* tradition, however, at least in its medieval scholastic—and even Thomistic—forms, although it had laid down well the metaphysical foundations for the notion of person as intrinsically relational, in fact got so preoccupied in its technical analyses with determining in just what consisted the "incommunicability" or distinctness of persons from each other that it failed to develop and highlight with full explicitness the relational pole, equally intrinsic to all persons, that was already so richly imbedded in its own theological sources.

Conclusion

In our own time, however, there is no longer any need for us to get stuck exclusively in one or other of the two correlative poles of real being, substance *or* relation. It is high time to retrieve the full richness of the classical notion of substance as active center generative (and receptive) of relations and to restore the full polarity of the real, which flourishes only in the vital tension and mutual complementarity of substance *and* relation. In sum, *to be is to be substance-in-*

relation. And the ultimate reason for this is, in what to my mind is the essence of St. Thomas's metaphysical vision, that the *esse* (the "to be") or act of existing that is the deepest core of every real being is of its very nature not just presence but *active presence*: presence both in itself and actively presenting itself to others. "It is the nature of every actuality to communicate itself insofar as it is posible. Hence every agent acts according as it exists in actuality." "Communication follows upon the very intelligibility (*ratio*) of actuality."[27] This last text, terse though it be, seems to me one of the richest and most profound in all of St. Thomas, indeed in any philosopher, whether of East or West. In the last analysis, it sums up all I have been trying to say in this essay.

[*Author's Note*. Since the writing of this paper, David Schindler, Editor of *Communio*, has published a sympathetic but critical review (*Communio*, 20, Fall 1933, 580–92) of my writings on person and relation, which urges me to go even further in the relational aspect of the person. He thinks my "dyadic" notion of the person as existing *in-itself* and *toward-others* is too limited in perspective. It stresses the priority of the substance as actively generating relations through its own active initiative, as though action would come first in us and relations second. But in every finite (created) substance there is a more primordial relation of receptivity constitutive of its very being before it can pour over into action at all: namely, that it has received its very act of existence from another, ultimately from God, the Source of all existence. Thus we should describe every created being as possessing its own existence *from another, in itself*, and oriented *toward others*—a triadic rather than just a dyadic structure.

I think he is perfectly correct in this. I had not thought of this profound dimension of receptivity, hence relativity, in all of us, even preceding any action on our part. Hence I am quite willing to broaden my description of all—at least finite—being to include a triadic aspect: being from another, being in itself, being toward others, or, in the luminous terseness of the Latin, *esse ab, esse in, esse ad*. That is why the first appropriate response of a conscious being should in principle be gratitude for its own being as a gift from. . . .

Can we go further and assert that this relation of primordial receptivity of its own being is proper not only to created being but to all being, including the divine? We could not affirm this on the basis of philosophical inference about the divine, hidden in mystery from our limited concepts, extrapolated from our experience of finite beings. But the Christian revelation of God as Triune opens up to us a vision of the interior life of God as containing receptivity within it as part of its very being as divine life, i.e., it is of the very nature of the supreme divine being that the Second and Third Persons within possess the one, whole, and complete divine nature as gift *received from* the First Person through the eternal processions of the Son from the Father and the Holy Spirit from both. Thus this primordial relation of receptivity is somehow present in all being, though in a highly analogous way in God, freed from all limitation and imperfection.

I might add that in created beings this primordial relation of receptivity in being extends not only to God but also to many other preexisting beings, such as our parents, and indeed to the whole supporting environment of our tightly interwoven material cosmos. We are indeed *from* this whole material world in some significant way and should extend our gratitude appropriately to it. I am grateful to David Schindler for thus stimulating me to expand my own thought, as I have expanded St. Thomas's, as I have already partly expressed in my friendly exchange with him in the above-mentioned issue of *Communio*, pp. 593–98.]

NOTES

1. For a fine exposition of Aquinas's doctrine of substance, see L. De Raeymaeker, *The Philosophy of Being* (St. Louis: Herder, 1954), ch. 7.
2. *Summa contra Gentes*, III, ch. 26.
3. *Sum. c. Gent.*, I, ch. 45.
4. *Sum c. Gent.*, III, ch. 113.
5. *De Potentia*, q. 2, art. 1.
6. *Expositio in Libros Sententiarum*, Bk. I, dist. 4, q. 1, art. 1.
7. *Summa Theologiae*, I, q. 19, art. 2.
8. *Sum c. Gent.*, II, ch. 79.
9. *Sum c. Gent.*, II, ch. 94.
10. *Sum. Theol.*, I, q. 77, art. 1 ad 7.
11. Cf. De Raeymaeker, *Philosophy of Being*, pp. 174–77.
12. W. Norris Clarke, "Action as the Self-revelation of Being: A Central Theme in the Thought of St. Thomas," in L. Thro, ed., *History of Philosophy in the Making: Essays in Honor of James Collins* (Lanham, Md.: Univ. Press of America, 1982), pp. 63–80, reprinted as chapter 3 of this collection.
13. For the discussion of this whole question of the self-diffusiveness of the good and the freedom of creation, cf. M. J. Nicolas, "Bonum est diffusivum sui," *Revue thomiste*, 55 (1955), 363–76; Kevin Keane, "Why Creation? Bonaventure and Thomas Aquinas on God as Creative Good," *Downside*

Review 93 (1975), 100–21. The consistency of the two notions was given a famous challenge by Arthur Lovejoy in his *Great Chain of Being* (1946). The answers of Henry Veatch and Anton Pegis and his response can be found in *Philosophy and Phenomenological Research*, 7 (1946). Norman Kretzmann has reopened the question in his "Goodness, Knowledge and Indeterminacy in the Philosophy of Thomas Aquinas," *Journal of Philosophy*, 80 (1983), 631–49. See also Scott MacDonald, ed., *Being and Goodness: The Concept of the Good in Metaphysics and Philosophical Theory* (Ithaca: Cornell Univ. Press, 1990).

14. *Replies to the 4th Series of Objections* in Haldane & Ross, eds., *Philosophical Works of Descartes* (Cambridge Univ. Press, 1931), II, 101.

15. See the fine discussion of Whitehead on substance: James Felt, "Whitehead's Misconception of Substance," *Process Studies*, 14 (1985), 224–36.

16. For a useful study of Locke on substance, see Gregory Reichberg, "Nominalism and the Inscrutability of Substance in Locke's *Essay concerning Human Understanding*," *Proc. Amer. Cath. Phil. Assoc.*, 61 (1987), 122–32.

17. Cf. the fine study of Kenneth Schmitz, "Substance Is Not Enough. Hegel's Slogan: From Substance to Subject," *Proc. Amer. Cath. Phil. Assoc.*, 61 (1987), 52–68.

18. *A History of Western Philosophy* (New York: Simon & Schuster, 1945), pp. 201–2.

19. Cf. William Shearson, "The Common Assumptions of Existentialist Philosophy," *Internat. Phil. Quarterly*, 15 (1975), 131–47.

20. Cf. Richard Connell, *Substance and Modern Science* (Houston: Center for Thomistic Studies, 1988). This work is helpful for organisms, molecules, atoms, and elementary particles, but does not venture further into the more mysterious subatomic world of quantum physics, with its wave-particles, fields, etc. For a daring reinterpretation of substance, where substance in the quantum world becomes the whole integrated mathematical structure of the world realized as a concretized Platonic idea, a single unitary substance of which all the subatomic reactions are but accidents, see Joseph Zycinski, "A Return to Plato in the Philosophy of Substance," *New Scholasticism*, 63 (1989), 419–34.

21. *Sum. Theol.*, I, q. 78, art. 1.

22. Josef Pieper, *The Truth of All Things*, reprinted in *The Living Truth* (San Francisco: Ignatius Press, 1989), p. 83.

23. *De Veritate*, q. 2, art. 2.

24. As Maritain beautifully expresses it: "Thus it is that when a man has been fully awakened to the sense of being or existence, and grasps intuitively the obscure, living depth of the Self and subjectivity, he discovers by the same taken the basic generosity of existence and realises, by virtue of the inner dynamism of this intuition, that love is not a passing pleasure or emotion, but the very meaning of his being alive." *Existence and the Existent* (Garden City, N.Y.: Doubleday, 1957), p. 90.

25. Cf. Mark C. Taylor, *Erring: A Postmodern A/Theology* (Chicago: Univ. of Chicago Press, 1984), ch. 2: "The Disappearance of the Self."

26. Josef Ratzinger, *Introduction to Christianity* (New York: Herder & Herder, 1970), pp. 102–3; and the more fully developed exposition in "Concerning the Person in Theology," *Communio*, 17 (1990), 438–54.

27. See note 6.

7
Analogy and the Meaningfulness of Language about God

I must say that I feel considerable sympathy with Professor Nielsen* in his difficulties in making sense out of the Thomistic doctrine of analogy as a device for rendering language about God meaningful. In fact, for many years now I have been struck by the constantly recurring phenomenon of philosophers outside the Thomistic tradition trying to understand the doctrine of analogy as applied to God and being quite sincerely baffled in their attempts to see how it can do the job assigned to it. When this occurs so often, there is a good chance that the fault is not all on the one side. And, to be honest, I do not think Professor Nielsen gets adequate help from either Father Copleston or Professor Ross. He may not get adequate help from me either, but I would still like to try, since I consider the issue such an important one.

The main reasons for the obscurity surrounding the Thomistic theory of analogy seem to be three. First, *historically*, St. Thomas himself, ordinarily such a systematic thinker, for some unexplained reason was never willing to pin himself down to any one consistent terminology or structural analysis of the logical form of analogy. He simply used it, very sensitively but without any full dress explanation of what he was doing. When Thomistic commentators after him have tried to pin down the theory more precisely and technically, they too often have fallen into the straightjacket of Cajetan's oversimplified and restrictive systematization, in which the structure of proper proportionality is understood as a four-term proportion, a structure that St. Thomas himself quietly abandons as not adequate by itself after his early work, *De Veritate*.[1]

This article is a reply to the article of Kai Nielsen, which preceded it, denying the possibility of any meaningful language about God: "Analogical Talk about God: A Negative Critique," *The Thomist*, 40 (1976), 32–60. In his article Professor Nielsen makes reference to F. C. Copleston, *Contemporary Theology* (London, 1956) and James F. Ross, "Analogy as a Rule of Meaning in Religious Language," *International Philosophical Quarterly* 1 (1961), 468–502, and "A New Theory of Analogy" in *Logical Analysis and Contemporary Theism*, ed. John Donnelly (New York: Fordham Univ. Press, 1972).

Secondly, *doctrinally* speaking, Thomists tend too often to omit in their formal analyses of analogy the indispensable metaphysical underpinning that alone justifies the application of analogy when one of the terms is not known directly in itself. No purely logical or semantic analysis of the structure of analogous concepts can supply this extra-logical component. In addition, Thomistic commentators for the most part do not bring out clearly enough—if indeed they accept the point at all—the fact that analogy does not lie so much in any formal structure of concepts themselves as in the actual lived usage of meaningful analogous language, found only when the so-called analogous concepts are used in *judgments*.[2] In the light of the above comments I would like to see if I can shed some light of my own on Professor Nielsen's difficulties, so that at least the authentic and essential points of disagreement may be brought more clearly into focus and allow more fruitful dialogue thereon than usually seems to be the case in this elusive question of analogy.

Objections of Professor Nielsen

The three most crucial objections of Professor Nielsen against the explanations of Copleston and Ross seems to me to be the following. (1) The first concerns the distinction made by Copleston between the "subjective meaning" of an analogous term, i.e., our understanding of the meaning as drawn from instances in our experience, which he admits is anthropomorphic, and the "objective meaning," i.e., the objective reality referred to by the concept as found in God and affirmed of God, even though we do not know just what this is like, but only point to it in the dark, so to speak, and for good reasons, since it is an infinitely higher mode beyond the direct grasp of our experience and concepts. But the trouble here, as Professor Nielsen points out, is that, since we have no access to this objective meaning as it is verified in God, which is quite different from the subjective meaning drawn from our experience, this so-called objective meaning is vacuous, empty of meaningful content for us who are using the term. And the gap between the two meaning-contents indicates that the concepts predicated in each case are not the same, though the same word is used; hence there is equivocation. (2) The second concerns the very meaning of an analogous concept in itself. At the heart of every analogous concept, Professor Nielsen insists, there must be "a common core of meaning," which in turn necessarily implies that this core of meaning must be univocal. "Common core of meaning" and "univocal" are co-extensive and convertible terms. No merely formal struc-

Analogy and the Meaningfulness of Language about God

ture of isomorphic relations can supply such a common core. (3) Third, Professor Nielsen points out that there is no way of confirming or verifying the meaningfulness or truth of what is analogously predicated of God, since there is no way of verifying or falsifying it from experience or by any kind of testing for consequences.

Most of my reply will be directly concerned with the objections to Copleston, since the objections to Ross seem to me merely a more technical application of the same basic difficulties. And, besides, I agree with much of Professor Nielsen's dissatisfaction with any attempt to lay out analogy in some formal logical structure. No isomorphism of formal relations can supply for intrinsic similarity in content between the sets of relations compared. Since I do not think it feasible to separate out the answers to the three objections, for they all involve the same roots, I shall give my own account of how analogy works and pick up the objections along the way at appropriate points. I will not give any distinct answer to the third objection. Many have handled this already. And there is simply no testing from experience or from consequences of predications when one is discoursing about the attributes of God. The only testing is the metaphysical exigency of intelligibility itself: predications about God *must* have both meaning and truth if our own world is not to fall into unintelligibility. They are all metaphysical *musts* flowing from the primary *must* of the causal bond itself. Hence I will divide my exposition into three main sections: I. Must Analogy Be Rooted in Univocity? II. The Extension of Analogy beyond the Range of Our Experience. III. The Application of Analogy to God and Its Metaphysical Underpinning.

I. MUST ANALOGY BE ROOTED IN UNIVOCITY?

As we read through Professor Nielsen's criticism of both Copleston and Ross, we notice one crucial assumption functioning over and over again, at first more or less implicitly, then finally surfacing with full explicitness. It is this: if there is to be any genuine similarity within difference in the various predications of an analogous term, then this similarity necessarily involves some "common property" or attribute, even if only a relation, which holds in all applications; and the presence of such a common property necessarily involves a "univocal core of meaning." Analyzing one of St. Thomas's descriptions of knowing (it should be noted, however, that this does not apply to all knowing but only to the knowing of another than oneself), that is, "the possession of the form of another as another, according to one's natural mode of possession," Professor Nielsen comments:

This last qualification presumably gives us the difference which keeps the predication from actually being univocal. But it remains the case that on the assumption (questionable in itself) that Aquinas' account of knowing is intelligible, it is true that in all cases of 'knowing' there is a property that remains common to and distinctive of all these uses. That is to say, we could construct a predicate signifying the *res significata* of 'knowing' that would be predicated of all cases of knowing. This would be a univocal predication. (p. 50)

In other words, whenever there is a common property predicated, there must be a univocal core of meaning. Hence even the qualifying phrase added by St. Thomas, "according to one's natural mode of possession," must leave intact the univocal core of meaning, "possession of the form of another as another."

Here is the central and clear-cut point of contention between Professor Nielsen and the Thomistic tradition in the very meaning of analogy itself. Thomists would admit—though a few, like David Burrell, seem unduly squeamish about doing so—that in some significant sense there must be some common core of meaning in all analogous predications of the same term, for otherwise it could not function as one term and concept. But they insist, on the other hand, that this common core of meaning is not therefore univocal, but remains analogous, similar-in-difference, or diversely similar. If it is any consolation to Professor Nielsen, his objection is exactly the same as that brought against Thomistic analogy by Duns Scotus and William of Ockham shortly after the time of Thomas himself. For them the sufficient requirement that a term be univocal is that it be able to function as a middle term retaining the same meaning in both premises of a syllogism, enough to avoid equivocation. An analogous term was for them really a verbal unity of two distinct, though related, concepts, and if used in both senses in the same argument would introduce a fourth term and invalidate the argument.[3]

Yet this is definitely not the Thomistic understanding of univocity and analogy. The difference in approach between the two positions might be summed up thus: The Scotus-Ockham analysis is geared primarily to the demands of deductive reasoning and the logical functioning of concepts. It also takes the word and concept as the fundamental unit of meaning, which remains intact in its own self-contained meaning no matter how it is moved around as a counter in combination with other concepts, including its use in a judgment, which is interpreted simply as a composition of two concepts, subject and predicate, without change in either. The Thomistic analysis is

Analogy and the Meaningfulness of Language about God 127

geared much more to the actual lived usage of the concept in a judgment, interpreted as an intentional act of referring its synthesis of subject-predicate to the real order, as it is in reality. Hence it tends to look right through the abstract meaning of the concept to what it signifies, or intends to signify (*intendit significare*), in the concrete, and so adjusts the content of the concept to what it knows about its realization in the concrete. The difference in perspective—and in theories of the relation of concept to judgment—leads to quite different conclusions, which I think are considerably more than a merely verbal dispute over different terminologies for the same thing, though there is some of that hanging like a cloud over the scene too, causing the opponents to pass each other in the fog without meeting.

Let me explain now how I think Thomistic analogy actually works, building it up genetically from its actual origin and use in living language. I take it as understood that from now on when I speak of analogous terms and concepts I am referring only to what Thomists identify as properly and intrinsically analogous terms, i.e., those that are intended to express a *proportionate intrinsic similarity* found in all the analogates (hence not analogies of the so-called "extrinsic attribution," such as "healthy" applied to man and to food, which is not designed to express similarity but some relation of causality, belonging to, etc.). Such intrinsic analogies are found in terms like "knowledge," "love," "activity," "unity," "goodness," "being," and the like.

We construct and use analogous concepts in our language-life to fit occasions wherein we cannot help but use them. This occurs when we notice some basic *similarity-in-difference*, or proportional similarity, across *a range of different kinds of subjects* (or on different levels of being, of qualitative perfection), such that the similarity we notice does not occur in the same qualitative way in each case but is noticed to be found in a *qualitatively different way* in each case. When we form a univocal concept, on the other hand, we pick out some similarity, usually some form or structure or quantitative relation, which we judge or notice to be found without significant qualitative variation in each case, usually falling within the same species or a genus with closely related properties. In such a case we notice that, even though a few examples are needed to get started, the meaning content, what the term objectively signifies, once grasped, remains neutral, indifferent, unchanged with respect to any further instances. Such a content is thus quite well defined, determinate, and fixed.

Not so with an analogous concept. The similarity we notice here is not some one thing or characteristic that remains exactly the same in all cases, except for some new additional note being added on each time from the outside. It is rather that the similar property itself is more or less profoundly and intrinsically modified in a qualitatively different way each time, so that through and through the *whole* property is recognized as at once similar yet different (not just found in some new instance that in other ways is different). An analogous concept is not a composition of one part exactly identical and another part different, as Scotus, Ockham, and Nielsen seem to imply; rather it is an indissoluble unity where the similarity itself is through and through diversified in each case. As a result there is quite a bit of "give," flexibility, indeterminacy, or vagueness right within the concept itself, with the result that the meaning remains essentially incomplete, so underdetermined that it cannot be clearly understood until further reference is made to some mode or modes of realization.

This leads us to discover one of the most remarkable and distinctive features of analogous concepts, especially the ones of broadest range: it is in fact impossible to define what we mean by an analogous concept, to grasp the similarity involved, except by actually running up and down the known *range* of cases to which it applies, by actually calling up the spectrum of *different* exemplifications, and then *catching the point*. The similarity involved cannot be isolated from its qualitatively diversifying modes and expressed by itself clearly, as it can be in the case of a univocal concept. It can indeed be caught or recognized by an act of intellectual insight as we run up and down the scale of examples. It can be *seen*, and *shown forth* by our meaningful linguistic behavior, as Wittgenstein would say, but it cannot be *said* or expressed clearly by itself. Or, if you wish, it can be said by framing one linguistic term for use in all cases, but the meaning of the term cannot be grasped at all clearly without actually calling up a diversified range of cases. The meaning of the term, therefore, must be completed and made determinate in each case by reference to some concrete qualitative mode. That is why the notion always contains within it, at least in an implicit way—which can easily be made explicit, as St. Thomas does in the example of knowledge—the parenthetical indication (like a kind of metalinguistic instruction or warning) *that* the property in question will be present in each case "according to the mode proportionate to the nature of each." Yet the concept itself, as an abstract predicate by itself, fit to be used in many different predications as somehow the same one concept, does not mention or contain within its expressed content *any* of these particular modes in any of its predications, but is understood as transcending them all. Otherwise, it is clear, it could not be used to refer to any other instance with a different mode. However, when this indeterminate abstract concept, unified as such, is actually *used in a concrete judgment*, its meaning, as *understood* in the *whole concrete act of knowing that is the judgment*, then molds itself or shifts to take on the particular determination of the case in hand, while at the same time continuing to recognize the intrinsic proportional similarity-in-difference of this instance with all the others in the range outlined by the concept. This is the point of the very astute remark made by Gilson long ago, that "'analogy' for Aquinas refers to our ability to make the kind of judgments we do," that it is to be explicated "on the level of judgment" and "not of concept" alone.[4] Analogy is found and understood on the level of the *lived use* of concepts and terms, not in any formalizable logical structure of the concept in itself. Thus when I understand in an analogous way a proposition like "*x* is active," what I mean is, "*x* exhibits or realizes in this different but still sufficiently similar way the same similarity-in-difference which I have already noticed running through a certain range of cases, so much so that I feel justified in expressing this case by the same analogous term as the others."

I have laid special stress in the above on the importance of the lived use of concepts in judgment, because it is not always brought out sufficiently by Thomists, and is one of the distinguishing marks of the approach of St. Thomas when compared to that of Scotus and Ockham. A Thomistic analogous term does indeed contain a certain genuine unity, though heavily laced with indeterminacy at its core, enough unity to function *logically* quite like a univocal term. And, of course, if one considers an analogous concept from a comparative or negative point of view with respect to other concepts, it is quite determinate in what it *excludes* from consideration, in how it delimits its *whole range* from that of other concepts. But the point remains that when looked at in what it positively includes within its range it cannot express clearly by itself the similarity in isolation from the differences. When it tries to do so through so-called definitions it can only call up as paraphrases other equally analogous and indeterminate terms, which themselves require reference to a range of diverse examples in order to be meaningful. And whenever it tries to become too precise, it contracts to become identical with just one of its modes and loses its analogical function.

Let me illustrate what I have been saying above by taking the same example used by Professor Nielsen, that of knowledge, defined by St. Thomas as "the possession of the form of another as another, according to one's natural mode of possession." Let us say that we have already recognized as included within its range of proper instances the dim knowledge through touch of the environment around it by an oyster or snail; the more complicated integration of visual, tactile, and audible sense images by a dog or other higher animal; the intellectual insight of man into justice or the inner law of operation of a typewriter or Einstein's Theory of Relativity; the Zen master's empty, imageless, supra-conceptual awareness of reality; the mystic's awareness of God in the "fine point of the soul" beyond all concepts and faculties. All are judged to be genuine though highly different instances of knowing. Now suppose we try to say or describe just what is the similarity amongst all of them, in itself. And suppose the person to whom we are trying to describe it says "I don't want you to do it by examples; just tell me what it is in itself." What could we possibly tell him that could capture the commonness by itself? We can only run through the spectrum of examples on different levels and then appeal to the person's own experience. "Do you know what I mean? Do you get the point?"

Professor Nielsen, it seems, would like to insist: "But there is a common univocal core: possession of the form of another as another. . . ." Yet suppose we try to apply this even to only two cases, such as a dog's "possession" of the "form" of a typewriter in the mode of a visual image of its external shape and color, compared with a man's "possession" of the "form" as intellectual insight into the inner law of operation of the machine. What in the world does "possession" mean here? How can we describe it in itself? Is it like the possession of a marble in one's pocket? No. Or having a cast in one'e eye? No. Is it possessing a visual image in consciousness? Aside from the problem of defining "consciousness," this is *one* example, but not one that adequately circumscribes the meaning, since having an intellectual insight into the intelligible form or law is vastly different, even though somehow similar—it is impossible to *specify* just how. The same difficulty would occur in trying to explain "form." The only thing one can finally do is call up the whole range of examples and ask, "Don't you catch the point? Do you see what I mean?" This is not an evasion; it is precisely the intelligent (in fact, the only effective) way to do it. The same with other analogous concepts, such as unity, activity, love, goodness, power, perfection (imagine trying to describe precisely what is similar in all instances of activity or unity). In a word, although one can indeed say that in some true sense (analogous) there is a common core of meaning in an analogous concept, it is nonetheless clear that the concept functions quite differently—if we look at it from within *as used*, not just from without *as a logical counter* in an argument—from a univocal concept with its common core.

This leads me to one more distinctive characteristic of the analogous concept which I think it most important to mention, since it too is frequently not made explicit by Thomist commentators. What kinds of things, or aspects of reality, or properties are thus amenable to, even necessarily require, expression through analogous terms? As I see it—and I am willing to defend this, even though it is not commonly mentioned—there is only one "dimension" of reality or "kind" of property that is capable of truly analogous expression: this is the realm of activities or dynamic functions, what we might call "activity properties" understood in the widest possible sense (plus, of course, the opposite correlative properties of receiving, being acted on, etc.: loving and being loved, causing and being caused are equally analogous). All such properties are expressed originally and primarily by *verbs*, not nouns, or are in some way reducible to verbs. Analogous terms can of course be nouns, but then the noun presupposes the verb—e.g., it signifies a subject, but as the doer of *such and such an action*, which aspect alone is made explicit (knower, lover . . .).

The reason why activity properties are such fit candidates for analogous expression is that the same general "kind" of activity can be performed quite differently by different kinds of agents or subjects without destroying the similarity-in-difference of the activity aspect itself. This is not true of forms, structures, quantitative relations, and the like, which are not thus elastic in their realizations. Different kinds of things in the universe, different levels of being, are not like each other in their essential specific forms or essences considered statically. But they are proportionally alike in their modes of *activity*, in their *dynamic functions*. Different forms themselves can only be compared as alike insofar as they are forms or structures for similar actions. If there is any formal structure to analogous concepts, it is not a strictly logical or formal structure, but the structure of an activity situation: an analogous term expresses *this general kind of activity x*, recognized as carried on in one distinctively different proportionate way by subject *b*, etc. The subjects and modes of acting are quite different in each case; the activities themselves are *recognized* as proportionately similar, similar-in-difference, although it remains impossible to state just *what* this similarity is apart from its range of varied modes. Let me add that if the term "activity" itself here is allowed to expand to its full analogous breadth of illuminative meaning, existence itself then not only can be described but is uniquely appropriate to be described as the most radical kind of activity or act, the act of "presenc*ing*." This is the Thomistic analogous notion of being itself: "that which has, or exercises, the act of existing."

II. The Extension of Analogous Terms beyond the Range of Our Experience

So far we have been analyzing how analogy functions within a range where all the main levels of exemplification lie within our experience, hence where the different modes can be directly known to us. The next phase of our investigation, crucial for the application to God, concerns the extension of analogous concepts beyond our present range of known examples, i.e., the formation of "open-ended" concepts whose range extends indefinitely beyond our present experience, at least in an upward direction. The ranges of analogous concepts can be roughly classified as follows: (1) those having *a ceiling but no floor* (no lower limit) in their application: terms like physico-chemical activity, whose upper limit is biological activity, or perhaps consciousness, but that extend downward to unknown depths of matter still hidden from us and perhaps very strange indeed compared with what we know; (2) those having both *a floor and a ceiling*, say, biological activity, or sense knowledge, limited by the non-living or unconscious below and intellectual knowledge above; (3) those having *a floor but no ceiling*: intellectual knowing, love, life, joy, etc.; (4) those having *neither ceiling nor floor*: the all-pervasive "transcendental properties" applicable across all levels of being, such as being, activity, unity, power, intelligibility, goodness (in the widest sense). Our special concern will be with numbers (3) and (4), as alone applicable to God.

How in general do we go about opening up an analogous concept beyond its presently known range of examples? Let us take the example of knowing. Suppose we reflect on how remarkably diverse are the modes we already know, and how impossible it is to deduce from a lower level what a higher level will be like; it then appears to us, when reflecting on the analogous meaning of knowing, that we have no good or decisive reasons for closing off its possible range at the level we know; in fact, there is some plausible suspicion that there may be higher kinds of intelligence on other planets or perhaps even beyond all corporeal entities (not yet God). We decide we should remain prudently open to the possibility of higher intelligence trying to communicate with us through some kind of signal. We have no idea what kind of communication or signals—they would not even have to be through material signs but might be by direct telepathy or thought-communication—or what the mode of intelligence involved might be like or how it might function in itself, even when not attached to a body. Yet it makes perfect sense, and in the concrete it is quite easy—we are actually doing it already—to open up the range of meaning of what we now experience and understand as intelligence to include in expectancy some possible level at present quite unknown and uncharacterizable by us. The new extension of the term, though empty of any precise content describable by us now, is not simply empty. It gets its new and very useful content of meaning from *its place on an ascending* (it might also be descending) *scale*, which serves as guide for *evaluation assessment* (respect, awe, fear, caution, etc.). Such a role as guide to evaluation procedures, and their practical consequences, is an indispensable one for our concrete life of the mind in the midst of a reality that is always partly known, partly concealed in relation to us.

Another example arises from the new scientific interest in parapsychology and psychic phenomena of various kinds. There is widespread talk of some new kind(s) of force that produces effects in the material world, yet seems to operate in ways thus far unknown to us and is quite different from the other physical forces we know— "psi-forces," some call them. They may be a new kind of physical radiation, or more probably psychic energy fields, or what have you. The point is that we quite readily enlarge the notion of force to make room for the *possible* discovery of a new mode, concerning which we can say nothing clear as yet, not even that it really exists. It may be objected that there is a univocal core in all description of such forces, in that they produce observable effects in the material world. There may, it is true, be one element of their definitions that has a univocal cast: the material effects produced. But the notion of force does not *mean* the effects produced. It means the *power producing* such effects, and as long as this central part of the meaning is variable in its mode the meaning must remain analogous.

In both of the above, and many other possible examples, in order to extend the range of an analogous concept we must "purify" its meaning-content, what it explicitly signifies, making it indeterminate enough so that its range of application will not be restricted within present limits. If we judge that this cannot be done without a violent and arbitrary wrench in the meaning that renders the term no longer comfortably serviceable, we judge the proposed extension inviable, too confusing, and devise an entirely new term to express the additional range of cases presumed to exist. This is a matter of good judgment, of a sense for successful living language, not a matter of the logical structure of concepts.

It is within the context of this extension of an analogous concept to a new application whose mode of realization is unknown to us that the traditional distinctions arise between "objective meaning" and "subjective meaning" (Copleston), the *res significata*, or the objective property signified by the term, and the *modus significandi*, or the modes by which we express to ourselves this property (St. Thomas), and other similar semantic devices. There is unfortunately much confusion in terminology here (and not infrequently in thought too, I fear), and I am not happy with either of the above ways of trying to spell out the same general point. St. Thomas's way is clear enough in itself—though often misunderstood, as it clearly is here by Professor Nielsen—but is so narrow in scope as he uses it that it does not do the entire job that has to be done. Copleston's way is, I fear, open to serious misunderstanding and seems to me to be inadequate to its task. So let me first state the job to be done, and how I think it best to express it, and then return to assessing the two sets of distinctions mentioned above.

In such a context of using analogous language, we must separate out the following: (1) the *res significata*, i.e., the "thing" or common property signified, which is what is actually predicated in each case, whether previously known or not. Its meaning-content as expressed in the analogous concept is deliberately or systematically vague and indeterminate, not restricted to any of its modes so as to be truly predicable of all cases. (It does not mean, by the way, the actual concrete *referent* of this predicate in a given judgment, although the terminology of "thing"—*res*—has misled some into thinking so.) (2) The *real modes*, or modes of being, in which this common objective property or attribute is understood to be realized in given applications, as we apply the term in concrete complete acts of knowing in the judgment. These modes may already be known to us, as the animal and human modes of knowing, or they may as yet be unknown to us, in which case we intend to signify what is there in the concrete but through a vague and incomplete act of knowing. Or, if you wish, we intend to refer to what is really there, but through a vague and incomplete mental sign, recognized as such, although we do recognize clearly *that* we are referring to a mode different from the others we know. These modes, however, are not part of what is actually predicated by the abstract analogous predicate itself, as is (1) above, although we *understand* the indeterminate content to take them on in the concrete, as we actually use the term.[5] (3) *The modes of our understanding* of the *res significata*, which are the best known modes of concrete realization of the common property, considered as ways or

Analogy and the Meaningfulness of Language about God   135

media *through which we first come* to lay hold of the meaning of the property and *upon which we fall back* as the clearest examples when we wish to evoke its meaning for ourselves anew—since, as we noted above, it is always necessary to call up some examples across a range in order to grasp or recall the meaning of an analogous concept. Among these there is usually—not necessarily always, it seems—one or more that stand out as prime analogates for us, i.e., as focal meanings or privileged exemplars closest to us by which we most easily and immediately grasp the meaning experientially, and out from which as from a center we extend it in lessening degrees of clarity. This usually means the properties as experienced and lived in our own selves, whether in body, psyche, or spirit. But it should be clearly understood that these ways of our coming to understand most vividly the common property do not themselves enter into the object meaning of the term when it is predicated analogously, in *any* of its predications. They are modes of *revealing* the analogous meaning of the term; they do not *constitute* its objective meaning itself—otherwise they would restrict it and destroy its analogical spread. Its objective analogical meaning as predicated is deliberately expanded, enlarged, made more vague and indeterminate than these modes of discovery, so that it will be able to transcend them in scope of application. Thus at the same time that we call up these privileged modes in order to evoke the meaning of the concept for ourselves, we *understand* (at least implicitly, but in a way that effectively controls our use of the term) *that* the meaning of the analogous term is being left open for further application, that it is not tied down to these modes of discovery. Thus if we were asked, in the example of speaking of hypothetical higher forms of "intelligence" that might communicate with us from outer space, what we mean by "intelligence," we would say something like this: "You know, the kind of thing we do, being self-conscious, comprehending the natures and properties of things, making signs or communicating in some way, in a word, understanding, but probably in quite different ways from ours." We do not confuse our modes of understanding with the content understood, or signified.

We could add another aspect (4) which would correspond exactly to St. Thomas's *modus significandi*, or modes of signifying the *res significata*. These are often misunderstood as signifying aspect (2), the actual modes of concrete realization of the common property in particular cases, as Professor Nielsen seems to understand them. This is quite incorrect. They are also sometimes extended to coincide with our (3), man's modes of *understanding* the *res significata*. There is no great harm in deliberately using *modus significandi* with this meaning, and one does need some appropriate term to express these. But it is still not what the expression itself means as Aquinas uses it. It refers only to our human modes of expressing the *res significata*, i.e., conceptual-linguistic modes. It was originally intended to take care of the obvious difference between the way God's perfections are found in him and our way of expressing the perfections of God through multiple verbal predicates, each distinct from the other, which are predicated of a subject as though they were accidents inhering in a distinct substance: "God is wise, *and* loving, *and* powerful." This is the way they are found in us, where wisdom can come and go and where a man can be wise but not powerful or vice versa. But what they signify as found in God himself is that God *is* identically all the positive perfections signified by these terms but united together in a single simple plenitude of perfection. Similarly we speak of God, who is beyond time, through verbal forms with tenses. Yet St. Thomas is quite clear that, although our *modes of expressing* these attributes bear the mark of their origin in our experience, these modes are not *what is expressed and predicated* by the concept itself, in any of its predications.[6] To say that John is wise and powerful does not *mean*, though it may indeed be understood to be also true, that wisdom in John is an accidental attribute really distinct from his power and his own essence. It is simply stating that it is true that he is wise and it is true that he is powerful, without stating how these are related. Hence our modes of expression do not corrupt with anthropomorphism our predications about God, or about anything, for that matter.

This is as far as St. Thomas's *modes of expressing* take us, though he also speaks of the "modes in which a perfection is found" or realized in its subject, which are not quite the same thing, but correspond rather to our *modes of realization* in (2) above. Where do Copleston's "objective meaning" and "subjective meaning" fit in here?[7] It is not entirely clear to me from his text how they do, and it is no wonder to me that Professor Nielsen had serious—and to my mind quite justified—difficulties with his explanation. For Copleston, the "objective meaning" means "the objective reality itself referred to by the term in question," which in his example, "God is intelligent," he maintains is "the divine intelligence itself," as it is in itself. The "subjective meaning" is "the meaning-content in my own mind . . . primarily determined for me by my own experience . . . of human intelligence." But here it seems that "intelligence" means in this predication "divine intelligence" and yet the only meaning-content in my mind in all predications is "human intelligence." This opens up a yawning gap between the two which Professor Nielsen has very astutely seen, and it

Analogy and the Meaningfulness of Language about God

is not at all clear from this text alone just how one crosses the gap. What Copleston fails to explain is that what he calls the "subjective meaning" is not really the *meaning-content* in my mind at all which I mean to signify by the analogous concept. It is my *way of discovering* the meaning but not the purified more indeterminate analogous *meaning* itself. He needs another intermediate term in his discussion to indicate this. He comes close to it, in fact, when he adds at the end of his text, not quoted by Nielsen, "But seeing that human intelligence as such cannot be predicated of God, I attempt to purify the 'subjective meaning'. . . . And in so doing we are caught inextricably in that interplay of affirmation and negation of which I have spoken." It is this "purified meaning," purified by being made more indeterminate and open, that is the one actually predicated of God, which is not Copleston's objective meaning either, since that is already determined to fit God only. He does not make this clear enough in his text. (I fear there is some confusion too in Father Copleston's text between meaning and reference, when he speaks of the meaning as "the reality *referred* to.") Thus it should be clear that I dissociate myself from Father Copleston's explanation and consider it an inaccurate rendering of St. Thomas's teaching, or at least an easily misleading one. Professor Nielsen has good reasons for finding it unsatisfactory. There is in fact no gap between the meaning of "intelligence" as predicated of God and its meaning as predicated of man. But there is a gap between the modes of realization which I *understand* this attribute will take on in the concrete in each case, as well as between my mode of coming to understand this meaning and the mode I affirm in God.

III. Application to God

Let us now take brief stock of what we have accomplished. We have tried to explain what the structure of analogous predication is in general, how it works, and what it means to extend the range of an analogous concept beyond its ordinary range in our experience. But the actual extension of our analogous language to some new entity, such as God, that is beyond the range of our experience requires three further steps: (1) we must have good grounds for affirming that there *actually is* (or at least might be) such a new candidate for the application of our language; (2) we must have good grounds for affirming that this new candidate is actually *objectively similar* in some way or ways to the presently known beings in our experience—in other words, that there are good grounds for applying our concepts and language at all; (3) once we are in possession of these grounds we must then proceed to figure out just which of the attributes in our store of knowledge are apt to be extended meaningfully and legitimately to such an entity. But the first two suppositions cannot be provided by a theory of analogy itself. They must come from outside, to build a bridge across which our analogical language can walk. It is especially the lack of any awareness of the second point above, the establishment of a bond of similarity between God and creatures, that renders Professor Nielsen's exposition of Thomistic analogy so cripplingly incomplete. Let us now turn to each of these three points. The first two will be handled together under Section 1.

1. Causality as the Bond of Similarity between God and World

The first step is establishing the existence of God. This is done through a causal argument, which postulates that, under pain of our world of experience falling into unintelligibility, there *must* exist, as experience's ultimate condition of intelligibility, or adequate sufficient reason, one ultimate Source of all being, whose only intelligible mode of being must be infinite perfection—for otherwise it could not be the ultimate condition of intelligibility. I would not carry on this argument through the Five Ways of St. Thomas, since they are too incomplete by themselves and defective in structure to do the job for us today. I would use rather the simpler and more basic metaphysical resources of St. Thomas, not drawn on clearly enough in the Five Ways, to show that no being that begins to exist, or is finite in perfection, or composed in its radical being, or member of a system of dynamically interrelated elements—to sum it up most simply, no finite being or group of finite beings—can supply the sufficient reason or ground of its own existence and that such an ultimate condition of intelligibility is not reached until we posit an infinite being, a being infinite in perfection.

It is not my purpose to work out this argument here, since it would take another whole article, and our main aim here is explaining the function of analogy within such a framework. (For my own version of such an argument see chapter 8 of this book.) Let us therefore suppose that this step has been carried out successfully. If it cannot be, there is no point in discussing Thomistic analogy any further as applied to God. But as soon as we have established the argument, without paying any explicit attention to analogy in the process, we discover that a strange thing has happened. Analogy is already being used in the very formulation of the conclusion: there *is* an ultimate Source or Ground of intelligibility (= cause) for the existence of creatures. For to be intelligible to us, these terms themselves must all

Analogy and the Meaningfulness of Language about God   139

be analogous when applied to a being outside our experience. (This, by the way, is just what we *mean* by "cause" here in its widest metaphysical sense, namely, that which fulfills a need for intelligibility, which answers the question, "What is effectively responsible for this datum *x*, which has turned out to be non-self-explanatory?" The meaning is not one drawn from the specialized field of the natural sciences, but from our common life-experiences of solving problems in any domain.)[8]

Does this mean that a vicious circle is here involved, that analogy presupposes causality and causality itself presupposes analogy? This is an excellent and crucial question, which Professor Nielsen himself has certainly seen when he speaks of a circle where one religious statement backs up another. There is indeed a circle of mutual involvement, but it is not a vicious circle; it is a vital one. For it is the very thrust of the mind's search for intelligibility, reaching out into the unknown to postulate a sufficient reason somewhere in being, that both sets up a new beachhead in being for our knowledge to explore further and at the same time carries with it its own enveloping field of analogy. Immanent in the entire innate drive of the mind toward intelligibility is an unrestricted commitment to intelligibility, wherever it may lead, and simultaneously to its objective correlate, being itself, as the source of all answers to this quest. To this range of intelligibility and its correlate being it is impossible to set any limits, since the mind, as soon as it becomes aware of these limits as limits, immediately transcends them by this very awareness. Our own inner *experience* of this quest for intelligibility that defines the very life of the mind reveals to us that both the quest itself and the answers to it are infinitely Protean, taking on endlessly different forms and modes. In a word, we experience the field of intelligibility, enveloping our own minds and reaching out beyond into its correlate, being, as *intrinsically analogical*, open-ended but somehow all bound together in some vague unspecifiable unity. The first and all-embracing analogous field which we discover—not by constructing it deliberately but by waking up within it, so to speak—is the correlation *intelligibility-being*.

Hence it is that when, as in the case of the affirmation of God, the mind is convinced—for what it believes are good reasons—that it can save the intelligibility of the world of our experience only by positing or postulating as existent outside this world (i.e., transcending its limitations) an ultimate infinitely perfect source of all being, it necessarily envelops this term that it posits with its own pre-existent and potentially all-embracing field of analogy, at once positing it as a *real* condition of intelligibility and as *necessarily analogous* in the same movement of thought. This initial analogy is extremely vague, not yet extending beyond the immediate correlates of the intelligibility-being field itself, together with the index of location within this field at the supreme apex of perfection, whatever that may be. For all the terms used to describe God in this initial stage, "ultimate ground *of intelligibility* for the existence of the world=cause," are nothing but reaffirmations of the general principle of the intelligibility of all being in principle, tailored to the particular situation where the beings we start with do not contain their own sufficient ground of intelligibility within themselves, hence force us to look beyond them.[9]

Thus the very initial positing of God as cause of the world situates this cause within the primary a priori (a dynamic and existential, not a logical, a priori) analogous field of both intelligibility and being—of being precisely *because* this is demanded by intelligibility. From the very beginning of our intellectual life there is a necessary mutual co-involvement of intelligibility, being, and analogy. This very vague initial analogous beachhead of knowledge about God is now ready to be expanded by further judicious search for more determinate valid analogies.

It is at this point that a second crucial corollary of the causal bond comes into play, one that is too often neglected in expositions of analogy and of which there is likewise no hint in Professor Nielsen's discussion. This is the principle, handed down to St. Thomas by both the Neoplatonic and the Aristotelian traditions, that *every effect must in some way resemble its cause*. In a word, every causal bond sets up at the same time a bond of intrinsic similarity in being. In the Platonic-Neoplatonic tradition this took the form of the principle that every higher cause communicated something of its own perfection to its effect beneath it, which participated in the latter as much as its own limited nature allowed. In the Aristotelian tradition it took the form of the principle that no being can cause any perfection in another unless it already possesses in act (in some equivalent way) this same perfection. These two strands were joined together in a single synthesis of *causal participation* by St. Thomas and other medieval thinkers; and the same *general* principle of causal similitude has been accepted by most realistic metaphysicians ever since, in one form or another.

The philosophical reason why every effect must in some way resemble its cause, at least analogously, is this: since all the positive perfection of the effect, as effect, derives precisely from its cause(s), the latter cannot give what it does not have; the effect must in some way participate or share in the perfection of the cause that is its

Analogy and the Meaningfulness of Language about God 141

source. If the cause does not possess in an equal, or some higher equivalent manner, the perfection it communicates to its effects, then the perfection of the latter would have to come from nowhere, have no relation to its cause. Where there is no bond of similarity whatever between an effect and its cause, there can be no bond of causality either.

The similarity in question, however, could be of two main kinds. If both cause and effect were of the same species the similarity would be on the same level and kind, that is, univocal. If the cause were a higher level of being than the effect, then the similarity could not be strictly univocal but would have to be at least analogous. In this perspective, the very fact of establishing a causal link between a lower effect and a higher cause at once *ipso facto* generates an analogous similarity, a spectrum of objective similarity extending from the known effect at least as far as the cause, whether the latter is directly known or only postulated as a necessary condition of intelligibility for an already known effect. Whether both terms of the relation are known or only one, every effect has to be similar in some way to its cause, or it could not be a real effect, and the same holds for the cause. As St. Thomas sums it up:

> Effects which fall short of their causes do not agree with them [i.e., are not exactly like them] in name and nature. Yet some likeness must be found between them, since it belongs to the nature of action that an agent produce its like, since each thing acts according as it is in act. The form of an effect, therefore, is certainly found in some measure in a transcending cause, but according to another mode and another way [i.e., analogously]. For this reason the cause is called an equivocal cause [a term that is "equivocal by design" in Aristotelian terminology is the same as what was later called "analogous"—opposed to "equivocal by chance"]. . . . So God gave all things their perfections and thereby is both like and unlike all of them.[10]
>
> An effect that does not receive a form specifically the same as that through which the agent acts cannot receive according to a univocal predication the name arising from that form. . . . Now the forms of the things God has made do not measure up to a specific likeness of that divine power; for the things which God has made receive in a divided and particular limited way that which in Him is found in a simple and universal unlimited way. It is evident, then, that nothing can be said univocally of God and other things. . . . For all attributes are predicated of God essentially. . . . But in other beings these predications are made by participation.[11]

It is because of this metaphysical context of causality and causal participation undergirding the Thomistic theory of analogy that the most recent and authoritative—in the sense of being almost universally accepted among Thomists—commentaries on St. Thomas's theory of analogy now all agree that despite his many changes in terminology he fairly early drops the structure of proper proportionality, taken by itself alone, for a richer structure involving both immanent proportionality among the analogates of a term *and* a reference to the causal source from which the analogous perfection in question is communicated to all the participating analogates. This fuller metaphysical-semantic structure of analogy as applied to the relation of God and creatures is most aptly called "the analogy of causal participation." The previously long accepted "orthodox" explanation of Cajetan in terms purely of proper proportionality without reference to a source is now recognized as inadequate to handle the application of analogy to a being not accessible to our experience, as is the case with God. A purely formal isomorphism of relations can supply no positive content of knowledge about the term of comparison otherwise unknown to us unless some positive intrinsic bond of similarity has already been established between both ends of the comparison. Cajetan presumed this had been done elsewhere, but his omission of this step from his formal and explicit analyses of analogy leaves a very serious gap in his formal theory of analogy when *taken by itself*, as most non-Thomistic thinkers, if not forewarned, would naturally tend to do. St. Thomas himself apears to have come to recognize this, since after his early work *De Veritate*—the main source for Cajetan's systematization of all Thomistic texts—he never again uses the formal structure of proper proportionality by itself to express his own thought.

Thus it is not surprising that when non-Thomistic thinkers like Professor Nielsen come to the theory of Thomistic analogy through older traditional expositions in the mode of Cajetan, which omit the context of causal participation as part of the doctrine itself as applied to God (or to any unknown cause), they find the structure of the analogy of proper proportionality by itself quite inadequate to perform the role claimed for it. Their critical insight is quite accurate.[12]

2. Which Attributes Can Be Applied to God?

Once we have set up this basic framework of causal similitude between all creatures and God, from which it follows that there *must* be some appropriate analogous predicates that can be extended properly and legitimately to God, the next step consists in determining just *which* attributes can, in addition to the initial most indeterminate attributes of being and perfection, allow for open-ended extension all the way up the scale of being, even to the mode of infinite plenitude, without losing their unity of meaning. This is the search for the "simple or pure perfections," as St. Thomas calls them, which are purely positive qualitative terms that do not contain as part of their *meaning* any implication of limit or imperfection. Once we have located one of these, even though we enter into its meaning in first discovering it or in re-evoking it through the limited and imperfect modes (i.e., our privileged modes of *exemplifying* it to ourselves) belonging to the things we find in our experience, *what we intend or mean* directly by the concept, once we have purified or enlarged it for good reasons into an analogous concept, is a flexible, broadly but not totally indeterminate core of purely positive meaning that transcends all its particular possible modes, both those we know and those we do not know.

We can recognize that we have effected this purification when we can meaningfully affirm, as we certainly do, that *all* the *experienced* modes of these open-ended perfections, such as unity, knowledge, love, and power, are *limited*, not yet perfect modes. For to affix the qualification "limited or imperfect" to any attribute is already to imply that our understanding of this attribute transcends all the limiting qualifiers we have just added to it. Any attribute that cannot survive this process of purification, or negation of all imperfection and limitation in its meaning (and of course in its actual mode of realization when applied to an infinite being) without some part of its very meaning being cancelled out, does not possess enough analogical "stretch" to allow its predication of God. The judgment as to when this does or does not happen is of course a delicate one that requires careful critical reflection, along with sensitivity to the existential connotations of the use of the term in a given historical culture.[13]

Two types of attributes have been sifted out as meeting the above requirements by the reflective traditions of metaphysics, religion, and theology: (1) those attributes whose meaning is so closely linked with the meaning and intelligibility of being itself that no real being is conceivable which could lack them and still remain intelligible, i.e., the so-called *absolutely transcendental properties* of being, such as unity, activity, goodness, and power; and (2) the *relatively transcendental properties* of being, which are so purely positive in meaning and so demanding of our unqualified value-approval that, even though they are not co-extensive with all being, any being higher than the level at which they first appear must be judged to possess them—hence a fortiori the highest being—under pain of being less perfect than the beings we already know, particularly ourselves; such are knowledge (particularly intellectual knowledge), love, joy, freedom, and personality, at least as understood in Western cultures.

a) The Absolutely Transcendental Properties

Once established that God exists as supreme infinitely perfect source of all being, it follows that every attribute that can be shown to be necessarily attached to, or flow from, the very intelligibility of the primary attribute of being itself must necessarily be possessed in principle, without any further argument, by this supreme Being, under pain of its not being at all, let alone not being the supreme instance. Thus it is inconceivable that there should exist any being that is not in its own proportionate way *one*, its parts, if any, cohering into one and not dispersed into unrelated multiplicity. Hence God must be supremely one. Such all-pervasive properties of being are few, but charged with value significance: e.g., unity, intelligibility, activity, power, goodness (in the broadest ontological sense as having some perfection in itself and being good *for* something, if only itself), and probably beauty too.

Since these properties are so general and vague or indeterminate in their content—deliberately so to allow for their completely open-ended spectrum of application—we derive from this inference no precise idea or representation at all as to what *this mode* of unity, etc., will be like in itself. But we do definitely know this much: *that* this positive qualitative attribute or perfection (in St. Thomas's general metaphysical sense of the term as any positive quality) is really present in God and in the *supreme degree* possible. Such knowledge, though vague, is richly *value-laden* and is therefore a guide for value assessment and for value responses of reverence, esteem, etc. I am puzzled as to why Professor Nielsen would consider such value-laden and value-guiding concepts simply empty and hence apparently able to serve no cognitive purpose at all. For if there is one thing we know about God with unambiguous clarity is that such a being is *No. 1* on the scale of all purely positive values. What more valuable bit of knowledge can we possess for wisely guiding our lives in the light of Reality?

b) The Relatively Transcendental Properties

There is a second genre of transcendental attributes of being that are richer in content and of more immediate interest and relevance in speaking about God. These are terms that express positive qualitative attributes having a floor (or lower limit) but no ceiling (or upper limit), and hence are understood to be properties belonging

Analogy and the Meaningfulness of Language about God 145

necessarily to any and all beings above a certain level of perfection. Their range is transcendental indefinitely upward but not downward. Such are knowledge (consciousness, especially self-consciousness and intellectual knowledge), love, lovableness, joy (bliss, happiness, i.e., the conscious enjoyment of good possessed), and similar derivative properties of personality in the widest purely positive sense (not the restrictive sense it has in many oriental traditions). All such attributes appear to us as purely and totally positive values in themselves, no matter how imperfectly we happen to possess them here and now. As such, they demand our unqualified approval as unconditionally better to have than not to have. Hence we cannot affirm that any being that exists higher than ourselves, a fortiori the supremely perfect being that God must be, does not have these perfections in its own appropriate mode. To conceive of some higher being as, for example, lacking self-consciousness in some appropriate way, i.e., being simply blacked out in unconsciousness, would be for us necessarily to conceive this being as lower in perfection than ourselves. Nor is there any escape in the well-known ploy that this might merely mean inconceivable *for us* but in reality might actually be the case for all we know. The reason is that to affirm that some state of affairs *might really* be the case is to declare it in some way conceivable, at least with nothing militating against its possibility. This we simply cannot do with such purely positive perfection-concepts.

What happens in our use of these concepts, as soon as we know or suspect for good reasons that there exists some being higher than ourselves, is that, even though *our discovery* of their meaning has been from our experience of them in limited degree, we immediately detach these concepts from *restricting* links with our own level, make them more purified and indeterminate in content, and project them upward along an open-ended ascending scale of *value appreciation*. This is not a logical but an existential move, hooking up the inner understanding of the conceptual tools we use with the radical open-ended dynamism of the intellect itself. One way we can experience this power of projection of perfections or value attributes beyond our own level is by experiencing reflectively our own poignant awareness of the limitations and imperfection of these attributes as we possess them now, even though we have not yet experienced the existence of higher beings. We all experience keenly the constricting dissatisfaction and restlessness we feel over the slowness, the fuzzy, piecemeal character of our knowing and our intense longing, the further we advance in wisdom, for an ideal mode of knowledge beyond our present reach. The very fact that we can judge our present achievement *as limited*, *imperfect*, implies that we have reached beyond it by the implicit dynamism of our minds and wills. To know a limit *as limit* is already in principle to have reached beyond it in dynamic intention, though not yet in conceptual representation. This point has for long been abundantly stressed by the whole Transcendental Thomist school, not to mention Hegel and others, who bring out that the radical dynamism of the spirit indefinitely transcends all finite determinate conceptual expressions or temporary stopping places.

The knowledge given by such projective or pointing concepts, expressing analogous attributes open-ended at the top, is again very vague and indeterminate, but yet charged with far richer determination and value content than the more universal transcendental attributes applying to all being, high or low. By grafting the affirmation of these attributes, as necessarily present in their appropriate proportionate mode in God, on to the lived inner dynamism of our spirits longing for ever fuller consciousness, knowledge, love (loving and being loved), joy, etc., these open-ended concepts, affirmed in the highest degree possible of God, can serve as very richly charged *value-assessment guides* for our value-responses of adoration, reverence, love, longing for union, etc. But note here again that the problem of the extension of analogous concepts beyond the range of our experience cannot be solved by logical or conceptual analysis alone, but only by inserting these concepts into the context of their actual living use within the unlimitedly open-ended, supra-conceptual dynamism of the human spirit (intellect and will), existentially longing for a fullness of realization beyond the reach of all determinate conceptual grasp or representation. Thomistic analogy makes full sense only within such a total notion of the life of the spirit as knowing-loving dynamism. The knowledge given by these analogous concepts applied to God, therefore, though extremely indeterminate, is by no means empty. It is filled in by a powerful cognitive-affective dynamism involving the whole human psyche and spirit, which starts from the highest point we can reach in our own knowing, loving, joy, etc., from the *best* in us, and then proceeds to project upwards along the line of progressive ascent from lower levels towards an apex hidden from our vision at the line's end. We give significant meaning to this invisible apex precisely by *situating* it as apex of a line of unmistakable direction upward. This delivers to us, through the mediation (not representation) of the open-ended analogous concept, an obscure, vector-like, indirect, non-conceptual, but recognizably positive knowledge-through-love, through the very upward movement of the dynamic longing of the spirit towards its own intuitively felt connatural good—a knowledge

Analogy and the Meaningfulness of Language about God 147

"through the heart," as Pascal puts it, or through "connatural inclination," as St. Thomas would have it.[14] Such an affective knowledge-through-connatural-inclination is a thoroughly human kind of knowing, quite within the range of our own deeper levels of *experience*, as all lovers and artists (not to mention religious people) know. Yet it is a mode of knowing that has hitherto been much neglected in our contemporary logically and scientifically oriented epistemology.

CONCLUSION

It is time to conclude this already too lengthy response. To sum up, analogous knowledge of God, as understood in its whole supporting metaphysical context of (1) the dynamism of the human spirit, transcending by its intentional thrust all its own limited conceptual products along the way, and (2) the structure of causal participation or causal similitude between God and creatures, delivers a knowledge that is intrinsically and deliberately vague and indeterminate, but at the same time richly positive in content; for such concepts serve as positive signposts, pointing vector-like along an ascending spectrum of ever higher and more fully realized perfection, and can thus fulfill their main role as guides for significant value responses, both contemplative and practical. Such knowledge, with the analogous terms expressing it, is, and by the nature of the case is supposed to be, a *chiaroscuro* of light and shadow, of revelation and concealment (as Heidegger would say), that alone is appropriate to the luminous Mystery which is its ultimate object—a Mystery which we at the same time judge that we *must* reasonably affirm, yet whose precise mode of being remains always beyond the reach of our determinate representational images and concepts, but not beyond the *dynamic thrust* of our spirit, which can express this intentional reach only through the open-ended flexible concepts and language we call analogous. Such concepts cannot be considered "empty" save in an inhumanly narrow epistemology.

NOTES

1. For a summary of these developments, see David Burrell, *Analogy and Philosophical Language* (New Haven: Yale Univ. Press, 1973), ch. 6 on Aquinas, and George Klubertanz, *St. Thomas and Analogy* (Chicago: Loyola Univ. Press, 1960).

2. Although I had come to this conclusion some time ago myself, I am deeply indebted to Father Burrell for his fine elucidation of this point, one of the main contributions of his valuable book, cited in note 1.

3. Cf., on Scotus, Burrell, op. cit., ch. 5 and 7; C. Shircel, *The Univocity of the Concept of Being according to Duns Scotus* (Washington, D.C.: Catholic Univ. of America Press, 1942); on Ockham, Burrell, op. cit., ch. 7; M. Menges, *The Concept of the Univocity of Being Regarding the Predication of God and Creatures according to William Ockham* (St. Bonaventure, N.Y.: Franciscan Institute, 1958).

4. Etienne Gilson, *The Christian Philosophy of St. Thomas Aquinas* (New York: Random House, 1956; rpt. Notre Dame, Ind.: Univ. of Notre Dame Press, 1994), pp. 105–7.

5. St. Thomas himself is quite clear about this. See his sensitive basic treatment in *Summa Theologiae*, I, q. 13 entire, especially art. 3: "Some words that signify what has come forth from God to creatures do so in such a way that part of the meaning of the word is the imperfect way in which the creature shares in the divine perfection. Thus it is part of the meaning of 'rock' that it has its being in a purely material way. Such words can be used of God only metaphorically. There are other words, however, that simply mean certain perfections without any indication of how these perfections are possessed—words, for example, like 'being', 'good', 'living', and so on. These words can be used literally of God" (Blackfriars trans.).

6. See his text in note 5.

7. The main part of the text of Copleston that Professor Nielsen is quoting (*Contemporary Philosophy* [Westminster, Md.: Newman, 1956], p. 96) runs as follows: "By 'objective meaning' I understand that which is actually referred to by the term in question (that is, the objective reality referred to), and by 'subjective meaning' I understand the meaning-content which the term has or can have for the human mind . . . i.e., my understanding or conception of what is referred to. . . . If this distinction is applied to the proposition 'God is intelligent', the 'objective meaning' of the term 'intelligence' is the divine intellect or intellect itself. . . . And of this I can certainly give no positive account. . . . The 'subjective meaning' is the meaning-content in my own mind. Of necessity this is primarily determined for me by my own experience, that is, by my experience of human intelligence. But seeing that human intelligence as such cannot be predicated of God, I attempt to purify the 'subjective meaning'. . . . And in doing so we are caught inexorably in that interplay of affirmation and negation of which I have spoken."

8. For this whole question of the meaning of "cause" in the context of the mind's quest for intelligibility and its necessarily analogous character as a correlate of the inquiring mind at work, see my own fuller development in "How the Philosopher Gives Meaning to Language about God," in *The Idea of God*, ed. E. Madden, R. Handy, M. Farber (Springfield, Ill.: Charles Thomas, 1968), pp. 1–28; and ch. 2 of my book, *The Philosophical Approach to God* (Winston-Salem: Wake Forest Univ. Press, 1979).

9. It is very important to make the point here that according to St. Thomas's metaphysical method—and any sound metaphysical method, it seems to me, which seeks to achieve knowledge of some being beyond our experience—it is a fatal error to accept the demand so habitually made by ana-

lytic philosophers and others that one must first define what one means by "God" *before* undertaking to establish God's existence. This stand is not an evasion; it is a question of proper method. For it is impossible philosophically to give any definition of God that can be shown to make sense before actually discovering such a being as an exigency of the quest for intelligibility. The meaning of "God" emerges only in function of the argument that concludes to the need for a being to which we then can appropriately give the name "God" or not, according to our culture and religious tradition. The *philosophical* meaning of God should be exclusively a function of the way by which such a being is discovered. Hence a properly philosophical approach to the existence of God should not ask, "Can I prove that God exists?" but rather, "What does the world of my experience demand in order to be intelligible?" Following out this exigency rationally, we "bump into" God, so to speak, as a being all of whose properties are defined exclusively by what it needs to fulfill its job of satisfying the exigencies of the quest for intelligibility. Hence any philosophical proof for the existence of "God" has already taken the statement of the question from some non-philosophical source, usually a religious one, and this cannot be philosophically justified.

10. *Summa contra Gentes*, I, ch. 29, n. 2. Cf. also *Sum. Theol.*, I. q. 13, a. 5.

11. *Sum. c. Gentes*, I, ch. 32, nn. 2 and 7. He goes on to say in ch. 38, n. 2: "For in equivocals by chance there is no order or reference of one to another but it is entirely accidental that one name is applied to diverse things.... But this is not the situation with names said of God and creatures, since we note in the community of such names the order of cause and effect...."

12. It is because of this basic similitude between all creatures and God that the phrase so often used by theologians, philosophers of religion, and spiritual writers, describing the divine transcendence over creatures, namely, that God is "totally Other," is really, if taken in unqualified literalness as a metaphysical statement, quite unacceptable as sound philosophy, theology, or spirituality. For if God were literally totally other, with no similitude at all with us, there could be no bond whatsoever between us, no deep affinity drawing us toward union with our true Good, no image of God deep in the soul, etc. God might be totally other in essence or *mode* of being, since God is beyond all form, but not totally other in the divine *being* itself or the activity properties that flow directly from its fullness of perfection.

13. For a fuller development, cf. my articles cited in n. 8.

14. Cf. *Sum. Theol.*, I, q. 1, a. 6 ad 3; I–II, q. 45, a. 2. See also J. Maritain, "On Knowledge through Connaturality," *Review of Metaphysics*, 4 (1950–51), 483–94; Victor White, "Thomism and Affective Knowledge," *Blackfriars*, 25 (1944), 321–28; A. Moreno, "The Nature of St. Thomas' Knowledge *per connaturalitatem*," *Angelicum*, 47 (1970), 44–62.

8

Is a Natural Theology Still Viable Today?

The enterprise of natural theology (or philosophy of God) is a particularly difficult one to carry out in our day. Philosophically, it has come under heavy attack from empiricists and Neo-Kantians, from analytic philosophers tinged with both of the above, from historical and linguistic relativists, appealing to hermeneutics, and more recently from Deconstructionists and Postmodernists in general. On the other hand, its relationships with contemporary science, in particular theoretical physics and cosmology, have warmed up considerably in recent times. Let us begin with a brief look at these varied relationships.

Relation to Science

In relation to contemporary science, natural theology is, from one point of view, on better terms with it than it has been for a long time. The notion that mind has a place in nature, that nature points to mind as its completion, is much more acceptable, even plausible, to many scientists today, especially theoretical physicists and cosmologists. A cosmologist like Fred Hoyle, for example, once a self-proclaimed atheist, now speaks of *The Intelligent Universe*. Many are favorably impressed by the now famous Anthropic Principle, which seems to point to an extremely precise fine-tuning of the four basic forces of the material universe, with its enormous statistical improbability, as a sign that the universe was planned from the beginning in view of the presence of conscious observers like ourselves in it. Very significant is the recent text of the physicist Arthur Dyson:

> I conclude from the existence of these accidents of physics and astronomy that the universe is an unexpectedly hospitable place for living creatures to make their home in. Being a scientist, trained in the habits of thought and language of the twentieth century rather than the eighteenth, I do not claim that the architecture of the universe proves the existence of God. I claim only that the architecture

Is a Natural Theology Still Viable?

of the universe is consistent with the hypothesis that mind plays an essential role in its functioning.[1]

Two points are noteworthy here. The first is the openness or "compatability" of the scientific picture with the theistic hypothesis, rather than the closedness that used to predominate. But the second is the warning that from within the scientific outlook this hypothesis is only *compatible* with the results of contemporary science, not authorized or established by them. As Ernan McMullin's fine recent paper has shown us, theistic philosophers in the past have persistently tried to argue to the existence of God from some gap in the existing scientific picture of the universe, from some need discovered within the web of scientific explanation for a further grounding that the scientific explanation itself could not supply. Thus, Newton believed that God's intervention was necessary to keep going the constant motion of the heavenly bodies. Paley and others argued from the marvelous adaptation of the various species of living organisms to their environment—given the common pre-Darwinian acceptance of the fixity of species—to a Cosmic Planning Mind that had thus ordered them; and so on. But in each case science eventually closed the gap in its web of explanation, and in so doing closed out the argument to the existence of God based on this gap. The "God of the gaps" has been progressively put out of a job.[2]

The same kind of process seems to be at work again today. Despite the initial plausibility and strong suggestiveness of arguments for the need of a world-ordering Mind from unfilled gaps in the current scientific picture, especially those based on the statistical improbability of our present world order,[3] this foundation does not seem to me a secure one for building a cogent natural theology. The figures are indeed impressive: for example a Princeton scientist, Don Page,[4] recently calculated that the odds against our present universe are something like one in $10,000,000,000^{124}$. But our opinions continue to vary as to the basis for making such calculations, given the unique situation or "singularity" of the earliest stages of the cosmic system. Others have put forward ingenious hypotheses, such that no choice is needed for the peculiar initial conditions of our universe, since an infinite number of *all possible* universes actually exist, so that ours is bound to turn up somewhere without the need for any calculus of probabilities or selective agent. Others try to argue that ours is in fact the only possible universe that can be actualized (given in quantum physics that many of the conjugate properties of subatomic particles can only be actualized by conscious observers like ourselves). Others weaken the base of the impressive argument from the fine-tuning of the four basic forces and other precisely balanced constants of the universe, by reducing the four forces first to three, then to two, then hopefully, in the light of some highly controversial hypotheses like superstring theory, to one simple, all-embracing one from which all else can be deduced. Some suggest tracing the beginning to a mere chance fluctuation of a primordial quantum field, emerging out of a pure, formless, high-energy vacuum state or pre-space-time "foam," which they ambiguously identify as "nothing."[5] In view of the intense ferment of speculation going on at this time in high-level theoretical physics, it does not seem to me possible yet to find any secure foundation within the exigencies of scientific explanation for the postulation of a Transcendent Mind as the only adequate cause of the origin and structure of our cosmos.

Others from within the biological community, or philosophizing on its data, suggest there is even stronger evidence for the need of a Cosmic Planning Mind to explain the origin of life and the large jumps to new species in the course of evolution. They argue from the huge statistical improbability of the passage from a nonliving molecule to a living cell—Fred Hoyle and his associate have calculated it to be 1 in $10^{40,000}$—the failure thus far of all attempts (despite some initial apparent successes) to reproduce successfully the conditions of such a passage, and the now widely conceded breakdown of Darwinian chance selection as an adequate explanation for the passage from one species to another of a higher order.[6] But again, such gaps in current explanations might possibly be filled in by some future hypothesis. And I might add that reductionist materialism still seems to have strong support in the biological sciences, more so than in physics today.

So, somewhat reluctantly, and without denying the powerful suggestiveness of inferences from the apparent enormous improbability of our present universe, both in its origins and in the evolution of life within it, I think it wiser to agree with Ernan McMullin in the paper just mentioned, that natural theology today should avoid any attempt to build its foundations on apparently unfillable gaps in the scientific picture of the universe. The "God of the gaps" has so often been put out of a job in the past that I think he should be, for the time being if not permanently, retired. Only a radically metaphysical argument, from the very existence of any determinate world at all, or from the existence of any dynamic order at all, has a fair chance of succeeding, as I see it.

PHILOSOPHICAL OBSTACLES

There have been many attempts in modern and contemporary philosophy to block any project of constructing valid philosophical arguments for the existence of a Transcendent Reality. There are, of course, both older and newer, more sophisticated forms of *empiricism* and *Kantianism*, whether in scientific, linguistic, or phenomenological versions, that are still tenaciously pervasive in contemporary thought. All these are fundamentally anti-metaphysical, in the sense that it is impossible to move, by philosophical reason, beyond the world of human experience, inner or outer, to affirm legitimately the existence of some reality transcending this experience. Then there are the newer movements of historical, cultural, linguistic, or hermeneutical *relativism*, together with the latest "demolition squads," known as *Postmodernists* and *Deconstructionists*.

For the *relativists*, all our expressed knowledge claims are history-, culture-, and language-bound, meaningful only within a given historical and linguistic framework of inquiry and expression, but never allowing any unconditional truth statements which, with appropriate translation, are capable of transcending the limitations of such frameworks. This at least seems to cripple any attempt to construct a natural theology with any cogency outside its own narrow tradition—if it can be done there.

For the *Postmodernist*, there is "no meta-narrative legitimation of first-order narratives."You have your story; I have mine (or my group and your group). But there is no norm beyond the individual stories by which to judge their truth or value. We must allow neither political nor conceptual tyranny: both are functions of the will to power, not truth. "Let all flowers bloom."[7]

The *Deconstructionist* calls on us to resist—and sabotage—the arrogant "logocentrism" of the West, with its pretensions to capture reality adequately in all-inclusive, totalizing conceptual systems, transparently reflecting the nonlinguistic real, à la Hegel. They propose a "heterology" (championing the Other, the different, the exception, the marginalized) in opposition to a "henology" (the reduction of the many, the different, the unique to some all-inclusive, all-explanatory One), as has been customary in Western metaphysics. The more radical versions, which Jacques Derrida, the most visible "father" of the movement, often makes gestures of repudiating, maintain that no expressed signifiers ever connect up unambiguously with the truth, or nonlinguistic reality, that there is no unambiguous dividing line between metaphor and objective concept, literature and philosophy, that all signifiers trail off into an endless labyrinth of reference to other signifiers and these to others, into traces of traces of traces. . . . In place of so-called truth claims, they unveil the hidden pretensions of the philosophers to impose their metaphorical schemas on others by the "will to power" (the influence of Nietzsche is clear here, and often explicitly avowed). In addition, all texts can be cracked open to reveal a hidden subtext that works against the surface text to undermine it. The radical Deconstructionist is a "double-agent and a nomad," who infiltrates one system to blow it up from within, then, with no "home" (or position) of his own, moves on to blow up another. It is obvious that an effective natural theology—or any kind of theology, it turns out—is, in such a context, a logocentric illusion.[8]

CLEARING THE OBSTACLES

Let me indicate briefly how I would go about removing or circumventing the above philosophical roadblocks to the positive construction of a natural theology. First, as to the contemporary relativists, Postmodernists, and Deconstructionists. I think it would be a serious mistake—an intellectual loss of nerve—to allow ourselves to be intimidated by these movements, with their often strident proclamations of the end of Western logocentric reason. My reason is this: Whenever these positions move to a really radical stance, blocking all access to objective truth, they promptly self-destruct and become inoperative as a critique. For either they are claiming to be informing us of some truth—what *is* the case—about all linguistically expressed human thought, and then their assertive performance contradicts the content of their assertions, namely, that *all* such assertions are culture- and language-bound so that they cannot connect up unambiguously with the truth; or, if they are not really claiming to tell us some significant truth about all of us, then their own position immediately becomes relativized and turns into just another late-twentieth-century culture-bound opinion, perhaps even localized to a small group of thinkers in a few large cities, and there is no reason for the rest of us to bother our heads about it; we are free to go on in our own contexts happily asserting our objective truth claims.

In short, the natural, spontaneous, and, in the last analysis, inextinguishable drive of the human mind to discover and give recognizable expression to the truth, to what is the case in reality, cannot tolerate for long any attempt at systematic self-sabotage of its own natural drive and innate cognitive structure of experience-insight-judgment as to what is the case about ourselves and the world we live in. As Derrida himself has well said somewhere, understanding this as a pragmatic necessity of actual human living, "Il faut la vérité" (There must be truth).

If the above movements are taken in moderation, however, they can lead us to an important, more realistic understanding of what in fact is the case about our human reason. There is no going back to a pre-hermeneutic understanding of human thought and language. What has really been demolished is the old and indeed arrogant Cartesian and Enlightenment ideal of human reason as pure, impersonal, autonomous, self-sufficient Reason, independent of any tradition, culture, historical perspective or authority, that will in principle be able to gather into itself unaided and with perfect transparency all the real, knowable, or worth knowing, with special priority given to *the* scientific method, specifiable according to rules, as the ideal method of reaching any truth available to us.

Accordingly, a self-aware contemporary thinker in any field should be willing to admit (1) that our human reason must always see the world from some limited (incomplete) historical perspective or vantage point; (2) that what is seen from other vantage points is—if we have done our work carefully—complementary, not contradictory; (3) that we cannot come intellectually naked to understand the texts of man and his world, but must go through some apprenticeship in a living hermeneutical tradition; (4) that the reliable knowledge we can indeed attain about the real is not the Cartesian ideal of absolute certitude such that the opposite can be shown to be a logical contradiction—this is attainable only in mathematics and logic—but is "reasonable affirmation," as Bernard Lonergan puts it, achieved not by impersonal, automatic, clearly specifiable rules for correct thinking, but by personalized responsible thinking (taking possession of oneself and one's drive to know and committing oneself to it), striving for intelligent insight into the meaning latent in the data and for personally responsible judgment based on evidence recognized as sufficient for its purposes; (5) finally, that all of our perception, concepts, and understanding are, as Polanyi has shown so well, a synthesis of focal and peripheral (or background) knowledge, such that it is neither possible nor necessary to make formal and explicit all that is in this background knowledge (for it is a mode of existential lived knowledge, acquired by sharing in a practical "form of life" never fully susceptible of explicit conceptual formulation), and that this is not, as Deconstructionists so often overlook, crippling to our capacity to understand, but positively enabling.

On the other side of the picture, however, it should always be remembered that no matter how limited or incomplete a perspective may be, it is still an opening onto something beyond the viewer. A perspective that opens onto nothing, or only inward into the viewer, is not a perspective at all, but a hall of mirrors. Similarly, no matter how much one may have to start within a hermeneutical tradition to learn a tradition and skills of inquiry and interpretation, a hermeneutics that effectively does its job is one that enables us to understand a situation or text that needs interpretation and, by a sensitively intelligent "fusion of horizons," come to understand significantly—though never totally—a different or older tradition. A hermeneutical viewpoint is a vantage point from which to discover and understand something—although not all that is to be seen, to be sure; it is not a labyrinth or prison in which one gets to know only the prisoners.

As for the *Deconstructionists*, Polanyi's theory of focal and peripheral knowledge, appropriately amplified for the study of texts, already takes care of many of their significant warnings—without the skeptical consequences. As for the claim of the Other, the absent, and so on, to deserve equal status with the One, being, presence, and so forth, it is my impression that Deconstructionists often exhibit a systematic blind spot to what St. Thomas was so well aware of, namely, the distinction between the mode of discovery of a concept as explicitly distinct from others and the content signified by it. Thus, in a realistic metaphysics like that of St. Thomas, the metaphysical notion of being, like most metaphysical concepts, is intrinsically analogous, that is, pregnant with one and many, sameness and difference, remaining systematically vague, so that all that is in it can never be made fully explicit; furthermore, the notion itself is indeed brought to explicit possession by contrast with partial absences, particular instances of nonbeing, etc. But all these differences, absences, partial nonbeings, and so on are always enveloped within the overall horizon of being, differences within being, not outside of it in a radical or unqualified sense. There is no warrant to argue, as it seems to me Deconstructionists persistently tend to do, from the mode of discovery of our concepts to the conclusion that in the real order nonbeing and absence can claim independent equality, much less priority, with respect to being, presence, unity, and so forth. All truly analogous concepts contain the many within the womb of the one from the outset.

As for *empiricism*, even in its various diluted contemporary forms, our basic response to it is that it cannot make stick its claims to block any ascent of rational human intelligence to transcendent reality, either within us or above us. It is in essence an arbitrarily restrictive theory of knowledge, attempting to constrict the natural dynamism of the mind to know and understand the real in all its fullness, attempting to tie it down merely to the realm of experience. It would allow description and correlation of the data of experience, with a privilege given to sensory data, but no explanations reaching beyond experience to fill the gaps of intelligibility found within experience. As many metaphysicians in the analytic tradition, like Strawson—who do not, by the way, consider themselves card-carrying empiricists of the Humean type—have put it succinctly: Descriptive metaphysics (description of the basic linguistic categories of our experience) is in. Explanatory metaphysics is out.[9]

But, in addition to an impoverished theory of efficient causality, the radical weakness in this procedure is that the knower itself cannot be caught adequately in the empiricist's net of all that is knowable. The intelligent knower who is looking at the data attentively, striving to gain insight into its meaning, interpreting and judging it, discerning value or disvalue within it, is not out there among the sensory data. The knower cannot "look" at itself as self-conscious, self-possessing, responsibly judging, self-governing "I," if empiricism is true. But, in fact, we do just this all the time in our conscious rational life. The knower transcends all its empirical data, is not reducible without remainder to all or any part of its empirically given data. This surplus between the knower in all its depth and its empirical data opens the way to a nonempirical (i.e., metaphysical) ascent of the mind through the exigencies of intelligibility to whatever transcendent reality is needed to fill the gaps in intelligibility found in the empirical data taken by themselves alone.

But there is one principle of explanation that must be explicitly rescued from the straightjacket of empiricism if our ascent is to be viable. That is the principle of efficient causality. The empiricist would have us believe that the foundational and only legitimate meaning of causality is simply the regularly observed succession in time of empirically observable antecedent and consequent events, such that from the first one can predict the second according to some law. Any further intrinsic link between cause and effect, such as the active production or bringing into being of the second by the first, the fact that the cause is responsible for the effect, which therefore has an ontological—though clearly not sensibly observable—link of dependence on its cause—all this is declared to be later, unnecessary, and unjustifiable baggage added on by the metaphysicians.

The opposite is in fact the case. Our modern natural sciences have indeed good reason, for methodological purposes, to restrict the meaning of efficient causality in practice to "predictability according to law," whether deterministic or, more often today, statistical. But the original meaning of the term, deriving from the Greek law courts, and its flourishing continued use today in ordinary life situations for explaining why things happen, is the notion of "that which is responsible (originally 'guilty,' in courtroom use) for" the given occurrence of some event, the presence of some entity, and so on, that of itself needs explanation, is judged (not empirically observed) not to make sense by itself alone.[10]

The principle of efficient causality, thus understood in ordinary life and more self-consciously and abstractly in realist metaphysics, is really, in the last analysis, simply a function of the inquiring mind at work, with a flexible analogous aplication just as wide as the reach of the mind itself. It is nothing more, but nothing less, than the reaffirmation of the basic commitment of the inquiring human mind to the unrestricted intelligibility of the real, tailored to fit a particular situation. When allowed to operate without arbitrary restrictions, the search for the efficient cause (or causes) is simply the search for whatever is needed to fill a discerned gap of intelligibility in the data of our experience. Wherever this search leads, to whatever is shown to be indispensable to fill this gap, whether a cause in the empirically given world or beyond, this can be affirmed legitimately under pain of allowing the initial data we are trying to explain to remain with a declared unfillable hole or "wound" in its intelligibility. In its wide-open scope, as wide as being itself, this principle contains no restrictions such as empiricism would force upon it.

As to the last of our roadblocks, *Kantianism*, two brief remarks will have to suffice. Kant is indeed a great thinker, especially in ethical matters. But we have been too long intimidated by his long shadow in epistemology, in particular his anti-realist and anti-metaphysical stance, which claims to bar the way to a rational affirmation of anything beyond empirical appearances. In the first place, his refutation of the so-called "Cosmological Argument" for God is flawed by a serious misreading of the traditional argument as presented by realist metaphysicians like St. Thomas. In the last crucial step of the argument, Kant distorts it to become an attempted deduction of the existence of a Necessary Being (I would prefer to call it a Self-Sufficient Being) from the idea of the *Ens Realissimum* (or infinitely perfect being). St. Thomas would indignantly repudiate such a procedure, all too easily refuted by Kant. The traditional procedure is precisely the opposite. Once the reality of a Self-Sufficient Being has been established from causal arguments, it is then argued that such a being could not be at once self-sufficient and finite, for the latter by nature requires a cause of its being as finite. Therefore the Self-Sufficient Being must be infinite, and so, by an easy step, unique. There is no deduction from the idea of perfection or from any mere idea in itself, although some such procedure may have been invoked by some of the rationalist metaphysicians of the Wolffian type just before Kant.

As to Kant's attempt to bar access to any valid affirmation about a real world beyond the knower, it suffers from a fatal flaw, a massive blind spot that has also plagued most of modern Western epistemology since Descartes, as pointed out insightfully by John Dewey, as well as by Thomists: namely, overlooking the key role of action as the self-revelation of being in our human knowing—an absolutely central theme in the epistemology of Aristotle, St. Thomas, and Dewey himself. For, on the one hand, Kant must admit action coming from the real world of things-in-themselves into the human knower, since he insists that he is not an idealist, that we do not create by thought the objects of our knowledge. On the other hand, he will not admit that this action is revelatory of anything objective in real things, anything true of them—not even their real existence, since "being" itself represents only the positing by the mind of its own synthesis of the unordered appearances in the sense-manifold and the innate, a priori forms of sense and intellect. But action that is totally non-revelatory of the nature of the agent-source from which it comes is itself unintelligible, cannot be truly action.[11]

Kant cannot have it both ways. Either there is no real action of the real world upon us—and he is forced into idealism, which he rejects vehemently—or he accepts the fact of real action of the real world upon us—and then this action is necessarily revelatory, a manifestation—incomplete indeed, but authentic in what it does manifest—of its real agent-source. As a thing acts, so must it be—*agere sequitur esse*, as the ancient Scholastic adage goes.

The root of the trouble lies, I suspect, in Kant's implicit rationalist ideal of knowing the real as knowledge by a detached, uninvolved pure knower of a real being as it is in itself independent of any action upon others, including the knower himself. Of course, such a knowledge is impossible save for a purely creative knower, which we are not. But the whole key to an action-based realist epistemology is that our knowledge, involving incoming action from the thing known, received according to the mode of receptivity of the knower, is through and through relational; but this relation itself is thoroughly real, what is the case, necessarily revealing something real about the other end of the relation. For it reveals the known as actor, as in itself this kind of actor—which is precisely, in the last analysis, just what an essence (i.e., a nature, an abiding center of action) should really mean in a realist epistemology, I would maintain. Thus, St. Thomas himself is not in the least reluctant to admit—in a text that astonishes many contemporary epistemologists—that "[t]he substantial forms of things as they are in themselves are unknown to us, but they shine forth to us through their accidents [i.e., their operations] . . . as through doors surrounding them," so that our mind points back to their hidden natures through their manifestations in "a kind of discursive movement"[12]—which I interpret as the intentionality of judgment, as opposed to a direct intuition.

Such a relational knowledge through action is necessarily perspectival and incomplete, proportional to the conditions and limitations of the receiver, but it is a genuine perspective on the known as self-revealing actor. And in the last analysis isn't that what we most want to know about other real beings: what *characteristic actions* can we expect of them? Given this umbilical cord to the real world through action on us, we can follow up any gaps in the intelligibility of the world thus revealed to us to affirm the existence of whatever is needed to fill these gaps, empirical or transempirical, as the case may be. This is precisely the path of efficient causality, of causal explanation, freed of arbitrary empiricist shackles.

Kant's attempt to block the use of causal explanation as a path to God has no more authority than that of his arbitrarily restrictive epistemology, according to which causality is an a priori form of understanding, simply given in the mind, whose *sole function* is to make intelligible connections between events in our material world empirically given to human sensibility—which would of course prevent its extension beyond the empirically given world. But this is precisely one of the fundamental flaws of the Kantian epistemology (with all its historical progeny), that it simply posits the a priori forms of understanding as given, universally and immutably, in all human minds, without any attempt to justify or ground them, either in the basic dynamism of the mind to know and the questions this generates about what is given to it in experience or in insight into the intelligible patterns already immanent within this expeience. Kant believed he had to do this in order to protect his theory of the apodictic certainty of modern (Newtonian) science, which could only be based on a priori factors. But now that our contemporary science has itself repudiated this claim to apodictic certainty in favor of a hypothetical mode of knowing with ever revisable conclusions, the Kantian apparatus of a priori concepts is no longer needed. Freed of this Kantian straightjacket, realist metaphysicians should reclaim without intimidation the principle of efficient causality as the natural birthright of the innate drive of the mind to know and the indispensable instrument for carrying out the mind's natural commitment to the intelligibility of being—a commitment of "natural faith," as Einstein and other great scientists have put it, that is really the inner dynamism and soul of all serious intellectual inquiry, scientific or otherwise.

To sum up now what has gone before, all attempts to lay mines that will definitively block the modest but real access of the human mind to the real and to whatever is needed to fill the gaps in its intelligibility succeed finally only in blowing up the mine-layers with their mines, leaving the rest of us free to navigate with critical care between the rocks and through the rapids. The metaphysical hypotheses worked out along the way, including arguments for the existence of God such as I will present presently, are not Cartesian absolute certitudes, but explanatory hypotheses that recommend themselves as worthy of reasonable affirmation because they fill the gaps in the intelligibility of the real world we experience in a more illuminating and adequate way than other, competing hypotheses—or lack of them—which either leave out something significant from our experience or leave gaps in its intelligibility unfillable in principle from their perspective. Now to our positive task.

CONSTRUCTING A NATURAL THEOLOGY

From all that contemporary philosophical discussion has taught us, it should be clear that it is not realistically possible to construct a purely objective philosophical argument for the existence of God—or for anything else, indeed—floating free from all personal roots, one that is capable of convincing by its pure impersonal cogency any intelligent hearer whatever, irrespective of all predispositions and presuppositions, moral and intellectual, of all cultural and conceptual frameworks—all hermeneutical traditions, if you will. As Polanyi, Gadamer, and others have shown, there is no presuppositionless thought, in any field. We do presuppose, therefore, in anyone who is willing to give sympathetic consideration to the arguments we are going to propose, a certain familiarity with—or at least willingness to enter into—what I would call a metaphysical type of thinking, that is, one that is open to asking radical questions about the very existence and intelligibility of the world we live in, following out the discovered exigencies of intelligibility (of making good sense), wherever they may lead, and not cutting short, a priori or arbitrarily, the innate drive of the mind to understand the real as fully as possible.

Our metaphysical procedure will be, first, to identify significant gaps in the intelligibility of our universe as a whole, if we can find them, then to propose in a kind of branching technique the main options for filling these gaps, and to try to eliminate all of these options, or explanatory hypotheses, save one. By "gap in intelligibility" I do not mean merely something I do not yet understand, some mystery; I mean that one must show positively that given the nature of the data there is something in them that excludes any adequate explanation of them—or rendering of any sufficient reason for their existence—if taken by themselves alone; in a word, that they just cannot, because of some built-in deficiency of their being, be self-explanatory, but demand the help of some further real being, which fulfills the role of efficient cause, that is, that which is *responsible* for their actual being or their coming into existence. In a metaphysical type of inquiry, because of its vast generality—and therefore elimination of details—it is possible to reduce the relevant options for explanation to a very few at one step, then move onto the next and do likewise—something that is rarely possible in the natural sciences because of the complex details to be explained and the wide range of hypotheses open. The elimination of all options but one can rarely be done by purely logical means, but usually requires metaphysical insight into intrinsic idea-connections, which cannot be commanded but which can afford, if carefully checked, sufficient grounds for reasonable affirmation of what it reveals.

I agree with Charles Hartshorne in his later works that it is more accurate these days to speak of "arguments" rather than "proofs" for the existence of God, since "proof" as understood today has become so rigorous in its requirements that it is impossible, properly speaking, to prove the existence of any real being (outside the knowing "I"), let alone the existence of a transcendent reality like God. Secondly, I agree with him that such arguments (or "reasonable ascents of the mind to God") exhibit a certain cumulative effect, one argument opening one side of the intelligibility needed; another, another side, or perhaps one argument for one type of mind, another for another. I believe, too, that a well-rounded and effective natural theology should proceed in a two-pronged approach: one that I would call the "Inner Path," through the exigencies of the inner life of man as intellect, will, and moral person; and the other the "Outer Path," through the exigencies of the entire cosmos (including man). The Inner Path would proceed from reflection on the innate drive of the human spirit toward the unlimited horizon of being as truth and goodness, such that one is faced with the option that either an Infinite Fullness of Being as truth and goodness actually exists as the only adequate goal of this innate drive, a drive that is constitutive of the human—hence not capable of being substituted for by any finite goal or set of them—or our human spirit is radically absurd, oriented toward what does not and cannot exist. And since there is no good reason for opting for the absurd, the unintelligible, and every good reason for opting for the existence of the Infinite as closing the gap in intelligibility in us—with room to spare!—it is uniquely reasonable to opt for the latter, though the opposite can never be shown to be a logical contradiction (it may be a "lived" one, however). I fear we will have no further space to develop the Inner Path argument in the present paper.[13] The reason I choose the Outer or Cosmic Path for fuller development here is that the Inner Path can indeed reach an Infinite Good as *my* final good, *my* God, but not as the Ultimate Source of *all* being, which is necessary for an adequate notion of God. I have also chosen this path because the original context for this paper was a discussion with scientists.

I. Argument from Any Conditioned Being to a Single Infinite Source of All Being

Let me start with my own adaptation of a classical argument of St. Thomas, combining three essential steps, which he stretches out over some nine questions in his *Summa Theologica*, Part I (beginning at question 2, article 3, and finishing at question 11—a point too often overlooked by those who look only to the Five Ways in question 2 for his complete proof). This argument, the longest one I shall give, will at least serve the purpose of initiating readers into a metaphysical type of inquiry, even if it does not convince them.

It is important to note the question we are asking as we begin this "ascent of the mind to God." The basic question we are raising about the beings of our experience is not: What are they? What are their properties? How do they operate? It is rather the radical question about their very existence: Why do they exist at all in this way that they do exist? What is the ultimate intelligibility, or sufficient reason, why they in fact exist at all? It is important not to short-circuit this question from the start, as Bertrand Russell and many empiricists have done. "Explanation," for them, as one told me, "means to relate the parts of the universe to each other *within* the system as a whole. But one can't raise questions about the system itself *as a whole*." As Russell put it in a nutshell in his famous BBC debate with Father Copleston some years ago, when the latter pushed him on this point:

"The world as a whole just is, that's all. We start there." Scientific explanation, it is true, must start there; a science can use its methods only on some subject matter already given to it in existence and cannot answer questions about the very existence of its own subject matter. But philosophically speaking it is an intellectual cop-out, an arbitrary restriction of the natural drive of the mind to know, to refuse to raise the most radical of all questions, the question of the very existence of our universe and ourselves as knowers within it. The primary theme song of all metaphysical inquiry, we might say, is, "Don't fence me in!"

The argument unfolds in three steps: (1) Given any conditioned being, there must exist at least one absolutely unconditioned, or self-sufficient, being; (2) No being can be self-sufficient unless it is qualitatively infinite or unlimited in perfection; (3) There can be only one such being infinite in all perfections—which therefore must be the unique Ultimate Source of all being. Such a being we can appropriately call "God."

Step one: There must exist at least one self-sufficient being. Let us begin with the beings around us. All of these manifest themselves to us as *conditioned existents*. That is to say, they are not self-sufficient, but depend on other beings outside them as conditions for their own existence, either to bring them into existence or to maintain them in existence, or both. Thus all human beings depend on their parents for initiating their existence, and on the air, temperature, nourishment, and many other factors around them to maintain themselves. The same is true of all living things, down through animals, plants, and whatever other intermediaries there may be. The same is also true of all molecules, which depend on the atoms composing them and on many other conditions of space-time, fields of force, temperature, and so on, without which they could not hold together with their specific properties. The same now appears to be true of the whole domain of atoms themselves. All depend on external conditions; for example, they could not hold together until the initial temperature of the cosmos cooled enough to allow it. The same seems to be true also of the primordial particles making up atoms, although we cannot directly corroborate this yet scientifically. Thus what many believe to be the most elementary particles, quarks, cannot exist alone but need always to be joined with two or three others. Everywhere around us, then, as far as our experience can reach, is a vast web of conditioned existents, none of which is self-sufficient for its own existence.

Now the question arises: Can all the entities of our universe be thus conditioned, non-self-sufficient, dependent on others for their

Is a Natural Theology Still Viable? 165

existence? On reflection the answer must be "no." Take any conditioned being A. It must depend on another entity B in order that its own conditions for existence be fulfilled. But now in our search for intelligibility we must ask the same question of entity B: Is it conditioned or not? If so, we must look further to entity C in order to explain B. And the same question will arise for C, D, and all other members of this causal chain. Can there be an infinite regress in this chain, so that the causal chain of dependency would extend endlessly, with all its members having the same existential status of conditioned existents, none of them self-sufficient for its own existence? Whether the chain extend backwards in time or simultaneously across the universe makes no difference; the problem is the same. Again, the answer must be "no." For if all the beings in the chain remain conditioned, dependent on another, then nowhere will the conditions for the existence of any member be adequately fulfilled. The search for the necessary fulfilling conditions will endlessly go on and in principle be impossible of completion. For in principle the necessary conditions can never be fulfilled. Hence the entire chain remains suspended without a sufficient reason, or adequate grounding, for any of them to exist. But the original beings we started with do in fact actually exist here and now—which means that in fact all their necessary conditions must be already fulfilled. Hence, under pain of the entire chain of conditioned existents remaining unintelligible in their actual existence, there must be somewhere in existence at least one absolutely unconditioned being, completely self-sufficient for its own existence, either at the beginning of the causal chain or outside of it, supporting the whole. There can be no conditioned beings unless there is at least one unconditioned one, which is the initiator (not necessarily in time) of the causal flow of existence into all the others in the series. (As far as we know at present, there may be many such series.)

Nor can it be objected that, even though all the parts of the world system may be conditioned, the system as a whole may be unconditioned, self-sufficient. Once the system is actually there, with its energy within it, it might be self-maintaining—that is another question we need not go into at present. But it cannot be the self-sufficient reason for its being there in the first place. For such a system that is made up of parts, even though a higher mode of being may emerge from the union of the parts, still depends on its parts, presupposes them as that out of which it emerges. It cannot operate as a whole at all unless the parts are already there. If it is the final source that generates its own parts, then it must be ontologically prior to and independent of them for its own existence. The question then must be raised whether it is self-sufficient or not, as before.

Nor can it be argued that the causal dependence might be circular: A depends upon B, B upon C, and C in turn upon A. For C must then be prior to A and B ontologically (not necessarily temporally), in the order of existential dependence, and yet must be posterior to A as depending on it. But it is contradictory for the same entity to be at once prior and posterior to another being in the same order of dependence. Such a circular system can be placed there all at once as a unity by an independent cause, and then might maintain itself by reciprocal support. But none of the parts can generate their own mutual togetherness as an existing whole.

The rejection of an infinite regress might be put in another, perhaps more austerely logical, way. Given that being A here and now exists, categorically and unconditionally. Now suppose one tries to explain A thus: A exists only if B, and B only if C, C only if D, and so on to infinity. In this case, since each one depends upon the conditions of its cause being fulfilled, and these conditions remain endlessly unfulfilled, the entire series remains conditional in its existence. Unless somewhere along the line one of the members exists unconditionally, that is, with no more conditions to be fulfilled, then the original existence of A itself becomes only conditional. There can never be a categorical affirmation of anything at all (nothing but "only ifs"). But the original A does categorically and unconditionally exist, as a fact, not "iffily." Hence we have failed in our search for the intelligibility of its existence—unless we go on to posit the unconditional existence somewhere along the line of a real cause that is self-sufficient, self-explanatory of its own existence, uncaused.

Many arguments stop here—as for example do three of St. Thomas's Five Ways (four in fact, since the third gives no reason for its final step). But there is much more to be done. What sort of being will qualify for being self-sufficient? And how many such can there be? The great Aristotle himself thought finally that there must be 55 unmoved, uncaused Prime Movers. So we must put an appropriate question to the self-sufficient being we have discovered that will smoke out its significant attributes further. The crucial one is this: Is it finite or infinite in perfection?

Step two: Any being self-sufficient for its own existence must be infinite in perfection, that is, unlimited in its qualitative fullness of all perfections. Or: *No self-sufficient being can be finite*. Why? Let us suppose it were finite. This means it would be one determinate, limited mode of being (limited in qualitative intensity of perfection) among at least

Is a Natural Theology Still Viable?

several other modes possible, such that at least one higher mode were possible (i.e., this one does not exhaust all possible fullness of perfection). Otherwise it would not be finite or limited. Now there must be some sufficient reason why the being in question exists in this particular limited and determinate mode of being and not in some other possible. Why *this* being, or *this* whole finite world-system, in fact, and not some other? A principle of selection is needed to select this mode of being from the range of possibilities and give actual existence (energy-filled existence) to it according to this limited mode (or "essence," as the metaphysician would say). But no finite being can do this selection of its own essence and conferral of existence on itself. For then it would have to preexist its own determinate actual existence (in some indeterminate state), pick out what it wills to be, and confer this upon itself. All of this is obviously absurd, unintelligible. It follows that no determinate finite being can be the self-sufficient reason for its existence as this determinate being. Therefore it requires an efficient cause for its actual existence as this being. But since we cannot go on to infinity in caused causes, we must eventually come to some Infinite Cause of these finite beings.

The same conclusion can be reached through a slightly different approach. Suppose that a finite being were self-sufficient. This would mean that it would have to be the total, ultimate source of all the positive attributes within it, including the central, all-embracing perfection of actual existence, energy-filled existence itself. Now it does not make sense that the ultimate source of a perfection should possess this perfection in some limited, imperfect way, less than the full plenitude possible of the perfection in question, when it is the very source of this perfection itself. Nor does it make sense that it should deliberately restrict its own possession of this perfection of which it is the ultimate source to some limited degree when it could enjoy the full plenitude of it. The notions of ultimate, self-sufficient source of a perfection and limited possession of it clash irreconcilably and cancel each other out. No being self-sufficient for its own existence, therefore, can possess existence only in some limited, incomplete, imperfect way.

Conclusion so far: every finite being, not only each one in particular, but any system as a whole that is finite and determinate in its mode of existence, as ours clearly is, needs a self-sufficient infinite being to draw it out of the range of possibilities and make it to *be* in this particular way and no other. It does not matter, in fact, how many other modes actually exist, or even whether all possible ones exist. Each one needs to be given actual existence according to its determinate mode, and no one can do it for itself.

Step three: There can be only one such infinite being. This is a quick and easy one, admitted by just about all metaphysicians, I believe, once the existence of an absolutely infinite being is granted. For suppose there were two such. Then one would not be the other. But this is impossible unless at least one of the two lacks something the other has. Otherwise they would coincide into total indistinguishable identity. But if one lacked some positive perfection, it could not also be absolutely infinite in all perfections. Also, as Duns Scotus has pointed out, at least one would be unable to know the other—a great imperfection; for either one would have to create the other or be acted on by the other; and in either case one of the two would have to be dependent on the other, hence not self-sufficient—which we already established.

Conclusion of whole argument: If anything at all exists, then there must exist one and only one Infinite Source of all being. This we may call an apt philosophical definition of "God."

II. Argument from Any Finite Being to a Single Infinite Source of All Being

It may have occurred to the alert reader that it is possible to condense the above long argument into a much simpler and more elegant one beginning with Step Two and proceeding directly from any finite being to the necessity of a single Infinite Source of all being. This is perfectly true. One has only to find a limited being in our experience—and God knows there are all too many around us, including ourselves—and immediately proceed from finitude itself as the ground for the need of a cause, as the gap in intelligibility needing to be filled by another. To avoid an infinite regress of finite causes one would have to bring in again the elimination of this possibility outlined in Step One. Step Three—that there can be only one Infinite in perfection—follows immediately as above to cap off the argument. This is a classic Neo-Platonic procedure, often used by St. Thomas himself (as in *De Potentia*, q. 3, art. 6), and echoed in his Fourth Way (though the order of parts is inverted—unfortunately, to my mind). Every finite being, St. Thomas says, by the very fact that it is limited, indicates that it is a participated perfection, and points beyond itself to an unparticipated infinite Source.[14]

Instead of starting from some particular finite being, one can also make this into a more powerful and impressive argument, simply by stepping back and taking as our starting point the entire system of our material cosmos as a whole. This is clearly a determinate limited system, whose basic constants are precisely limited—for example, the four basic forces, the speed of light, Planck's constant h, and so on (whether or not there is some infinity on the purely quantitative level can be left open for settlement either way). Therefore the entire system as a limited whole can provide no sufficient reason why it actually exists as this determinate system and no other. Physicists have been able to show that it is possible to vary the values of the basic constants of our universe (e.g., the speed of light, the force of gravity, etc.) and still get a consistent system. Why, then, this determinate one rather than some other? The system itself can provide no answer. The only conceivable way one could do so would be if one could show that this particular material universe was absolutely and in every respect the only one possible—that is to say, there could be not only no other material universe, but no other universe of any kind at all, including all possible modes of higher spiritual beings (for, although something would always have to have existed, there is no way of showing that a material universe must exist, if other modes of being exist). It is clearly impossible to make any such all-inclusive claims, particularly from the point of view of any natural science, or science of any kind we know.

The argument holds firm, I believe. There is no way for the system itself to fill the gap in its own intelligibility, to illuminate the sheer brute fact of its own limited existing thisness. Note, too, that this argument is a purely metaphysical one, quite independent of any changes or progress in the content of the sciences. For the natural sciences by their very nature must always be dealing with new patterns and systems of determinate, finite—and probably measurable—entities, of whatever sort. Science and the determinate finitude of its objects are by necessity always linked together.

It is noteworthy, too, that the whole process of scientific inquiry implicitly reaffirms the philosophical claim that our finite universe as it manifests itself to us does not contain within it the sufficient reason for its own existence in this particular way, is not self-explanatory. For at each stage of explanation, science keeps raising new questions why the system should be such—which is an implicit admission that it is not self-explanatory. It keeps seeking for the ideal goal of a single ultimate unifying principle from which all else may be derived and a principle that is as simple as possible. But is not this an implicit admission that, as long as we remain with some determinate complexity, we have not yet reached the end of the line in intelligibility? No finite determinate mode of being, that is *this* and not *that*, can ever be ultimately self-explanatory. Only an unqualifiedly infinite fullness of existence can ever be the final resting place of the search for intelligibility. Science itself cannot formulate this last step of its search, for there is no scientific way of giving meaning to it or solving it in terms of scientific data or empirical verification. This is precisely where science points the way toward metaphysics as the next stage of the journey toward the fullness of meaning of our always question-laden universe.

III. Further Reflections on the Contingent Existence of Our Universe

I would be reluctant to describe this reflection as another independent "argument" for the existence of God in the strict sense. It is rather a deeper reflection on the profound gap in intelligibility that lies between the possible existence and the actual existence-with-energy of our universe, in short, a reflection on its radical contingency in the order of existence. It would thus be in the order of a metaphysical insight, or "musement," in Peirce's sense. It was stimulated by some of the highly theoretical—and still very controversial—speculations of some cosmologists about the Big Bang origins of our material universe. Some have speculated—and tried to work out mathematical hypotheses expressing this—that ours might be, in some significant sense, the only possible universe (in its large lines of course, not in all the details of its evolution). In the Vatican observatory symposium that was the original context of this paper, Frank J. Tipler has in fact formulated a hypothesis along these lines and drawn the implications for a natural theology:

> In this paper I shall discuss two recent developments in physics which have important implications for religion.... The second development is the possibility of a Theory of Everything (TOE). A TOE might imply that there is only one logically possible universe. This would refute the Cosmological Argument and, more importantly, its premise that God had some freedom of choice in creating the universe. The traditional God would be made superfluous, but an evolving God might be made necessary.[15]

That such an objection should even be formulated reveals a profound metaphysical insensitivity to the abyss between mere possibility and actual existence. Even if it were proved—which it certainly has not been—that this was the only possible material universe (nothing, of course, could be said by science about other higher levels of spiritual existence), this would still leave our universe a merely possible plan, or model for a real universe. It would in no way necessarily entail that such a universe actually existed, endowed with power and energy, that the model or "essence" was *actually* instantiated in the

Is a Natural Theology Still Viable? 171

real order. Actual existence is a wholly different order from mere possibility, no matter how beautifully intelligible the latter may be in itself. The essential insight here is that there is nothing in the intelligible plan, model, or "essence" (essential structure) of our universe that demands or prescribes its own actual existence-with-energy. There is nothing in its laws that prescribes that they must be instantiated. In fact, no determinate model, especially a mathematical one, can ever specify its own instantiation. It is merely a formal structure of relations of laws, properties, and so on, which of itself is timeless and unmoving. It cannot *do* anything actually, cannot deploy the energy its laws regulate. In short, our universe is radically contingent: it can exist (because it does) but cannot ground or explain its own actual active presence. Stephen Hawking, the great British physicist, seems to have a keen sense of this point in his best-selling book *A Brief History of Time* when he remarks:

> Even if there is only one possible unified theory, it is just a set of rules and equations. What is it that breathes fire into the equations and makes a universe for them to describe? The usual approach of science of constructing a mathematical model cannot answer the questions of why there should be a universe for them to describe. Why does the universe go to all the bother of existing? Is the unified field theory so compelling that it brings about its own existence? Or does it need a creator, and if so, does he have any other effect on the universe? And who created him?[16]

Well said! (except for the last question, which we have already taken care of). What is needed to close this gap between possibility and actuality is some cause that is already firmly planted in actual existence and can confer it on others, in fact—to avoid an infinite regress—one that does not just *have* existence as a sheer brute fact but one for whom actual existence is a part of its very essence, whose very essence *is* the fontal plenitude of actual power-filled existence itself, an existent self-explanatory of its own existence. But this is precisely for St. Thomas the proper philosophical name of God, Subsistent Existence itself (*Ipsum Esse Subsistens*), interpreting the biblical name of God given to Moses, "I am Who am." This must be ultimately the actualizing-energizing cause of all whose essence is not identical with existence itself. And such a cause, since it is the very source of all possible modes of real perfection, cannot but be unique and beyond all limitation.

The same argument would hold against the other leading claim, inspired by scientific speculation, that no higher cause is needed to choose this universe out of other possible ones. According to this hypothesis, at the moment of the Big Bang, an infinite number of *all possible* universes blew out like bubbles from the initial energy point, each independent of and not communicating with the others. Since *all* possible universes actually exist, there is no need of any higher cause to choose between them, hence no God is needed. But here again the objection starts too late, with all the universes *already existing*. The question still arises, Why should any of them at all actually exist? Just because they are possible in no way grounds or necessitates that they be actually present with built-in energy. They cannot of themselves cross the abyss between possibility and actuality. A self-existent, actualizing-energizing source transcending them all is needed. In a word, our universe is contingent in its very being and can never be self-explanatory.

Note that none of our arguments above is build on the supposition of a beginning of our universe in space and time, but only on the actual existence of some limited determinate system of active beings. Contrary to common belief, a beginning in time is not the only reason—in fact not even the principal one—why our material universe needs a transcendent, self-existent Ultimate Cause. The question whether something is self-explanatory of its own existence is not answered by asserting that it has always existed. An eternally dependent universe is no less dependent just because it has always been around.

IV. Argument from Order in the World

This ancient argument from order or design in the world, now more commonly known as the teleological argument (teleology = activity ordered towards an end), St. Thomas calls the most widespread and most efficacious path to God (*via efficacissima*) for all peoples, in all times and all cultures. And I think he is right. Such an argument, however, needs special adaptation to be effective in the light of contemporary science, both evolutionary and cosmological. In the brief space at my disposal let me indicate how I think it can be adapted.

One classic form of the argument, sketched by St. Thomas in his Fifth Way, argues from the regular action of natural agents producing their effects (unless hindered) to a dynamic orientation built in to their natures.[17] The reason is that such regularly repeated action cannot be the result of mere chance. All chance, in fact, must be built upon some matrix of built-in, regularly acting natural properties, or nothing will happen at all. But such a built-in dynamic orientation toward a not-yet-existent future effect requires making this not-yet-existing future present as a guide or focus in the very structuring of

Is a Natural Theology Still Viable? 173

the nature toward action. And such making the future present, or taking into account a not-yet-existing future, can only be the work of a mind ordering means to a possible future end through a creative idea. Hence the ordered activity of nonrational nature must at least ultimately be the work of a creative Ordering Mind transcending nature itself.

This argument, I believe, is a sound one in itself. But it runs into complications when applied to the evolutionary development of living organisms (a fact unknown to the originators of the argument), because of the large interweaving of chance involved, as we see the process today—although it is now well known that the original Darwinian hypothesis of evolution by pure random selection and survival of the fittest has proved to be seriously, if not irretrievably, flawed. It is wiser today to restrict the argument to the great underlying physico-chemical laws of the universe that in fact remain stable throughout all the evolutionary development of living organisms, as the necessary permanent matrix of order upon which the latter build. For unless there were some basic ordering of the fundamental active elements of the universe to interact with each other in some definite ways, nothing would ever happen; they would simply pass by or through each other like ships in the night, uncommunicating, with no interactions at all. There would be no foundation for chance itself to work on, since chance is always parasitic on some stable properties of several different items in order to start off its calculus of probable interactions. Furthermore, unless this basic matrix of physico-chemical laws were stable, it would be impossible for living organisms to learn from experience. They must lean on the stable to build the new.

I would like now to present what I think is a more powerful adaptation of the argument, fitting more closely the way we understand nature today. (St. Thomas himself did indeed lay down the basic principle, namely, that when many nonrational agents cooperate together to form a single world order, some unifying mind must be the source of this ordered system. But he developed it differently in detail, applying it only to the relations between species and levels of being [e.g., plants and animals, not the basic physical elements themselves]).[18] My form of the argument runs thus:

Take any dynamically ordered system of active elements, such as our own material cosmos, such that the various constitutive elements are ordered toward regular reciprocal interaction with each other. For example, all hydrogen atoms are ordered toward combination with all oxygen atoms in the fixed proportion of 2 to 1, whereas all oxygen atoms are in turn ordered towards all hydrogen atoms in the reciprocal proportion of 1 to 2, to form water (H_2O); the same holds for the fixed chemical valences of all atoms, the mutual gravitational attraction of all particles in the universe with mass, the strong force holding together the particles in the nucleus of atoms, electromagnetic laws, and so on—all of these laws combining to form a unified cosmos-wide order. Now in such a system, where each active element's basic properties (their natures, in metaphysical terms) are defined by relation to the others in the system, no one element can explain its own nature, be the sufficient reason for its own active nature as existing and operating, unless it is also the sufficient reason for all the others reciprocally related to it. But this is impossible. For then this element would have to be both prior (in causal, not necessarily temporal priority) in its activity to the others and responsible for them, and at the same time presuppose them, since its active properties are all ordered to interaction with them according to law. It would thus in its very nature as active presuppose the others as reciprocally constituted in relation to itself and yet be independent of and responsible for these correlated properties in others by which its own active nature is defined. Clearly this will not work.

Such a cosmos-wide order, therefore, is one in which many are brought together under the unity of great overarching laws of mutual interaction. But such an all-inclusive order, which is a form of unity, can have its ultimate sufficient reason, its intelligible grounding, only in some cosmos-wide unifying cause, capable of thus ordering many active agents into the unity of one order. Such a unifying, ordering agent, which is needed to set up the system-wide unity of reciprocal interactions of the multiple elements of the system, can only be a Mind.[19]

There are two reasons for this, closely intertwined but helpful to distinguish. (1) These overarching laws of reciprocal interaction are each a one-over-many, gathering many different elements into an intelligible unity that is system-wide, yet without collapsing together the real distinctness and separation in space and time of each element. This is a space-and-time-transcending unity that can only be constituted by an idea—which in turn can only be generated by a mind. Such a unity of many in one, leaving intact the distinction of each, is almost a definition of an idea. And an idea must originate from a mind.

(2) The ordering of the natural properties of these elements toward dynamic interaction must be constituted prior (priority of causal dependence, not necessarily temporal priority) to their actual operations of interacting, since they interact according to their (already constituted) natures. But this means that they must be ordered

toward, constituted in view of, not yet existing future actions, or possible future actions. Now only a mind can constitute out of possibility a future order, can "order means to an end," as St. Thomas likes to put it. Only a mind can thus make present in its field of consciousness the future and the possible, which do not exist in themselves and can have only a mental presence. A purely material being without consciousness is locked into the here and now of its place in space and time. To order possibilities with a view to future action is again almost a definition of mind, or certainly one of its most characteristic functions. Thus the cosmos-wide dynamic order of our world system necessarily requires a cosmos-ordering Mind to constitute its order.

It follows by immediate inference that such a Mind must transcend the system that it has constituted, that is, not be dependent on the system itself for its own existence and operation. For if it did thus depend, it could not exist or operate unless the system were already set up and operating, whereas in fact the system itself cannot exist or operate unless the ordering Mind has already set it up. Both the Mind and the system, then, would have to be both prior and posterior (in the order of dependence) to each other at the same time. This is obviously a contradiction. Hence the world-ordering Mind must be outside of, or transcending, this cosmos of ours that it has constituted. To sum it up, the last word about this or any cosmos must always be (to paraphrase philosophically the beginning of St. John's Gospel): "In the beginning was the Word." Before all action, there must always be the inner word, the creative thought, the *Logos*.

Theoretically speaking, of course, to complete the search for the intelligibility of the universe, we must raise the further question whether the Mind we have discovered as the ground of the universe's order is one or many, finite or infinite. Recourse must be had here once again to the earlier—and, in the last analysis, indispensable—argument from finitude to one Infinite Source of all being (second and third steps of Argument I). But it should be noted that even without taking this last step explicitly, we have already reached a Transcendent Reality upon which our whole cosmos and ourselves within it depend for our very natures. This already gives a sufficient basis for a basic religious attitude of gratitude, reverence, love, and obedience toward the Author of our nature and destiny. This is enough for the ordinary nonphilosophical person, who probably makes the leap to a single Infinite Source implicitly and spontaneously. At any rate, we are already out of the world of the secularist and the materialist into the religious.

The beauty of this argument is that it works for any basic dynamic order in our or any universe whatever. For without some primal ordering of the basic elements in a system to mutual interaction, prior to their actual operation, nothing would happen at all, not even by chance. There simply would not be a world at all.

Does this argument lose its power when set in the context of current discussions of theoretical physics and cosmology, all of which are attempting to reduce the present complex order to an original simpler order, or possibly to some absolutely simple primal state? Thus some speculate that our present cosmos came about as a chance fluctuation in a primal quantum energy field or high energy "vacuum." This does shift the ground of the argument significantly, and one must think hard about its implications.

But it seems to me that the argument still holds firm. For no matter how simple the original energy state may be, it does evolve into, or give rise to, a system of determinate active elements that exhibit a built-in dynamic orientation to combine together in mutual interaction in regular determinate ways to form an ordered system. Some prior dynamic orientation must have existed within the original energy state to thus evolve into determinate dynamic order. Otherwise the latter would arise with no intelligible grounding in anything prior at all, as a sheer brute fact in total discontinuity with what precedes it, as totally unintelligible, with no sufficient reason whatever. This is not an explanation at all, but an intellectual cop-out. Note, too, that even if the particular cosmic order that emerges from the original simple energy state emerges purely by chance—which is highly controversial—it still remains that any ordered system whatever would have to be internally ordered within itself if any reciprocal interaction is to take place within it, if it is to be a determinate cosmic order at all. And therefore an ordering Mind would have to be somewhere at the origin of the unity of its order. It seems, then, that the principle of the Argument from Order holds firm: any determinate dynamic order at all, whether primal in itself or originating from some previous physical energy state, must be grounded ultimately in an ordering Mind transcending the system itself.

With regard to the evolutionary development of living organisms, let me add: No matter how much chance there may be in the external conditions of the environment that these organisms exploit to evolve, what remains as the essential prior condition for the whole process is the built-in *inner dynamism*, the unflagging *dynamic drive* of the organisms toward intereacting in determinate ways with the other agents in the universe around it, toward actively exploiting the opportunities offered them by chance. This innate positive drive to survive, to act, to interact, cannot be supplied by any chance exterior conditions. It must be built in to the active potentialities (or dispositional properties) of the very natures of the organisms, prestructured from the beginning to interact with other natural agents in some basic determinate ways. It is this innate drive that is not supplied by evolutionary theory, but must ultimately be predetermined by some creative ordering Mind, the only power that can transpose intelligible possibilities from creative idea into actual entities endowed with focused energy.[20]

V. Derivation of the Divine Attributes

Since it is impossible to condense a whole course in natural theology into this one paper,[21] let me sketch out with extreme brevity the general procedure for determining which attributes (or predicates) can legitimately be applied to the God we have discovered at the term of our quest for the intelligibility of our universe: one single, self-existent Source of all being, endowed with the infinite qualitative fullness of all possible perfection.

Two basic principles are involved. One is a corollary of the nature of efficient causality—understood, of course, in its active productive ontological sense, not as mere Humean succession with predictability. This is the similitude that must exist in at least some analogous way between an effect and its cause. For, since the effect as effect receives its being from its cause, and the cause cannot give what it does not possess at least in some higher equivalent way, there must be some bond of real similitude between them. This can then serve as the bridge by which we can link our knowledge of the effect with what we can affirm of the cause.

The second principle is that we cannot without further analysis transfer any attribute found in the effect directly and literally to its cause. In the case of God, for example, any attribute (or predicate) containing in its very meaning some limit or imperfection must be winnowed out as implying some contradiction if literally applied to God—this is what St. Thomas calls "the negative moment" in the process. The attribute in question must be reduced to some broader, more universal one that is purely positive in its meaning, containing no limits or imperfections in the core meaning of the term, including the lower limited attribute as only one of its limited modes or degrees and calling for our unqualified approval such that were God to lack it, He-She would be less perfect than we are. Thus visual power in a creature would be transposed into knowledge in God and so on. A small number of basic attributes survive this purification process and can be applied literally, though analogously, to God, with the index of infinity added.

Such viable attributes turn out to be a small number of basic ones, like existence, unity, activity-power, goodness, intelligence, will, love, and a few others derived from these. A central one would be God as supremely personal being, although we could not philosophically derive the intersubjectivity within God (God as Triune). This derivation procedure is not a simple logical, deductive one, but a very delicate one, requiring careful reflection as to what we truly value with unqualified approval. We can and must affirm these as necessarily true of God, that is, we must affirm that the divine being possesses them in an infinite way, while at the same time we recognize that just *how* God possesses them (God's own proper essence or mode of being) is totally beyond the grasp of our abstract concepts. As St. Thomas tells us, constantly insisting on the unknowability of the divine essence in itself, we know "*that* God is intelligent, but not *how*." Our own natural dynamism of intellect and will toward the Infinite must be brought into the process here; for it illumines obscurely but richly this mystery-shrouded essence of God by a certain "connatural affinity" with Him (St. Thomas) as His lovingly created images, that is, by a "knowledge of the heart" (Pascal) through longing and love, as magnetized in the depths of our being by this Infinite Good that is our final End—a "knowledge" through longing and love, I repeat, not through vision—at least in this life.

Let me point out, finally—a point too often overlooked in discussions of the divine attributes and the difficulty of knowing the divine essence—that there is one thing that we do know with absolute precision about this mysterious Ultimate Reality: that it is Number One on the scale of value of any and all positive attributes, and alone there, the unique supremely perfect one in any line of perfection. But is not this all we really need to know in order to give it, without reservation, the fullness of our religious adoration, reverence, love, trusting commitment, and so forth? As long as we know this being is the Number One in wisdom, power, love, and so on, and therefore uniquely worthy of our religious worship, do we really need to know just how our God exercises these various attributes? Do we really need a do-it-yourself kit for the divine attributes? What we do know is something of supreme importance for the meaning of our lives, something we do not know of any other being in the universe (in fact, we know it cannot be true of any other). It seems to me this is to have found the pearl of great price, which is more than enough for the truly religious person in quest of final meaning for his or her life.

Let me conclude by suggesting as a fascinating task-challenge-opportunity for natural theology today to speculate creatively and imaginatively on what the "personality" or "character" must be like of a Creator in whose image this astonishing universe of ours is made, with its prodigal abundance of energy, its mind-boggling complexity yet simplicity, its fecundity of creative spontaneity, its ever-surprising fluid interweaving of order and chance, law and apparent chaos, and so forth. Must not the "personality" of such a Creator be charged not only with unfathomable wisdom, power, and exuberant generosity, but also with dazzling "imaginative" creativity—might we say a daring Cosmic Gambler who delights in working out His-Her providence by a creative synthesis of both law and order, on the one hand, and chance, risk, spontaneity, on the other—a "coincidence of opposites," as St. Bonaventure put it long ago?[22]

To return now to the question with which we began: "Is a Natural Theology Still Viable Today?" I am prepared to answer with modest conviction that it certainly is, if one asks the right questions, the most radical ones about existence itself, and does not short-circuit the process by an arbitrarily restrictive epistemology or metaphysics and gives full rein to the deep dynamism of the human mind in its quest for total intelligibility of the real.

NOTES

1. Arthur Dyson, *Disturbing the Universe* (New York: Harper & Row, 1979), chapter on "The Argument from Design," p. 251.

2. E. McMullin, "Natural Science and Belief in a Creator: Historical Notes," in R. Russell, W. Stoeger, G. Coyne, eds., *Physics, Philosophy, and Theology: A Common Quest for Understanding* (Rome: Vatican Observatory, 1988—dist. by Univ. of Notre Dame Press), pp. 49–79.

3. A valuable survey of details on this can be found in L. S. Betty and B. Cordell, "God and Modern Science: New Life for the Teleological Argument," *Internat. Philosophical Quarterly*, 27 (1987), 409–55.

4. See D. E. Thomsen, "The Quantum Universe: A Zero-Point Fluctuation?" *Science News*, 128 (Aug. 3, 1985), 7.

5. It would be more accurate, it seems to me, to describe it as an absence of *form*, not of energy, which is still very much in the real order. See, in the Vatican Symposium (above, n. 2), John Leslie, "How to Draw Conclusions from a Fine-Tuned Cosmos"; C. J. Isham, "Creation of the Universe as a Quantum Process"; Frank Tipler, "The Omega-Point Theory: A Model of an Evolving God."

6. Cf. the article of Betty and Cordell cited in note 3, and C. Thaxton, W. Bradley, R. Olsen, *The Mystery of Life's Origin: Reassessing Current Theories* (New York: Philosophical Library, 1984).

7. For typical examples, see *After Philosophy: End or Transformation?* eds. K. Baynes, J. Bohman, T. McCarthy (Cambridge, Mass.: MIT Press, 1987),

in particular the essay by J. F. Lyotard, leading French Postmodernist, "The Postmodern Condition," pp. 67–94.

8. On Deconstruction, see the essay by Derrida in the collection cited in note 7; also John Caputo, *Radical Hermeneutics, Repetition, Deconstructionism, and the Hermeneutical Project* (Bloomington: Indiana Univ. Press, 1987); John Sallis, ed., *Deconstruction and Philosophy* (Chicago: Univ. of Chicago Press, 1986); Hugh Silverman and Don Ihde, eds., *Hermeneutics and Deconstruction* (Albany: SUNY Press, 1985); Christopher Norris, *Deconstruction: Theory and Practice* (London: Methuen, 1982).

9. Similarly Anthony Quinton, definitely a metaphysician in the analytic mode, maintains this stricture on the use of causal inference: "For a causal inference is only legitimate if it is at least possible to obtain evidence for the existence of the cause which is independent of the events it is said to explain," in "The Problem of Perception," G. Warnock, ed., *The Philosophy of Perception* (New York: Oxford Univ. Press, 1967), p. 62. All the classical metaphysicians in their ascent to God by causal inference have systematically violated this unduly restrictive rule, one of the many implicit hangovers from the empiricist mentality often found still imbedded in analytic thought.

10. For the origin of the term "cause" in the Greek law courts, see H. Boeder, "Origine et préhistoire de la notion philosophique de l'AITION," *Revue des sciences philosophiques et théologiques*, 40 (1956), 421–43. For a defense of the common-sense notion of efficient causality as active, causal efficacy, see R. Harré and E. Madden, *Causal Powers* (Totowa, N.J.: Rowman & Allanheld, 1975); Dorothy Emmet, *The Effectiveness of Causes* (Albany: SUNY Press, 1984); Galen Strawson, "Realism, Causal Efficacy, and Causation," *Philosophical Quarterly*, 37 (1987), 255–77; John Wild, "A Realistic Defence of Causal Efficacy," *Review of Metaphysics*, 2 (1948–49), 1–14. For a fuller treatment of efficient causality as applied to arguing to the existence of God, see my book, *The Philosophical Approach to God: A Neothomist Perspective* (Winston-Salem: Wake Forest Univ. Press, 1979), ch. 2: "The Metaphysical Ascent to God through Participation." For another robust defense of active efficient causality and its application to proving the existence of God, see an important book of David Braine, *The Reality of Time: The Project of Proving God's Existence* (Oxford: Clarendon Press, 1988), ch. 3.

11. For the philosophical significance of action in St. Thomas's metaphysics and epistemology, and its relevance to Kant and modern epistemology, see my essay, "Action as the Self-Revelation of Being: A Central Theme in the Thought of St. Thomas," in Linus Thro, ed., *History of Philosophy in the Making* (Lanham, Md.: Univ. Press of America, 1982), pp. 65–81— reprinted as chapter 3 in the present collection. For John Dewey's reference to action as the key to epistemology and its neglect in modern philosophy, see his 1897 lecture, "The Significance of the Problem of Knowledge," *Early Works of John Dewey* (Carbondale: Southern Illinois Univ. Press, 1972), pp. 295, 297.

12. I have joined together two texts, one from *Summa Theologiae*, I, q. 77, a. 1 ad obj. 7, the other from *Expositio in Libros Sententiarum*, III, d. 35, q. 2, a. 2, sol. 1.

13. I have developed this path at greater length in my book, *The Philosophical Approach to God* (n. 10 above), ch. 1: "The Turn to the Inner Path in Contemporary Neothomism."

14. *Summa Theol.*, I, q. 93, a. 6; q. 44, a. 1 ad obj. 1.

15. Frank Tipler, "The Omega-Point Theory: A Model of an Evolving God," in the symposium, *Physics, Philosophy, and Theology* (n. 2 above), pp. 313–14.

16. Stephen Hawking, *A Brief History of Time* (New York: Bantam, 1988), p. 74. In the light of this text, I find it a step backward and hardly consistent to read his earlier enigmatic statement: "the quantum theory of gravity has opened up a new possibility, in which there would be no boundary to space-time . . . no singularities at which the laws of science broke down and no edge of space-time at which one would have to appeal to God or some new law to set the boundary conditions for space-time. One could say, 'The boundary condition of the universe is that it has no boundary.' The universe would be completely self-contained and not affected by anything outside itself. It would neither be created nor destroyed. It would just BE" (p. 136). If he means only that the universe need not have had a beginning in space-time, this, though controversial, can be acceptable philosophically. But if he means that our material universe, determinate in structure and energy though it be, is totally self-sufficient for its own existence in this mode, this does not follow from the scientific hypothesis at all and stops short of the radical question we have raised of why it should exist at all.

17. *Sum. Theol.*, I, q. 2, a. 3.

18. Some samples are: *Summa contra Gentes*, I, ch. 13, n. 35; ch. 42, n. 7; *De Potentia*, q. 3., a. 6. For an analysis of all Aquinas's arguments to God from final causality and order, see Leszek Figurski, *Finality and Intelligence* (Lanham, Md.: Univ. Press of America, 1979), ch. 6.

19. Charles Hartshorne develops well a similar argument, using the felicitous phrase, "a cosmic-wide order needs a cosmic-wide orderer," *A Natural Theology for Our Time* (LaSalle, Ill.: Open Court, 1967), pp. 58–62, and in other later versions of the same, for which see Donald Viner, *Charles Hartshorne and the Essence of God* (Albany: SUNY Press, 1985), ch. 6: "The Design Argument."

20. For some recent attempts to build on the enormous statistical improbability of the passage from a nonliving molecule to a living cell, see Betty and Cordell, "God and Modern Science: New Life for the Teleological Argument" (n. 3 above), and *The Mystery of Life's Origin* (cited in n. 6). Despite their persuasiveness, however, I am reluctant to recognize this as a cogent argument in view of the new Chaos theories of Prigogine and others, according to which conditions of apparently chaotic high turbulence can give rise to unpredictable new forms on a higher level. See Arthur Peacocke, *God and the New Biology* (New York: Harper & Row, 1986), pp. 63–64.

21. I develop this whole theme of the divine attributes at greater length in ch. 2 of my *A Philosophical Approach to God*.

22. See the very suggestive essay of Robert Russell, "Quantum Physics

in Philosophical and Theological Perspective," in the symposium *Physics, Philosophy, and Theology" A Common Quest for Understanding*, pp. 343–74, and also the considerably more daring piece in the same collection by Sally McFague, "Models of God for an Ecological, Evolutionary Era: God as Mother of the Universe," p. 249, based on her books, *Metaphorical Theology: Models of God in Religious Language* (Philadelphia: Fortress, 1982), and *Models of God: Theology for an Ecological, Nuclear Age* (Fortress, 1987). I think she goes too far, however, in her metaphor of the universe as "the body" of God as Mother, where God combines in her one nature both matter and spirit, and thus "overturns the dualisms of body and mind, flesh and spirit . . . an explicit rejection of Christianity's long, oppressive, and dangerous alliance with spirit against body, an alliance out of step with a holistic, evolutionary sensibility as well as with Christianity's Hebraic background" (p. 260). The dispersal of parts outside of parts across space-time that seems essential to the notion of body as material seems to me incompatible with the infinite intensive unity and perfection proper to God as Infinite Spirit.

9
A New Look at the Immutability of God

Anyone who has even a superficial acquaintance with the field of philosophical theology today is aware that one of the most crucial areas of debate concerns the immutability of God and the reality of his relation to the world. The traditional Scholastic position (henceforth for greater precision we shall call it the Thomistic position) on the immutability of God and the absence of any real relation on his part toward the world has been radically challenged from two sources which at present we frequently find coalescing into one. These two sources are: (1) process philosophy, in terms of the speculative exigencies of its own metaphysics of reality, and (2) existential religious consciousness, with its strong emphasis on the truly personal relation which must exist between a religiously available personal God and finite persons he has created.

If the only challenge came from the first source, it might be relegated to the domain of just another technical dispute in the realm of purely speculative philosophy. But the challenge coming from existential religious consciousness seeking an intellectual understanding of itself adds a new and greater urgency to the question. For any sound philosophical theory must do justice to the basic phenomena of human experience which it is its task to illuminate.

Now, if we are to take seriously the religious dimension of human experience—and we are taking for granted here that this is the case, especially for a Christian philosopher—then it is clear that one of the central tenets of man's religious belief (at least in Judaeo-Christian religion) is that God is one who enters into deep personal relations of love with his creatures. And an authentic interpersonal relation of love necessarily involves not merely purely creative or one-way love, but genuine mutuality and reciprocity of love, including not only the giving of love but the joyful acceptance of it and response to it. This means that our God is a God who really cares, is really concerned with our lives and happiness, who enters into truly reciprocal personal relations with us, who responds to our prayers—to whom, in a word, our contingent world and its history somehow make a genuine difference. In short, the God of Judaeo-Christian religion must be a "religiously available" God on the personal level, as Whiteheadians put it.

There is no doubt that any adequate philosophical or theological concept of God must be such as to render intelligible such a personal relation between God and ourselves. Yet traditional natural theology insists that God is unconditionally immutable and has no real relation to the world, i.e., no relation which is a dimension of God's own real being, affecting his own real being, but only a "relation of reason" (*relatio rationis*), as it is technically called by St. Thomas—a relation which is not real in God objectively but is only attributed to him by extrinsic denomination because of the way minds have to think about him as cause. Now, this traditional doctrine of the God of philosophy seems to many to be in clear conflict with the exigencies of the God of personal religion. And since theory must always yield to life, they have rejected the above philosophical notion of God as unqualifiedly immutable and having no real relation to the world. In order to do justice to what they believe are the implications of religious belief and experience, many have substituted the theoretical framework of process philosophy. According to this philosophy, the "primordial nature" of God is immutable and infinite, but the "consequent nature" of God, as related to the ongoing world process by knowledge and love, is truly involved in this temporal process itself, affected by it in his life of knowledge and love, hence really related to it and truly changing and growing with it, as He knows it and responds to it. Hence God is mutable, finite, and really related to the world in his consequent nature—a view of God apparently in direct contradiction to the traditional Thomistic one.[1]

This process conception of God first arose among Protestant Christian thinkers, under the inspiration of Whitehead, but is now spreading among Catholic thinkers as well. As a result, we are witnessing a widespread rejection, among Judaeo-Christian religious thinkers of all persuasions, of "the immutable, unrelated, impassive, non-dialoguing, religiously unavailable God" of Thomistic metaphysics in favor of the involved, really related, changing God-in-process of process philosophy.[2]

The problem is clearly a crucial one for anyone concerned with thinking through his religious belief in some coherent intellectual framework. What I should like to do in this essay is to explore the resources of the Thomistic metaphysical system to see how far it is capable of making a place for a God who can enter into truly personal relations with his creatures. In the past Thomistic metaphysicians seem to have been content for the most part to assert and defend the absolute immutability of God and to relegate all change and diversity to the side of the creature. But they have not gone on to explain how God can enter into a truly interpersonal dialogue with created persons, how his loving of them and their response to him in the particular contingent ways which are proper to a free exchange between persons can truly make a difference to him, how he is not the completely impassive, indifferent metaphysical iceberg, or at least one-way unreceptive Giver, to whom my loving or not loving, my salvation or damnation, make no difference whatever, as Hartshorne and other process philosophers have objected. It does seem to me that they have a legitimate grievance against the way Thomists have handled, or failed to handle, this problem.

On the other hand, it seems to me that it is quite possible to draw upon the latent resources of the system, in particular by developing the traditional distinction between the orders of real and intentional being, hitherto very little exploited with respect to God, and by adapting the notion of immutability to fit the perfection appropriate to personal being, so that the loving dialogue of God with creatures becomes truly possible and intelligible, though always clothed in mystery on God's part. This seems to me a wiser strategy than simply to jettison the traditional doctrine lock, stock, and barrel before testing out its resources to the full and substituting a totally new metaphysical framework of process philosophy which, as I see it, introduces a host of new difficulties which might well leave us worse off philosophically than we were before.[3] In a word, let us try evolution first rather than an over-hasty revolution.

I should like to present this paper, therefore, as an essay in creative Thomistic metaphysics, an effort to adapt what still seems to me an incomparably rich and profound metaphysical system to the newly felt and now better understood exigencies of the domain of interpersonal being. (For reasons of space, this will have to be almost entirely a speculative presentation, with no attempt at detailed grounding in the texts of St. Thomas or discussion with his commentators.) But since every creative development and adaptation of one philosopher's thought by another always involves the risk of introducing such profound and sometimes unnoticed seismic tremors into the original system so that its own author might well repudiate it, I must take full responsibility upon myself for this "Thomistic adaptation" and not blame it upon St. Thomas, even though I believe it to be authentically and coherently Thomistic in its inspiration. Let me also acknowledge from the start that I owe a great debt in what follows to the inspiration, though not always the conclusions, of other Thomistically inspired contemporary Christian thinkers—such as Karl Rahner and others[4]—who in recent years have been trying to grapple in their own way with various aspects of this complex and difficult problem.

THE IMMUTABILITY OF GOD'S REAL BEING

In working out any treatise on the attributes of God, the central notion which must remain constant and command all the rest, setting limits to their meaning and application and ordering their mutual relations, is that of absolute or infinite perfection or, if you like, the fullness of perfection. Thus the affirmation that God is absolutely perfect functions as a kind of formal constant down through the history of philosophical conceptions of God, whereas philosophical and cultural evaluations of precisely what constitutes perfection often vary down the ages or across cultures, with corresponding variations in the set of other attributes which are affirmed of God in order to spell out the central exigency of perfection. Hence it is only because, and precisely insofar as, immutability is seen as a necessary corollary of this fullness of perfection that it should be affirmed of God, and not vice versa. Immutability is not an absolute self-justifying value in its own right to which the notion of perfection itself must be made to conform. This key point must be kept in focus throughout the discussion which follows.[5]

Why does St. Thomas affirm the immutability of God? Because mutability, as he understands it in the Aristotelian metaphysics of change, necessarily involves imperfection. In order to grasp the point of this conclusion, it is imperative to remember that the whole context of the Aristotelian doctrine of change as a passage from potency to act and requiring an extrinsic cause—which is St. Thomas's own context, too—is that of real change, or change in the intrinsic real being of a thing. To change in this context is to acquire (or lose) some new mode of intrinsic real being not possessed before. Hence it implies an increase (or decrease) in the ontological perfection of the being undergoing change, a passage from imperfection to greater perfection. It is for this reason that if the subject of change does not already possess, at least in some equivalent way, the new perfection it acquires, it must receive this from some extrinsic source, which is called the efficient cause of the change. For nothing can give to itself what it does not already have in some equivalent way.[6] It must be remembered, too, that in St. Thomas's theory of real relations every real relation must be founded in something in the intrinsic real or absolute being of that which is related. Hence every change or newness in the real relations of a being must be founded on something new in its intrinsic real being (unless the relations are in the purely static dimension of quantity or similitude—relations which St. Thomas, mistakenly to my mind, calls real—where only one term need vary).[7]

Now, if we interpret change in this strict Aristotelian sense, then for God to be mutable would mean that he could pass to some new higher mode or level of perfection of intrinsic real being which he did not possess before. But it is not at all clear how such a growth in God's intrinsic perfection makes any sense, or is needed for any religious or personalist purposes. For if one is to hold to any traditional concept of God at all, one must affirm that God is already and from all eternity positively infinite in the fullness of perfection. Would we want God first to be a non-loving type of person, then to grow or improve to become a loving type? Surely what we look for in God is to be loving, disposed to love by his very nature, to be the eternally steadfast, faithful, indefectible Lover, unchangeable, rather than inconstant and mutable, in the fullness of his loving goodness.

What we do indeed expect of God is that the *expression* of this love for us should be constantly growing and developing, unfolding throughout our lives to anticipate and respond to our own contingent history of unfolding—and highly variable—love-relations with him. We expect, therefore, that the field of his loving *consciousness* should be contingently other because of his personal relations to us. This is quite true, and we shall see how this must and can be taken care of by determinate contingent modifications of the field of intentional or cognitive being within God (or, more accurately, by determinate contingent *differentiation* of his intentional consciousness, since, as we shall see, we have no grounds for attributing real temporal succession to this consciousness).

But that the intentional content of God's loving consciousness should be contingently other because of the unfolding expression of unchanging personal love for us does not entail that God's own intrinsic real being, the level of his own intrinsic perfection, in any way undergoes real change to acquire some new higher mode of perfection not possessed before. Even in the order of knowledge and love God already knows and loves the highest possible fullness of being and goodness, his own self. Any further knowledge of a finite being will not be a passage to a higher fullness of knowing, but only an inner determination, or limitation of its focus, to some new limited mode of participation of God's own infinite perfection. It will be a numerically new item of knowledge, but not a passage to a higher or richer level of knowledge than that attained in knowing himself. Similarly, in loving some new created person in an unfolding sequence of ways, God is loving a numerically new object of love, but one which is only a limited participation and overflow of his own already totally loved infinite Goodness. No created object of God's knowledge and love adds any new *higher* dimension to the eternal fullness of being and goodness which he already knows and loves in himself. It adds only a new determinate sharing of this eternal plenitude, determinately known and loved, in a never-ending process of new *expression* of God's eternally infinite plenitude of goodness and love, but without the current's ever rising higher, so to speak, than its original source. In one word, to add a new finite content of knowledge and love to an already infinite plenitude of knowledge and love is not to pass from potency to act in the order of real being, to acquire a new higher mode of intrinsic perfection of being not possesed before. To add the finite to the infinite can only be in the mode of a sharing, an overflow, an expression of the plenitude which is already infinite. There is genuine novelty, to be sure, both in the real being God communicates to creatures and in the intentional content of the divine consciousness determinately knowing and willing them. But this is not change in God's own intrinsic being or perfection.

Much of the insistence on the mutability of God as implied in freely creating and loving these determinate creatures in time, rather than others equally possible, arises, it seems to me, from an anthropomorphic projection onto God of the mode of consciousness proper to us as finite consciousness incarnate in a body and thereby inexorably immersed in the flow of temporal succession. It is quite true that we, as finite, must unfold our knowledge in a succession of limited and incomplete acts, and that as incarnate or enfleshed spirit we have to receive the objects of our knowledge and love from without through action on our body which modifies our own intrinsic real being; in addition, every act of knowing or loving which we make is accompanied by and expressed through some intrinsic real change and motion in our bodies, if only in the constant firing of neurons in our brain cells.

But suppose we project knowing, loving, and efficacious causing (whether creation or some partial communication of new being makes no difference here) onto the level of a purely spiritual, infinite cause, where causing becomes simply efficacious spiritual willing. When a purely spiritual cause efficaciously wills (or loves) something or someone, there is clearly a focusing of the intentional consciousness of the willing agent on the object-term of its willing. This means that its field of intentional consciousness is modified, or, more accurately, is determinately other in its intentional content than it would be if it did not so will. But this determinate differentiation is in the order of *intentional being* or objective focus, the being of the *other* as held within consciousness. (We shall examine explicitly in a moment the difference between the orders of real and intentional being for St. Thomas.)

What about the intrinsic real being of the agent? In a purely spiritual willer there are no wheels to go round, no brain cells to fire, no physical motion to bring it close to its effect, since it is present wherever it wills to act. In a word, we can locate no grounds for internal motion or intrinsic change; there is only a pure, motionless, intentional ecstasy of the agent's conscious will focused on the intentionally represented objective term of its knowing-love. The only change is in the field of intentional consciousness, not in the "physical" or natural intrinsic being or perfection of the spiritual agent. This is precisely what it means for A to will X: it means to-will-X, not to change or move around inside A's own absolute being. This is precisely what the realm of interpersonal relations is all about in its pure essence, abstracting from the accidentally accompanying motions in us as finite and corporeal agents: it is concerned with the way in which the mutually interrelated persons focus on each other in their intentional consciousness, reaching out to each other, not physically but spiritually, in the immanent ecstasy of mutual inherence in each other's consciousness by knowing-love. Of course, this modification of intentional consciousness is important, "real" in this sense; it is precisely what determines the quality of our interpersonal relations, how we know and love. But this still does not permit us to attribute any further modifications or motion to the intrinsic real "natural being" of the agent, in the strict Thomistic sense of the terms. To love rather than not to love indeed makes a real difference in the intrinsic perfection of a person. But God is by essence always and totally loving, with infinite intensity and fullness, his own infinite goodness, both in itself and in all its participations. The only difference in such a love lies thus in the intentional focus applying it to this or that finite recipient. Hence the differentiation in the objective content of intentional consciousness does not *ipso facto* allow us to infer any change in the intrinsic or absolute real being of the willer. We must resolutely resist here the spontaneous tendency to project our own mode of incarnate willing onto a pure spirit and to picture all willing as such as some kind of physical "moving around" inside. The will as such has no "muscles" to flex—even in us.

Here is the place to recall the classic metaphysical position of both Aristotle and St. Thomas—still as valid and profound as ever, it seems to me—that efficient causality "takes place," or is ontologically "located," in the effect, not in the agent as such: *actio est in passo*.[8] For to cause is precisely to make *another* be (in whole or in part), to enrich *another*. It affirms nothing at all about enriching (or impoverishing) the agent. Change, on the other hand, is the exact opposite: it is enriching *oneself*, acquiring something new for *oneself*, and it says nothing at all about any enrichment of another. Hence the affirmation of a causal action, taken strictly and solely as such, gives no grounds for affirming any new intrinsic being in the agent. There is only one new reality resulting from a causal situation: this is in the subject or receiver of the action. And this one identical new reality simultaneously grounds three equally true and objective affirmations or attributions: (1) that there is real novelty, new real being, in the recipient Y, (2) that this is brought about by agent X, that X is the cause-of-Y, and (3) that there must be a determinate focusing of X on Y in the intentional order, the order of final causality, in X itself. No more can be affirmed without some added data outside the causal relation itself. And the presence of the final cause (the term-to-be-effected) in the dynamic intentionality of the agent is a presence in the intentional order only, and not in that of real being (otherwise the term would already be really present, and there would be no need to produce it at all). All this is traditional Thomistic metaphysical analysis, except that point (3) is too frequently omitted or left implicit in simplified expositions or in the heat of debate, thus giving initially plausible ground for the objections of process thinkers.

One more point. Real relation, in the strict Aristotelian-Thomistic meaning of the term, always requires some foundation in the intrinsic real being of the related subject; hence a new relation requires some new intrinsic change in the real or absolute being of the *relatum*. It follows that purely and simply from the attribution of causality to a being, with no further data added from the special mode of operation of the agent, one has no right to attribute any real relation in the agent toward its effect, though of course one can and must attribute a relation in the intentional order—a point consistently forgotten, it seems to me, in most disputes on this matter between Thomists and others. Thus St. Thomas maintains that creation as such, by a purely spiritual and infinite Cause, does not posit any real relation in God as cause, in Thomas's strong and technical sense of "real being."[9]

It follows from all this that the attribution of authentic loving and efficacious willing to God gives no grounds for affirming real

A New Look at the Immutability of God 191

change or mutability in God in the strict and strong sense of the term for St. Thomas—or for anyone, in fact, who holds the distinction between the orders of intentional and real being. But clearly if one says only this and no more, one has not said enough, and we would still remain in the dark about the way in which God can be said to be truly related to us in interpersonal relations of mutual love. Hence we must now turn our attention to the companion piece to the above doctrine of the real immutability of God, the otherness in the divine intentional consciousness which I am convinced we must affirm and which seems to me also authentically Thomistic in principle, though all too often it has been left totally in the shadow or even denied. I consider the explicit drawing-out of the implications of this distinction with respect to God the principal contribution of this essay.

CONTINGENT OTHERNESS AND PROCESS IN THE DIVINE CONSCIOUSNESS

Up to now we have tried to show why we have no good grounds for asserting real mutability in God, mutability of God's own intrinsic real being and perfection. But the reader will not fail to have noticed that we have been able to do this only by referring constantly to another and complementary order of being in God, that of "intentional being," to which we ascribed the contingent differentiation we excluded from God's intrinsic real being. We must now turn our attention explicitly to this order of being and its relation to that of real being.

St. Thomas distinguishes between (1) the being or existence of a thing in its own right, with its own intrinsic act of existence or "natural being," by which the thing exists with its own nature in itself and not merely as an object of thought in a mind (its *esse naturale, esse in re*, or *in rerum natura*) and (2) the mode of being which it has as an object of knowledge (or love) existing or present in the consciousness of a knower (or lover), which he calls its "intentional being," or being as the object of a consciousness "intending" it, or focusing its attention toward it, either as an object of contemplative knowledge or of actual willing of it as a real other (*esse intentionale, esse cognitum, esse volitum*).[10]

It is absolutely essential to distinguish these two orders of being in a realist epistemology and metaphysics, and for the following reasons. (1) If it is not distinguished, then we will have to say that when I—or any knower—know a raging fire outside of me, there is also a real raging fire existing in my consciousness, since the fire as known must be somehow truly present within my consciousness. This is patently absurd. (2) If the object known were in my consciousness in its own real being, then my knowledge would not be of the real fire outside of me at all but of a second real fire within my consciousness. But this would defeat the whole purpose of the act of knowledge in the first place, which is precisely not to create a second real world in duplication of the first, but to know one and the same identical real world already existing. In a word, knowledge is *of* a real other as present in the knower in the mode of a self-effacing cognitive duplicate or intentional representation of the real other. This cognitive presence of one real being in another is called "intentional being" because its whole being points or refers as a cognitive sign to the real object it stands for and makes present to the consciousness of the knower. This intentional mode of being, distinct from, but intrinsically related to, a thing's real being, is required for any act of knowledge where what is known is other in its real being than the knower itself; hence it holds even in the case of God, as knowing and loving a real world other than himself.[11]

Now, the only being of an object of knowledge, existing as such in a knowing consciousness, is, as St. Thomas puts it, its *being-known: esse eius consistit in ipso intelligi* (its to-be is its to-be-thought-about).[12] It has no real being of its own, but exists entirely within the consciousness of the knower, with an "existence" or presence given and maintained entirely by the real act of knowing in the knower, and only as long as the knower actually thinks about it. Hence its intentional mode of being is entirely according to the mode of being of the knower: if the knower is completely spiritual in its own being, then the mode of being of the object as known will also be completely spiritual, even though it may be *of* or *about* the most solidly material thing imaginable. And since the order of intentional being within a knower is intelligibly distinct from—although, of course, always inseparable from and dependent on—the order of its real being, it follows that multiplicity, materiality, or motion in the intentional objects of consciousness do not in any way of themselves divide up, materialize, or introduce change into the real being of the knower. (It should be noted, of course, that the distinction between the real act of a mind thinking and the intentional being of the contents of its thinking cannot be, for St. Thomas, a *real* distinction, since that would require that *both* terms be real. It is a *sui generis* "relation of reason," i.e., a relation of distinct intelligibilities holding between a real act of thinking and its idea-content. Hence when St. Thomas insists on the *real* identity in God of the intentional order with the one, simple, infinite act of existence that is God's real being, this should be taken in its strict technical meaning as denying all multiplicity of real beings or real acts in God. But this does not in the least deny the formal distinction of intelligibilities between the two orders: the one real act of divine thinking, on the one side, and the many distinct intelligibilities God is thinking *about* in the intentional order, on the other. Thus a spiritual knower can know a material object, without its own real being or its real act of knowing being material; it can know many objects without introducing multiplicity into its own real being or into the real act by which it knows them; it can know things in motion without its own being or its own act of knowing being in motion. If, however, it has to receive the content of its knowledge by action of the object itself on it from without, then the real being of the knower must itself undergo real change as the necessary complement of its new content of knowledge. This is not the case with God's knowing.

There are also two sources from which intentional being arises: from the objects toward the knower, and from the knower pointing outward toward its objects. The first occurs when the real object acts upon the knower from without, communicating an intentional extension of its own form to become an intentional presence of itself within the knower, molding the consciousness of the knower to its own form to make itself known there. The second occurs when the knower actively forms the objects of its thought within its own consciousness and uses them as self-determined intentional forms of its thinking and guides for its action.

Let us now apply the above ontology of intentional being to God. What follows has been developed only very sketchily by St. Thomas and little more by Thomists after him.[13] The main distinction of orders of being and its application to all knowers is explicit enough. But the further implications with respect to God, strangely enough, never seem to have been pursued. Following St. Thomas, Thomists have mostly contented themselves with saying that, since God cannot receive knowledge by being acted on by creatures from the outside but only by knowing himself as actively causing all creatures, God's own essence as acting must be the "species" or cognitive medium by which he knows all things. Creatures do not actively project their intentional being into God's consciousness by acting on it from without. Thus only the second mode of origin of intentionality is present in God: from his creative intellect-will constituting the intentional objects or terms of his active sharing of his own goodness with creatures. That this position raises problems about how God can know our free actions without totally determining them and how he can "receive" our love in return is clear. We shall consider these later. Let us proceed first to draw out the implications of the *fact*—which all must admit—of the intentional presence of all creatures in the divine consciousness as determinate objects of his knowledge and love.

1. God's intentional "field of consciousness," whose content is the order of intentional being, of intentional objects of God's knowledge and love, necessarily contains the whole multiplicity of all creatures in their unique individuality and distinctness; otherwise he would not be their intelligent and loving Creator and could not exercise providence over them. All admit this.

2. It follows that because of God's free decision to create this possible world rather than that, to respond lovingly to this person in this way rather than that, his field of intentional consciousness must be determinately and contingently *other* than it would and could have been had he decided in some other way. For free decisions are by definition contingent, could have been otherwise, and we should not have the least reluctance to affirm that in its creaturely *intentional objects* or terms the divine consciousness is contingently and determinately differentiated. Nor does this in the least militate against the necessity and immutability of God's intrinsic real being. (Remember that a spiritual willing as such is a pure motionless act of willing *this* rather than *that*.) Our God, therefore, the only God there is, is precisely the one who in intentional loving consciousness chooses us and not some others. It should be clear, therefore, that we must admit at least this much about God: that the divine consciousness, in its intentional content, is *distinctly, determinately,* and *contingently differentiated* or *other* with respect to creatures because God has freely chosen this world, than it would and could have been had he chosen a different world or none at all. (Whether or not this determinate otherness in divine consciousness is "from eternity" without change at all, or involves God in some kind of temporal succession, is a further question which must be treated in its own right.) Let us first see what implications are contained in what we have achieved already.

God Is Truly Related to Creatures by an Intentional Relation of Personal Consciousness

Let us presume for the moment that the above intentional differentiation in the divine consciousness does not involve temporal succession in God, but is eternally present in him, since it proceeds from and is grounded in God's own real being and real act of knowing, which exist in a timeless moment "outside" or independent of, and yet contemporaneous in every point with, all our temporal succession. Even granting this, without any concession to temporal process in God, it follows that God is truly related through intentional consciousness to us whom he has freely created and freely loves. For God's consciousness is truly other, determinately and contingently differentiated, precisely because of us, because of his free decision to create us, and all his subsequent knowledge and expressions of love of us are consequent upon these decisions and our own free response to them.

Thus we do make a difference to God, a very important difference in the domain of personal relations. But this, in St. Thomas's metaphysical framework, is still a relation in the intentional order, grounded in the differentiation of intentional terms in the divine consciousness, and not in any otherness of God's real being. Hence it cannot be properly called a "real relation" in his strict terminology. But it should definitely be called a relation of intentional consciousness, or, more briefly, an "intentionality relation," by which God is truly related to us. Accordingly, it is truly a personal relation. For where else does the quintessence of interpersonal relations as such reside save in the order of knowing and loving, of *conscious* relationship, which, for St. Thomas, is precisely the order of intentional being, of consciousness as differentiated by its intentional terms? Hence it seems to me perfectly legitimate and in fact necessary to say that God is truly related to creatures by a relation of personal consciousness (understood as the equivalent of the technical term "intentional" which so many non-Thomistic thinkers are unfamiliar with).

Here I should like to register my own criticism of the Thomist tradition in the way it has handled this problem of the real relation of God to the world. From St. Thomas on, Thomists have been content for the most part with insisting on the absence of any real relation (in St. Thomas's strict meaning of the term) in God toward the world, and with explaining and defending the reasons for this position. But this done, they have simply stopped there, and have not gone on to say anything further about what other kind of relation can be truly predicated of God, beyond predication by extrinsic denomination because of our way of thinking about him as cause; nor have they indicated how God can be said to be truly involved in a personal dialogue with us, in a mutual love relationship which is the ground of our religious devotion. In failing to draw the implications of intentional relationship in God, which is no less significant and important for not being "real" in the strict sense, it seems to me that they have not lived up to their full responsibility as philosophers of God sensitive to the exigencies of religious belief and experience. Hence it is with great satisfaction that I note that another philosopher speaking from within the Thomistic perspective has already come forward with the same suggestion as the one I have made. In fact I have borrowed his exact—and to my mind very felicitous—terminology in expressing my own independently-arrived-at conclusion: there is in God "a relation of personal consciousness" to the world (*relatio conscientiae personalis*).[14]

It seems to me that once one had admitted such authentic personal relation in God to us, so that God is truly other, different, in his consciousness, because of his relations with us, the essential demand of religious consciousness is satisfied. What we really want to know, what really matters to us, is: do we make a difference to God, is God truly related to us in the personal dimension of knowledge and love? Whether this relation is described as real or intentional is a technical speculative problem which can be left to specialists to argue over. And I see no compelling reason why the religious person should insist on going further and affirming some further "real change, real difference," in the intrinsic real being or perfection of God. "Truly related" seems to me to verify enough what the ordinary person means by "really related."

Of course, the process philosopher may here quite relevantly object that it is a peculiar, paradoxical, and unsatisfying terminology for the modern mind to call something as important as this personal relation of consciousness not "real." To the contemporary mind, oriented to value rather than to being, what is important should be termed "real," and what is most important, "most real." This is a legitimate criticism. One can simply step back from the whole conceptual framework and find it not wrong—for it does the job to be done in its own way—but unsatisfactory, aesthetically inadequate, if you wish. One certainly has the right to set up a new conceptual framework to handle the same problem. But in so doing, one must be careful to take care of all the key aspects of the situation handled by the old framework. For instance: should "the important" always be convertible with "the real"? Suppose that I am thinking about building a space ship or entering a Carthusian monastery. Surely how I think and decide about these possible goals of action is of great importance for my life. Yet clearly neither of the two goals is yet real, even when I decide on one before executing it.

Or suppose again that I decide that a difference in one's intentional consciousness is so important for personal life that intentional being should be called "real." Fine! But then one is going to have to invent a new distinction inside of real being to take care of the indispensable Thomistic insight that the being of something as known and loved, as in the consciousness of the knower-lover, is not identical with its real natural being as it exists in its own right, nor is it a second real being of the same ontological density. One is going to have to distinguish real being into (1) real intentional being, and (2) real natural being, or something of the sort. Otherwise we shall be thrown back again into the old unsolved problems of exaggerated realism which have plagued the Platonic tradition from its inception. And I must confess that I do not find process philosophers nearly sensitive enough, for my metaphysical taste, to the distinction between the real and the intentional order, or to the exigencies of pure spiritual knowing and loving which we must all postulate, even though we cannot directly experience it, when we are talking about God. Perhaps the root lies in the lack of an authentic analogy of being in Whitehead, though hints are certainly there to be developed.[15]

There is also the difficulty, I might add, that to speak of "real intentional being" brings the new disadvantage with it of being an expression considerably at variance with ordinary language use. In ordinary language, something is called "real" precisely to set it off from what is merely "ideal" or thought about, though I admit that the term has many fuzzy edges. Perhaps part of the trouble comes from the fact that "really" in ordinary language has gradually developed a weaker sense where it means simply "truly," as in the question: "Does this theorem in logic (or mathematics) really follow from these premises?" "Really" here surely does not imply that logical or mathematical entities or propositions are real beings. Perhaps all that people finally mean when they ask whether God is "really related" to them is whether God is truly related to them. And the answer in terms of my own exposition above would be a resounding "Yes."[16]

TEMPORAL SUCCESSION IN GOD

Our efforts to meet the challenge of process philosophy are by no means over with the above conclusion that God can be said to be truly related to us by a relation of personal consciousness, because his intentional consciousness is contingently different in view of us. A process philosopher might perhaps concede that by the distinction of the real from the intentional order Thomists can take care in their own way of the demand that the world make a difference to God. But the process philosopher insists on considerably more. He or she wishes to claim that a God who knows, acts in, and responds to a world unfolding as a process in time must also be involved in process, hence in temporal succession. God is thus a God who is in process, that is, changing, mutable. In a word, even if the process philosopher were to concede that the contingent otherness in the divine consciousness were only in the order of intentional and not real being, he or she would still maintain that this entails *temporal process* in the divine consciousness, at least in the order of intentional being. As some have put it, if God is a personal being who responds to created persons, then God cannot be a timeless being.[17] He can be an eternal being, but one whose eternity is that of an eternal duration, extending over all time and beyond, with temporal succession in it matching ours, and not the eternity of a timeless moment, outside of all duration and temporal succession. The latter is the classical Thomistic concept of the divine eternity (traditional also in most classical Christian thinkers from Boethius, through Anselm, down to the present).

We must now come to grips with this difficult problem of the timelessness or in-time-ness of God. Let us proceed step by step, following always the rule of metaphysical parsimony, namely, that one is not justified in affirming anything of God unless one must do so. What must we affirm of God with regard to temporal succession? First, what the problem is *not*: it is not that the real effective expresion of the divine causality and God's real response to us (the novelty in the order of real being) take place in time. Of course they do, and Thomists have always asserted this. For this effective action and response, following the classic axiom that causal action takes place *within* the recipient (*actio est in passo*), as *from* or *due to* the agent, occur precisely down in us, not back in God. This is precisely where it should be, where we would *want* it to be, immanent *in us*, communicated *to us*, not consisting of some moving-around of inner wheels in God or change in his own intrinsic real being. A response should be precisely *in* the one to whom the response is being given. So the real being of God's action on and response to us occurs down in our temporal process. Causality is the ecstasy of the agent present by its power *in* its effect. The failure to understand this key metaphysical point in the nature of causality invalidates a large amount of what seems to me simply uncritical "common sense" criticism of the divine-immutability position, as though it were obvious that to do something, to produce any change, in time necessarily puts change and time in the doer.[18]

Our problem, then, is concerned exclusively with the content of the divine intentional consciousness, which is truly in God and which is the point of origin of the real changes produced in us. What must we affirm of it?

(1) We must first affirm that for every knowable item in our world of process there is a corresponding cognitive content in the divine intentional consciousness, since God knows determinately in all its detail all that is. (Note that this does not yet allow us to infer a distinct real act of knowing corresponding to every distinct item known, since there is no difficulty in principle in one spiritual act's knowing many things in one act of vision if it is powerful enough to do so. And the divine act is infinite. We simply have no vantage point to do a "phenomenology" of the divine mode of knowing as it is in itself.)

(2) Since these created items known have as part of their intrinsic intelligibility their sequence in time, the content of the divine consciousness must contain or represent this internal time-sequence of the items as related to each other; in other words, it must be a cognitive representation of the time process, perfectly isomorphic in this cognitive content to the time process it represents. In this sense, therefore, one can speak of a "cognitive or intentional sequence" in God, or sequence within the *objective content* of the divine cognition.

(3) Does this introduce real process, and hence "real" time, into the divine consciousness itself? It must be recalled here that for St. Thomas, following Aristotle, time is present only as the cognitive measure of some real change or process of succession in the order of real being. "Time is the measure of motion"—i.e., real motion. Where there is no real motion there can be no time in the proper sense of the term, only understood sequence of cognitive contents. This cognitive sequence can be *correlated* with a real time-sequence by extrinsic intentional reference to the latter, but is itself of a different order (intentional and not real being) and hence incommensurable with the latter and unable to be timed by any time standard, since time is always the measure of real motion. In a word, it is impossible to time a pure cognitive sequence unless there is some real succession underlying it in the knower. Thus for there to be authentic time in God there would have to be some real change or succession underlying the cognitive sequence in his intentional consciousness and allowing us to spread out these contents in an *extended continuum* of succession and distinguish them as moments before and after in a process of real change.

But in the divine consciousness there is not the slightest real change or real motion going on *between* the successive items known, even though these do feed up to this consciousness earlier and later from really distinct moments down in the process from which they originate. But they coalesce in God's eternal Now outside of all and present to all moments. Let us call moments A and B two distinct moments in our temporal process, and A' and B' the corresponding "moments" in the divine cognitive field. We can distinguish A and B temporally because of the real motion going on between them. But how are we to distinguish A' and B' in God? How long is it between them? Since there is no motion going on in the real being of God (including the real being of his consciousness), there is absolutely no way to distinguish, by examining this inner being of God, whether a second has elapsed, or a million years, or any determinate length of time, or none—*between* or *within* the items of the intelligible sequence of God's world-directed consciousness. All the moments in God telescope into the single real moment of his motionless eternal presence, contemporaneous with all the moments of our or any other created time-sequences. For if there is no time between any two moments, they coalesce into the equivalent of simultaneity, a simultaneity not of distinct nows conceived on the model of temporal sequence in our world, where any two distinct nows *exclude* each other, but one of spiritual presence and consciousness that includes and mirrors perfectly, without in any way negating or dissolving, the internal sequence of time relations of the objects of its knowledge as they exist in their own order of real succession, which alone can generate time.

One can, of course, *correlate* this understood sequence of cognitive contents in God with the real temporal sequence to which they correspond and from which they come. They correspond item for item. One can also, if one wishes, measure the duration of the divine existence and cognition by an *extrinsic* standard or point of reference, namely, the motion going on outside of him in our world. Thus one can say that God has existed as long as the world has existed, or that God's knowledge of World War II took four years to complete, etc. We can "time" him by our clocks, if we wish. But this is in terms of pure extrinsic denomination, somewhat like the projection of a point onto a line in projective geometry. It posits no real time sequence, because it posits no real succession in God, only an understood sequence between the objects of God's consciousness in the order of intentional being, each referring to a really distinct point in our real temporal process. And these two orders of real and intentional being are simply incommensurable with each other in any time framework, since there is no change in real being in one of the terms of comparison and therefore nothing to be measured by any time standard. However, I am perfectly willing to admit that just as we have allowed an intelligible sequence in the order of intentional being in God, so too we can allow an intelligible or "intentional time" in the divine consciousness corresponding to this sequence. This intentional time would be analogous to our real time in the same way that intentional being is analogous to real being.

The position I am maintaining, therefore, is that there is a correlate in the intentional order in God of the real temporal succession in the world, but that this pure cognitive sequence cannot be called "temporal succession" in any proper meaning of the term, since there is no real change in God underlying it and spreading out its "moments" into an extended continuum. Now, if a process philosopher wishes to object that for him any kind of succession, whether in the intentional or the real order, is a time process, then of course he is at liberty to say that God is in time, or that there is process in God. But he must still respect the radical difference between the two kinds of process and time, one of objects as known, the other of intrinsic real being, and not immediately conclude *ipso facto* from the first to the second.

I see no serious difficulty for a Thomist to admit such a "process" or sequence in the intentional order in God with its correlate of "intentional time." For just as the traditionally admitted multiplicity of intentional being in God does not in the least prejudice the simplicity of his real being, and just as the contingent otherness of the divine intentional consciousness with respect to freely willed creatures does not prejudice the necessity of God's own intrinsic real being, so it follows that there is no reason why process or succession in the purely intentional order—understood sequence of objects as known—should prejudice the immutability and timelessness of God in his real being.

Perhaps the real difficulty which is disturbing those who insist on process and time in God is that they wish his knowledge and love of the world to be only *contemporary* with what is going on in the world and not prior to it in some predetermined eternity where all would somehow be pre-known and pre-loved independently of the actual course of created history (with the consequent endangering of true contingency and freedom), and actual history would make no difference to God, since he had pre-decided the whole thing on his own anyway.

This to my mind is a real misunderstanding of the theory of the divine knowledge and love as eternal. First of all, the notion of any "foreknowledge," properly speaking, in God must be rejected. God does not know anything, let alone a free action, "before" it happens (understanding "before" as before to God). It may be before to us, from our limited vantage point as fixed at one point in the process, although I am not sure how much sense that makes either. But God knows all real things, past, present, and future, St. Thomas says, in their actual presence as going on, in their *now*, by his "eternal presentiality" to the whole time process from the motionless Now of his real being outside of the process, though working immanently within it.[19] Hence God knows our free actions as *contemporary with them*, not before they exist in actuality. And being an infinitely perfect purely spiritual knower-willer, God can "improvise" his providence instantly, from his timeless Now outside our time, to match each unfolding phase of the world as it takes place, without any need of knowing "ahead of time" what is going to happen, as though he would somehow have to have enough time to plan things out well. To impose on God a process of first deliberation then later decision would be a pure anthropomorphic projection of our own body-bound consciousness into him.

For this reason it seems to me unwise, because it is easily misleading, to say that God knows our free future acts "from all eternity," as though from some eternal duration stretching out far back before creation. For where there is no real process (in fact, before creation there is not even any "intentional time"), there is no meaning to "before" and "after" and no standard for measuring it. Hence it would seem wiser to say that God knows my free actions and all of history not *from* all eternity but *in* his eternal, i.e., timelessly present, ever-contemporaneous Now.

At this point, however, we are faced with two different modes or conceptual models of the divine eternity, between which one must choose. Many, including myself, think that both are compatible with the minimum requirements of an authentic Christian notion of God, though the second is not compatible with the classical Scholastic tradition represented by Boethius and St. Thomas. The first or classical model is that of an absolutely durationless eternity, durationless even in the intentional order, where the whole history is seen *tota simul*, in a single simultaneous vision where all points of the temporal process are equally simultaneous to God as outside the whole temporal order, with no privileged ongoing "now" in God's knowledge matching the ongoing "now" of history itself. As Lonergan puts it, the whole of history is seen as a single strictly concrete actualized world order.

The other model of the divine eternity is a durational one—durational, that is, only in the intentional contents of the divine consciousness as directed toward the world of creation. In this model the divine field of intentional consciousness is constantly expanding to match the ongoing evolution of temporal history, in exact contemporaneity with the latter's ongoing "now." This does not entail, of course, any expansion or change in the qualitative level of the intrinsic real perfection of God. For the latter is eternally infinite in plenitude, and all the new finite determinations of the field of his intentional consciousness are but limited participations in the unlimited divine plenitude, never rising to a higher level than their original source, hence involving no real change in the Aristotelian sense. In this view, the ongoing now of actual history is normative for all thinkers who know it as it is, including God, and cannot be relativized into a simultaneous whole as an actual present. Such totalization can only be done when the history is all a finished past. Since the being of our evolving world is a not yet finished being in process, it cannot be known as finished without distorting the kind of being it is.

Such process and expansion in the intentional field of consciousness of God with regard to the world would not, however, constitute an imperfection in God's knowledge. For it cannot be an imperfection not to know what is not in itself knowable—i.e., the future, the not yet real, at least in its free or not yet determined aspects. Perfect knowledge of an evolving reality would by nature have to evolve with its object. And since the intentional content of this expanding consciousness would always be only more finite participations of God's own infinite plenitude, the perfection of the content would never rise higher than the ever-present primary object of the divine knowledge, God's own infinite intrinsic perfection.

This model of the divine infinity is certainly not a Thomistic one. Whether or not it is a more adequate model than the classical Thomistic one is an excellent subject for debate. When I first composed this essay in 1973, I was myself leaning somewhat toward this view, impressed by the suggestion of Hilary Armstrong in his recent study of Plotinus's unsuccessful attempt to handle the same problem, when in the last line of his discussion he raised the question "whether non-durational eternity is a concept which can be usefully employed in any philosophical or theological context."[20]

Now, twenty years later, revising this essay for the present collection, I have moved back again toward St. Thomas's position, that God acts and knows from an eternal Now entirely outside anything like successive duration. My main consideration is the incoherence of trying to locate God in any kind of time sequence or framework of real succession. (*Which* time frame in the universe, given Einstein's Relativity Theory, etc.??) And I no longer see any urgent need for the durational view of eternity in order to preserve anything significant that needs to be perserved. We do, of course, have to surrender considering the "now" of our own ongoing history as normative for the whole universe, including God. Another consideration has been the testimony of mystics in so many different traditions, which seems to point overwhelmingly to timelessness as a common characteristic of their union with Ultimate Reality.

But my main concern here is not to settle the question whether the durational or non-durational concept of God's eternity is the correct one. It is only to make the point that whether one is drawn to accept the durational concept or not, it is *possible* to adopt it without compromising the divine perfection of knowing and the immutability of God's intrinsic real being. By restricting the Thomistic metaphysics of immutability in God to the Aristotelian dimension of change in the intrinsic real perfection of a being, we have opened up the possibility of a whole new dimension of intentional process in God which leaves intact, while transcending, the entire Aristotelian dimension of real change and immutability. It may well be that the mystery of the divine consciousness is so beyond our human comprehension that we must be content to allow several different conceptual models of it without having any unambiguous decision procedure to decide between them.

How Can God Receive from Us in the Order of Knowledge?

Throughout this paper we have been taking for granted the *fact* that God knows our free actions, our free responses to him, which of course implies that this leaves their freedom intact and does not one-sidedly determine them. All accept this fact—at least those in the Catholic philosophical tradition, including, naturally, St. Thomas himself. But just *how* it is possible for God thus to know our free actions without either determining them or being acted on, and hence changed, by us constitutes a celebrated and very difficult classical problem, with various thinkers in the tradition presenting diverse and never very satisfactory solutions. St. Thomas, perhaps wiser than most, is very laconic on the subject, contenting himself with affirming that God knows all the actions of creatures by "moving them" to their actions, those which act by determination of nature to act by natural necessity, those which act freely to act freely.[21] The precise *how* he leaves a mystery.

We could also do the same thing. But process philosophers insist—and with good reason, it seems to me—that if God knows our free actions without determining them, he must be learning from us, receiving knowledge from us. They then argue that this necessarily implies that God is changed by us, acted on by us in time. Hence I feel obliged to say something on this point: is God's knowledge of our free actions *determined by us*, and if so, how?

A New Look at the Immutability of God

My answer is in brief outline as follows:

(a) It seems to me that one must resolutely affirm that God's knowledge of our free actions is determined by us in some significant sense. For the essence of a free act as *mine* is that it is self-determined by me, that I am responsible for the determination, not God, though he can positively cooperate with my action in carrying out the pursuit of the good once chosen.

(b) The whole question now comes down to *how*. The classical Dominican Thomist school rejects my above affirmation on the grounds that if creatures determine God in any way, then God will be causally dependent on them, contingent, etc., which is impossible for an infinite self-sufficient being. I do not accept this dilemma. The kernel of my solution is that there are *two ways* in which one's knowledge can be determined by another. In the first way the object known acts causally on the knower as on a passive recipient. This way is, of course, excluded in the case of God.

In the other way a superior agent freely offers its indeterminate abundance of power to a lower agent, allowing the latter to channel, or determine—which means here to delimit (partially negate)—the flow of the former's power along lines determined by the lesser agent, to help the latter execute its own limited operation. In this case the determination contributed by the lower agent does not add any new being to the power of the higher agent. It "adds on" only a partial negation or delimitation of the higher plenitude, hence does not introduce any change in, or addition to, the real being of the higher agent. In this situation the higher agent knows what the lower is doing, not by being positively acted on to receive new real being from the lower, but precisely by knowing *its own action*, by knowing just how its own power is allowed to flow through the lower agent, along the channel which the lower agent determines. So God can know my free action by knowing just how I allow his freely offered power, always gently drawing me through the good, to flow through me. God knows my choice by knowing his own active power working within me, as thus determined or channeled determinately here and now by me. Hence God knows by acting, not by being acted on, but I supply the inner determination or limit of this power at work—which I repeat is not a new positive being at all but only a limiting down of an indeterminate plenitude. Clearly I am not limiting the real being of God or the inner plenitude of power within him, but only the exercise of it in me.

A crude image might be of help here. Suppose a strong man pushing gently against two doors (not forcing them), which are being held by another man on the other side, while the latter deliberates which door he wishes to open. When the latter has made his decision he lets one of the doors go and the power of the one pushing immediately follows through to push it open. The pusher knows what decision the second man has freely made, not by being acted on by the latter, but by knowing where his own power is allowed to flow through. Only the negative determination or channeling of the offered power is provided by the decider. And to determine in this context is not to act upon—a point consistently overlooked, it seems to me, by those who refuse to allow that God's knowledge can in any way be determined by creatures.

I see no reason why the above-described conjunction of power and determination cannot be found analogously in the conjunction of the divine power with our free self-determination. God then truly "receives" the determination of his knowledge of our free actions from us, but without in the least being a passive recipient of a new mode of real being in himself, impressed thereon by any positive causal action of ours.

(c) The perceptive reader will surely have noticed that implied in the above theory is the assumption that the actual self-determination which is the heart of the human free choice is entirely caused by us and not by God, is not the "work" of God. This seems at first glance quite contrary to the traditional position: there is nothing we can do which God does not do with us. But this is precisely the key to the problem: the crucial moment in free decision is *not a doing at all*. It is precisely the moment of *negation* or *exclusion* of all possible avenues of choice save one, the saying "No" to all but one. For, given choices A, B, C, we cannot choose C unless we first negate A and B. This negation is not a positive *act* at all, producing anything new; hence it cannot be shown that it requires any causal cooperation of God. It is completely in "our power" thus to negate, i.e., to exclude from the focus of our intentional consciousness, all but one good. Then as soon as we have closed the door to all but one good—our responsibility alone—the active pursuing of this remaining good becomes a positive act and God's power immediately follows through to cooperate with us in this positive side of the coin of free decision, as in all positive actions of creatures. God only says "Yes" with us in our free choices; we alone say the "No" which is the necessary prelude to our combined "Yes."

Since the above hypotheses all seem to me to make reasonably good sense, I have sufficient grounds for affirming that it is not impossible (unintelligible)—though I cannot, of course, claim positive insight into how this is done—for God to "receive" knowledge of my free actions from me, to let it be determined by me, since this determination does not add on any new mode of positive being but only a delimitation (i.e., partial negation) or channeling of the way in which I allow his active cooperating power to flow through my will. Hence I neither need to, nor have the right to, affirm any *real change* (hence real temporal succession) in God, change in his own inner real being, in order to affirm genuine receptivity to me in the divine knowledge.

Once we have established this principle of determination of God's knowledge by limitation or channeling of his power flowing through us, determined by our free choice as "traffic directors'" so to speak, this opens up a rich new dimension of *receptivity* in God with respect to love relationships, allowing *mutual* relationships of friendship, both giving and receiving love, between God and ourselves. From all that we know about love as the highest perfection of personal living, it belongs to the very meaning of love at its richest to involve mutuality, not only a self-communicating giving love but also an active welcoming openness to receive love from the other. Love without mutuality always falls short of the full spendor of love. Love within the Trinity, as revealed to us by Jesus, is the supreme example of what the perfection of love is at the pinnacle of being, and our own should in some way imitate this as best we can. And in receiving our return of love with delight God is not being positively acted on by us, but allowing his loving power, working in us and through us, to be guided by our freedom, so that in the last analysis God can love himself in a new creative way through us, as we open ourselves freely to a new finite participation in God's own infinite power of loving his own infinite goodness. Receptivity, at the highest level of personal being, is not passivity, not an imperfection, but an aspect of pure perfection, as Hans Urs von Balthasar has so insightfully pointed out, and as I have taken into account in my latest book, *Person and Being*, and the briefer article, "Person, Being, and St. Thomas," now chapter 10 of this collection.[22]

CONCLUSION

All that we have done thus far really comes down to reinterpreting the immutability in God to fit the perfection proper to the dimension of personal—and therefore interpersonal—being, hence proper to God as truly, though analogously, personal. I grant that this is not the unqualified immutability in all domains which seems to have been the ideal of the classical Greek mind, conceived at least implicitly on the model of being as object rather than subject, and resulting in the self-absorbed, unrelated self-contemplation of the Aristotelian Prime Mover or the Neoplatonic One (the latter above all otherness even in its knowledge, since this would imply real duality). Such a notion of immutability simply does not fit our new sensitivity to the meaning of being as interpersonal, with its exigency of mutual relatedness and reciprocity—a notion which itself is perhaps largely the result of the "good news" of the revelation of the Judaeo-Christian God of love. The notion of immutability must always be controlled, as we said earlier, by the central normative notion of perfection as proper to a person.

Let us say, then, in conclusion, that the immutability which must be affirmed of God is the unchanging, indefectible steadfastness of an infinite plenitude of goodness and loving benevolence, but a benevolence which also *expresses* itself in a process, a progressive unfolding, of mutual interpersonal relationships, spread out in real temporal succession at our receiving end and matched by a distinct differentiation of intentional consciousness in God for each real external expression in us, in terms of which he is truly related to us by an intentional relation of personal consciousness. With less immutability we would not have a truly infinite God; with more, we would not have a truly personal God. And I cannot see the slightest imperfection introduced into God by the "intentional process" we have postulated in him— even from the point of view of Thomistic metaphysics and epistemology. Hence I conclude that it is perfectly legitimate, from the metaphysical point of view, quite adequately metaphysically grounded, even in a Thomistically inspired metaphysics, for the religious consciousness to speak in the warmest personalist terms of God's truly ("really") caring, personal relation of mutual love with us.

NOTES

1. See the well-known works of Charles Hartshorne, *Divine Relativity* (New Haven: Yale Univ. Press, 1964); John Cobb, *A Christian Natural Theology Based on the Thought of Whitehead* (Philadelphia: Westminster, 1965); E. H. Peters, *The Creative Advance: An Introduction to Process Philosophy as a Context for Christian Faith* (St. Louis: Bethany, 1966); *Process Philosophy and Christian Thought*, eds. D. Brown, R. James, G. Reeves (Indianapolis: Bobbs-Merrill, 1971); and the careful study of Alix Parmentier, *La philosophie de Whitehead et le problème de Dieu* (Paris: Beauchesne, 1969).

2. See, e.g. (in addition to note 1), James Felt, S.J., "Invitation to a Philosophic Revolution," *New Scholasticism*, 45 (1971), 87–109; J. C. Robertson, "Does God Change?" *Ecumenist*, 9 (1971), 61: "For a large number of both Catholic and Protestant theologians, of the younger ones at least who

are trying to disengage the Gospel from the classical world-view and to express it in terms of the modern one, the processive idea figures in their interpretation of Christian doctrine in a large way."

3. See Robert C. Neville, "The Impossibility of Whitehead's God for Christian Theology," *Proceedings of American Catholic Philosophical Assoc.*, 44 (1970), 130–40.

4. I am thinking in particular of the creative synthesis of Whitehead and St. Thomas which the late Walter Stokes, S.J., was in the midst of working out: "Is God Really Related to the World?" *Proceedings of Amer. Cath. Phil. Assoc.*, 39 (1965), 145–51; "Whitehead's Challenge to Theistic Realism," *New Scholasticism*, 38 (1964), 1–21; "God for Today and Tomorrow," ibid., 43 (1969), 351–78. I also call my readers' attention to the historical article of Gerald McCool, S.J., "The Philosophical Theology of Rahner and Lonergan," ch. 7 in *God Knowable and Unknowable* (New York: Fordham Univ. Press, 1973).

5. See Frederick Sontag, *Divine Perfection: Possible Ideas of God* (New York: Harper, 1962).

6. Cf. *Summa Theologiae*, I, q. 2, a. 3; q. 9, and parallel passages.

7. Cf. *Sum. Theol.*, I, q. 13, a. 7; *Summa contra Gentes*, II, ch. 12; *De Potentia*, q. 7, a. 10; and the first article of Stokes cited in note 4.

8. Cf. Francis Meehan, *Efficient Causality in Aristotle and St. Thomas* (Washington, D.C.: Catholic Univ. of America Press, 1940); W. N. Clarke, S.J., "Causality and Time," in *Experience, Existence, and the Good*, ed. I. C. Lieb (Carbondale: Southern Illinois Univ. Press, 1961), pp. 143–57.

9. For a careful study of the meaning and importance, for St. Thomas, of naming God "cause" by extrinsic attribution, and the absence of change or real relation in the cause formally as cause, see the Ph.D. dissertation of Thomas Loughran, "Efficient Causality and Extrinsic Attribution in the Philosophy of St. Thomas" (Fordham Univ., 1969).

10. See, e.g., *De Spiritualibus Creaturis*, a. 1 ad 11; *De Veritate*, q. 22, a. 10; q. 2, a. 2; *Sum. c. Gentes*, IV, ch. 11; I, ch. 55; *Sum. Theol.*, I, q. 14, a. 1; q. 15; *In II De Anima*, lect. 24, nn. 552–53; and the studies of André Hayen, *L'intentionnel selon S. Thomas* (2nd ed., Paris: Desclée de Brouwer, 1954), and L. M. Régis, *Epistemology* (New York: Macmillan, 1959), ch. 6, with the abundant texts of Aquinas cited there.

11. *Sum. c. Gentes*, I, ch. 55: "A knowing power does not know anything in act unless an intention is present."

12. See, among other texts, *Sum. c. Gentes*, IV, ch. 11.

13. See Stanislas Breton, *Conscience et intentionnalité* (Paris: Vitte, 1957), for a comparison of St. Thomas and Husserl.

14. Anthony Kelly, C.S.S.R., "God: How Near a Relation?" *Thomist*, 34 (1970), 191–229. See also the articles of Walter Stokes cited in note 4.

15. See H. R. Reinelt, "A Whiteheadian Doctrine of Analogy," *Modern Schoolman*, 48 (1970–71), 327–42.

16. I must come to grips here with the penetrating objection raised by my colleague, Joseph Donceel, S.J., to the effect that an increase in knowl-

edge through intentional being is certainly an increase of real perfection in us; otherwise growth in knowledge would be no growth in real perfection for us—which is clearly false and contrary to St. Thomas himself. I admit that such growth in knowledge *in us* is a growth in real perfection, a change to a higher level of perfection, precisely because it gives us knowledge of real beings we did not know before and which are not a limited participation in our own preexisting perfection but are quite independent of us in the source of their being. Were we, however, to know something we had totally thought up and totally produced in all its being from our own preexisting plenitude, then knowledge of such a being would not add to our real perfection, though it would add a new determination to our field of intentional consciousness. This is precisely the case with God.

17. See Nelson Pike, *God and Timelessness* (New York: Schocken, 1970). In this carefully argued book the author allows that the concept of a timeless God as a *cause* can be meaningful and correct, but not the concept of God as *both* personal and timeless.

18. See W. N. Clarke, S.J., "Causality and Time" (cited in note 8). From this point of view I also find the article of James Felt, S.J. (note 2) metaphysically defective in its criticism of St. Thomas, namely, in its apparent assumption that the act of creation, precisely as an act of causality, necessarily implies change in the cause.

19. See *Sum. Theol.*, I, q. 14, a. 13.

20. A. H. Armstrong, "Eternity, Life, and Movement in Plotinus' Account of *Nous*," in *Le Néoplatonisme*: Colloques Internationaux, Royaumont, 1969 (Paris: Centre National de la Recherche Scientifique, 1971), p. 76. In a subsequent letter to me, the author further clarified his suggestion—namely, that it may be necessary to use both models, durational and non-durational eternity, in dialectical complementarity, in order to speak properly about God.

21. *Sum. c. Gentes*, II, ch. 88–90; *Sum. Theol.*, I, q. 105, a. 4; *De Potentia*, q. 3, a. 7, and ad 12–14.

22. Cf. Gerard O'Hanlon, S.J., *The Immutability of God in the Theology of Hans Urs von Balthasar* (New York: Cambridge Univ. Press, 1990), nicely summed up in same author's "Does God Change? Hans Urs von Balthasar on the Immutability of God," *Irish Theological Quarterly*, 53 (1987), 161–83, at p. 171. I have tried to assimilate this into my own thought in my *Person and Being* (Milwaukee: Marquette Univ. Press, 1993), pp. 82 ff.; also in my article, "Person, Being, and St. Thomas," reprinted in the present collection.

10

Person, Being, and St. Thomas

The notions of person and being are in fact deeply intertwined, since personal being is the highest mode of being, the most perfect expression of what it means to be. As St. Thomas has put it, "Person is that which is most perfect in all of nature."[1] But too often the person is treated merely as a special mode of being, from the point of view of psychology, or ethics, or legal philosophy, or the phenomenology of interpersonal relations, and the like. Yet the person is not something added on to being as a special delimitation; it is simply what being *is* when allowed to be at its fullest, freed from the constrictions of subintelligent matter. So the notions of being and person can each throw much light on the other when brought together on the level of being itself.

My objective in this article is to work out what I might call a "creative completion" of St. Thomas's own thought on these two themes, or perhaps a "creative retrieval," as a Heideggerian might put it. For, on the one hand, Aquinas has an explicit, powerfully dynamic notion of being, of what it means to be, as intrinsically self-communicative and relational through action. On the other hand, he never quite got around to applying this in explicitly thematized fashion to his *philosophical* notion of person. Medieval discussions of the metaphysics of personhood tended to get fixated on the technical problems of the "incommunicability" of the person, i.e., what makes it unique, not a part of any other being, and distinct in some way from the rational nature which always accompanies it.

Drawing the distinction between person and nature was indeed necessary in the context of Christian theology because of the need to explicate, as far as humanly possible, the two central doctrines of God as Triune (i.e, one divine nature possessed equally by three distinct Persons, distinguished only by their relations of origin to each other) and Christ as God-man (i.e., one divine Person possessing two distinct natures, one divine, one human). The challenge of these two revealed doctrines forced a careful working out of the distinction between person and nature which might have taken much longer if left to purely philosophical inquiry into our ordinary human experience, and in fact might never have occurred at all—as is the case in the Chinese and Japanese traditions before their encounter with Western thought, where the notion of "person" as a distinct concept seems to have been lacking. But as a result, the relational, self-communicative dimension of the person, flowing from its very status in being, was left in the shadow. The two notions were ready and waiting to be brought together. But St. Thomas did not quite get around to making the junction explicit. The controversies of the day absorbed his attention elsewhere. The explicit philosophical thematizing of the relational, interpersonal dimension of the human person had to wait until the existentialist and personalist phenomenologies of the twentieth century for its full highlighting and systematic development.

It is one of the paradoxes of intellectual history, however, that St. Thomas and the other medieval scholastics did indeed develop a relational notion of the person for use in the *theological* explanation of the Trinity. But for some reason they did not exploit this remarkable intellectual achievement for the *philosophical* explanation of the person. Cardinal Joseph Ratzinger (in his previous "incarnation" as a creative and daring theologian) takes St. Thomas—and other scholastic thinkers—to task rather sharply for not developing this relational notion of the person within Christian philosophy but instead slipping back into the traditional Boethian definition of person as "an individual substance of a rational nature." And so St. Thomas failed to recognize that in the relational notion of person developed within the theology of the Trinity "lies concealed a revolution in man's view of the world: the undivided sway of thinking in terms of substance is ended; relation is discovered as an equally valid primordial mode of reality . . . and it is made apparent how being that truly understands itself grasps at the same time that *in* its self-being it does not belong to itself; that it only comes to itself by moving away from itself and finding its way back as relatedness to its true primordial state."[2]

I think the Cardinal has a point, and I would like to do for Thomistic metaphysics what Thomas himself could have done, but for various reasons did not get around to doing. I would like to join together his dynamic relational notion of being as active, already explicitly developed, with the notion of person, already rooted by him in the act of existence, to bring into the clear the intrinsically relational character of the person precisely as the highest mode of being. Person and being are, in a sense, paradigms of each other.

THE DYNAMIC, RELATIONAL NOTION OF BEING

One of the central themes in the thought of Aquinas is his notion of real being, i.e., actually existing being, as intrinsically active and self-communicating. A superficial reading of Aquinas might not notice this at first, because it is never thematized as the formal question asked in any question or article. But it runs all through his thought, both philosophical and theological, as one of the key mediating ideas in explanations and drawing of conclusions, as I have tried to show at greater length in my article on the subject.[3] A sampling of his texts will show this clearly enough.

> From the very fact that something exists in act, it is active.[4]
>
> Active power follows upon being in act, for anything acts in consequence of being in act.[5]
>
> It is the nature of every actuality to communicate itself insofar as it is possible. Hence every agent acts according as it exists in actuality.[6]
>
> It follows upon the suberabundance proper to perfection as such that the perfection which something has it can communicate to another. Communication follows upon the very intelligibility (*ratio*) of actuality. Hence every form is of itself communicable.[7]
>
> For natural things have a natural inclination not only toward their own proper good, to acquire it, if not possessed, and if possessed, to rest therein; but also to diffuse their own goodness among others as far as is possible. Hence we see that every agent, insofar as it exists in act and possesses some perfection, produces something similar to itself. It pertains, therefore, to the nature of the will to communicate to others as far as possible the good possessed; and especially does this pertain to the divine will, from which all perfection is derived in some kind of likeness. Hence if natural things, insofar as they are perfect, communicate their goodness to others, much more does it pertain to the divine will to communicate by likeness its own goodness to others as far as possible.[8]

Not only is activity, active self-communication, the natural consequence of possessing an act of existence (*esse*); St. Thomas goes further to maintain that self-expression through action is actually the whole point, the natural perfection or flowering of being itself, the goal of its very presence in the universe:

> Every substance exists for the sake of its operations.[9]
>
> Each and every thing shows forth that it exists for the sake of its operation; indeed, operation is the ultimate perfection of each thing.[10]

Thus there is an immense innate dynamism in the very nature of actual being as such, wherever an act of existing is found, participated or unparticipated, to pour over into self-expression, self-communication of its own inner perfection or goodness. Full credit must be given to Etienne Gilson for his role in rediscovering the centrality and dynamism of the act of existence in contemporary Thomism. As he puts it pithily:

> Not: to be, then to act, but: to be is to act. And the very first thing which "to be" does, is to make its own essence to be, that is, "to be a being." This is done at once, completely and definitively. . . . But the next thing which "to be" does, is to begin bringing its own individual essence somewhat nearer its own completion.[11]

Gerald Phelan, one of the early disciples of Gilson at Toronto, was also peculiarly sensitive to the expansive character of being through action:

> The act of existence (*esse*) is not a state, it is an act and not as a static definable object of conception. *Esse* is dynamic impulse, energy, act—the first, the most persistent and enduring of all dynamisms, all energies, all acts. In all things on earth, the act of being (*esse*) is the consubstantial urge of nature, a restless, striving force, carrying each being (*ens*) forward from within the depths of its own reality to its full self-achievement.[12]

Despite their sensitivity to the intrinsic connection between *to be* and *to act*, these comments of Gilson and Phelan limit their focus to the drive of each being toward fulfilling its own perfection, to its passage from its own potency to its own act—still in some respects an Aristotelian perspective. Aquinas, in the texts we have seen above, goes considerably further, speaking of an intrinsic dynamism in every being to be *self-communicative*, to share its own goodness with others, to pour over into the production of another actuality in some way like itself. This is what Maritain has aptly called "the basic generosity of existence."[13]

It follows that, for Aquinas, finite, created being pours over naturally into action for *two* reasons: (1) because it is *poor*, i.e., lacking the fullness of existence, and so strives to enrich itself as much as its nature allows from the richness of those around it; but (2) even more profoundly because it is *rich*, endowed with its own richness of existence, however slight this may be, which it tends naturally to communicate and share with others.

This innate fecundity and generosity proper to being as existent, by which it is naturally self-communicating to others, is St. Thomas's way of integrating into his own metaphysics of being the rich Platonic and Neoplatonic traditions of the self-diffusiveness of the Good (understood by them as more ultimate than being, which always meant limited intelligible essence). Existence itself (*esse*) now becomes for Thomas the ultimate root of all perfection, with unity and goodness its transcendental properties or attributes, facets of the inexhaustible richness of being itself. And once the Platonic realism of divine ideas is overcome, Thomas's Supreme Being, the pure subsistent Act of Existence, can become identically Intelligence and Will, and the intrinsic self-diffusiveness of the Good turns into Love, self-communicative Love. The ultimate reason now appears why all beings, by the very fact that they *are*, possess this natural dynamism toward action and self-communication: they are all diverse modes of participation in the infinite goodness of the one Source, whose very being is identically self-communicative Love. Dante, good Thomist that he was, was right after all when he summed it up in the *Paradiso*: "Love makes the world go round."

This understanding of being as intrinsically active, self-manifesting and self-communicating through action, I consider not merely as a position of historical interest for appreciating ancient and medieval thought, but also in its own right as one of the few great fundamental insights in the history of metaphysics, without which no viable metaphysical vision can get far off the ground. For consider what would happen if one attempted to deny that every real being is active, self-manifesting through action. Suppose a being that really exists, but does not act in any way, does not manifest itself in any way to other beings. There would be no way for anything else to know that it exists; it would make no *difference* at all to the rest of reality; practically speaking, it might just as well not be at all—it would in fact be indistinguishable from non-being. If many or all real beings were this way, each would be locked off in total isolation from every other. There would not be a connected universe (its root, *universum*, means in fact "turned toward unity"). The only way that beings can connect up with each other to form a unified system is through action. To be and to be active, though logically distinct, are inseparable. "Communication," as Aquinas says, "follows upon the very intelligibility of actuality." The full meaning of "to be" is not just "to be *present*," but "to be *actively present*." Existence is power-full, energy-filled presence. *Agere sequitur esse* (action follows upon being, as the medieval adage has it, although the interpretation varied according to the meaning given to *esse*). To know another being, therefore, is to know it as *this kind of actor*.

The innate dynamism of being as overflowing into self-manifesting, self-communicating action, is clear and explicit in St. Thomas.

What is clearly implied, however, though not as explicit, is the corollary that *relationality* is a primordial dimension of every real being, inseparable from its substantiality, just as action is from existence. For if a being naturally flows over into self-communicating action to and on others, it immediately generates a network of relations with all its recipients. Action, passion, and relations are inseparably tied together even in the Aristotelian categories. While all relations are not generated by action, still all action and passion necessarily generate relations.

It turns out, then, that relationality and substantiality go together as two distinct but inseparable modes of reality. Substance is the primary mode, in that all else, including relations, depend on it as their ground. But since "every substance exists for the sake of its operations," as St. Thomas has just told us, being as substance, as existing *in itself*, naturally flows over into being as relational, turned *toward others* by its self-communicating action. *To be* is to be *substance-in-relation*.[14]

In a creature it may well be accidental *which* particular other being it will be related to here and now. But *being related* in some way to the world around it, as well as to its various sources, will flow from its very nature both as an existent being and as material. Within the divine being, the relations of procession between the three Persons are not accidental but constitutive of the very nature of the divine substance. Substantiality and relationality are here equally primordial and necessary dimensions of being itself at its highest intensity. And the ultimate reason why all lower beings manifest this relationality as well as substantiality is that they are all in some way images of God, their ultimate Source, the supreme synthesis of both. Therefore, all being is, by its very nature as being, *dyadic*, with an "introverted," or *in-itself* dimension, as substance, and an "extroverted," or *toward-others* dimension, as relational through action.

Let us conclude this section with a quotation from Josef Pieper, who, more than most contemporary Thomists, has brought out the proportional connection between the substantial and relational aspects of being:

> To sum it up, then: to have (or to be) an "intrinsic existence" means "to be able to relate" and "to be the sustaining subject at the center of a field of reference." . . . Only in reference to an inside can there be an outside. Without a self-contained "subject" there can be no "object." Relating-to, conforming-with, being-oriented-toward—all these notions presuppose an inside starting point. . . . The higher the form of intrinsic existence, the more developed becomes the re-

latedness to reality, also the more profound and comprehensive becomes the sphere of this relatedness: namely, the world. And the deeper such relations penetrate the world of reality, the more intrinsic becomes the subject's existence.[15]

This dynamic polarity between substance and action-plus-relations was submerged and almost forgotten in the post-medieval period from Descartes on. Three major distortions of the classical notion of substance broke the connection: (1) the Cartesian notion of the isolated, unrelated substance, "that which needs nothing else but itself (and God) to exist"; (2) the Lockean static substance, the inert substratum needed to support accidents but unknowable in itself; and (3) the separable substance of Hume, which, if it existed, would have to be empirically observable as separated from all its accidents, and hence is an impossible fiction.

Because these emasculated versions of substance were the only ones familiar to them from classical modern philosophy, a large number of modern and contemporary thinkers have simply rejected substance entirely as a nonviable mode of being, e.g., Bergson, Collingwood, Whitehead, Dewey, Heidegger, most phenomenologists, and many others. As a result, the person tended to be reduced to nothing but a relation or set of relations. The difficulty, here, however, as Pieper warned, is that if the substance, or *in-itself*, pole of being is dropped out, the unique interiority and privacy of the person are wiped out also and the person turns out to be an entirely extroverted bundle of relations, with no inner self to share with others. But there is no need for this either/or dichotomy between substance and relation, once the notion of substance as center of activity—and receptivity—has been retrieved. *To be* is to be *substance-in-relation*.

APPLICATION TO THE PERSON

For St. Thomas, personality in the ontological sense, i.e., to be a person, is rooted in the act of existing: to be a person is to be an intellectual nature possessing its own unique act of existing so as to be the autonomous source of its own actions. Thus, in the theological application of the doctrine, the human nature of Christ is complete as a nature, but does not own its own act of existing, so it is not a *human* person, but is owned by the personal act of existence of the Second Person of the Trinity. Now the person, for Aquinas, "is that which is most perfect in all of nature." But since the act of existing is for him the root of all perfection, it follows that to be a person is not something added on to being from without, but is really only the perfection of being itself, being come into its own, so to speak, allowed to be fully what it tends to be by nature when not restricted by the limitation proper to the material mode of being, i.e., the self-dispersal over space that is characteristic of matter. In a word, when being is allowed to be fully itself as active *presence*, it necessarily turns into luminous *self-presence*—self-awareness, or self-consciousness—one of the primary attributes of person. To be fully is to be personally.

All this is clear enough in Aquinas himself. But another very significant implication follows from this rooting of personal being in being itself at its supra-material levels—an implication that was not brought out explicitly, or at least was not thematized or highlighted by him. Being is not just *presence*, but *active* presence, tending by nature to pour over into active self-manifestation and self-communication to others. And if personal being is really being itself only at its supra-material levels, then it follows that to be a person as such is to be a being that tends by nature to pour over into active, conscious self-manifestation and self-communication to others, through intellect and will working together. And if the person in question is a *good* person, i.e., rightly ordered in its conscious free action, then this active presence to others will take the form of willing what is truly good for them, which is itself a definition of *love* in its broadest meaning, defined by Thomas as "willing good to another for its own sake." To be a person, then, is to be a bi-polar being that is at once present *in itself*, actively possessing itself by its self-consciousness (its substantial pole), and also actively oriented *toward others*, toward active loving self-communication to others (its relational pole). To be an authentic person, in a word, is to be a *lover*, to live a life of *inter*personal self-giving and receiving. Person is essentially a "we" term. Person exists in its fullness only in the plural. As Jacques Maritain puts it felicitously:

> Thus it is that when a man has been really awakened to the sense of being or existence, and grasps intuitively the obscure, living depth of the Self and subjectivity, he discovers by the same token the basic generosity of existence and realizes, by virtue of the inner dynamism of this intuition, that love is not a passing pleasure or emotion, but the very meaning of his being alive.
>
> Thus subjectivity reveals itself as "self-mastery for self giving . . . by spiritual existing in the manner of a gift."[16]

Josef Pieper has also caught well the intrinsic bi-polarity of personal being as spirit, when, commenting on a brief sentence of St. Thomas, he unfolds it thus:

> The higher the form of intrinsic existence, the more developed becomes the relatedness with reality, also the more profound and comprehensive becomes the sphere of this relationship: namely, the world. And the deeper such relations penetrate the world of reality, the more intrinsic becomes the subject's existence. . . . These two aspects combined—dwelling most intensively within itself, and being *capax universi*, able to grasp the universe—together constitute the essence of the spirit. Any definition of "spirit" will have to contain these two aspects as its core.[17]

Transpose "spirit" into "person," as being itself existing on the spiritual level, and Pieper and I are both expressing the same insight.

Once the intrinsically self-communicating and relational notion of being has been integrated into the notion of person as its highest expression, the way is open to grafting the whole rich contemporary phenomenology of the person as essentially relational and interpersonal onto the more basic metaphysics of being as active presence. It also becomes clear that, viewed in this relational perspective, the person cannot be looked on as primarily an isolated, self-sufficient individual, with freely chosen relations added on as a merely occasional, accidental complement. The person is intrinsically ordered toward togetherness with other human persons—and any other persons accessible to it—i.e., toward *friendship, community,* and *society*. As Aquinas himself puts it in a beautiful little aside: "It is natural for man to take delight in living together with other human beings."[18] Thus precisely because to be a person is to be the highest mode of being, the fullest expression of what it means to be, person means at once that which stands in itself as a self-possessing, autonomous center and at the same time, by the very dynamism of its self-possession, that whose whole being is oriented toward others, especially other persons, in self-communicative expression and sharing of itself, as *interpersonal*. Thus one of the small but growing number of contemporary Thomists who have caught on to the intrinsically relational aspect of both being and person, Norbert Hoffman, can speak of "this movement of the *pro*, this self-openness towards the other" (most luminously manifested in the revelation of divine being as self-communicative interpersonal love), as "the primal mystery and the first of all impulses in the heart of being. All of its own, and not because of subsequent determination, Being posits itself as *communicatio*; its essential form is called 'love.'"[19]

RECEPTIVITY AS A PERFECTION OF BEING AND PERSON

So far I have developed the self-communicative aspect of the person as stemming from the intrinsic dynamism of being itself. I would now like to bring explicitly into focus another aspect of this same dynamism of being and the person which has not been developed, even implicitly, it seems, by St. Thomas himself. Yet, I think it deserves to be developed if we are to carry through all the way our "creative completion" of St. Thomas. The suggestion for this development I owe to two sources: one is John Cobb, representing the process point of view, who made the point during the question period after the initial presentation of this paper at the annual meeting of the Metaphysical Society of America at Villanova University in March 1992. The other is the profound and daring speculation of the Swiss theologian Hans Urs von Balthasar, whose thought on the subject has been made available to the English-speaking community by the work of Gerard O'Hanlon, *The Immutability of God in the Theology of Hans Urs von Balthasar*.[20]

In addition to Balthasar's creative rethinking of the notion of the immutability of God to allow in the Trinity an eternal dynamic "process" or "event" of interpersonal communication beyond time and change—but of which change and time in our world are an imperfect image—he makes the point that in an adequate notion of the perfection of love *receptivity* is the necessary complement of active self-communication and of equal dignity and perfection with the latter. Self-donation would be incomplete without welcoming receptivity on the other side of the personal relation. And this belongs to the very perfection of the love relationship itself. We have too long been accustomed to regard receptivity as passivity, associating it with the inferior status of potentiality as poverty which is completed by actuality as the perfecting principle. This is certainly the case with many lower-order examples of receptivity, particularly as connected with the passivity of matter. But the higher up one moves into the realm of spirit and person, the fullness of being as such, the more this "passivity" turns into an active, "welcoming" receptivity that is a mark of the perfection—not the imperfection— of interpersonal relations. As O'Hanlon puts it:

> This is shown most clearly at the top of an ascending scale of subject/object relationships in the created sphere when one arrives at the interpersonal relationship between two subjects, at the heart of

which is a welcoming, active receptivity. . . . the higher up the scale of created reality one goes the more this passivity (in the sense of an active receptivity) increases, and the more it may be seen, in the case of human inter-personal encounter, as a perfection.[21]

The proof that this welcoming, active receptivity is a mode of actuality and perfection, not of potentiality and imperfection, is seen clearly when we turn to the intra-Trinitarian life of God. Here it is of the essence of the personal being of the Son as such that it be totally and gratefully receptive to the gift of the divine nature from the Father; the personality of the Son might well be called "subsistent gratitude." So too with the Holy Spirit as the love image of both Father and Son, receiving its whole being from them as gift and reflecting that back as the pure essence of actively receptive love. Since all notion of change—with its accompanying imperfection of first a state of non-possessing potentiality, then a later state of possession—is eliminated from this eternal, ever actualized "process," all notion of imperfection disappears, too.

Thus in its highest and purest form, echoed analogously and proportionately, with increasing imperfection, down through creation, the radical dynamism of being as *self-communicative* evokes as its necessary complement the active, welcoming *receptivity* of the receiving end of its self-communication. Authentic love is not complete unless it is both actively given and actively—gratefully—received. And both giving and receiving at their purest are of equal dignity and perfection. The perfection of being—and therefore of the person—is essentially dyadic, culminating in *communion*.

I call this grounding of the person as relational—both self-communicative and actively receptive—in the very dynamism of being itself a "creative retrieval and completion" of the latent, implicit resources and implications of Aquinas's own metaphysics, lying just under the surface and waiting to be developed. But it must be honestly admitted that without the stimulus of contemporary phenomenological insights into the relational aspects of the person, the insistence of process thinkers, and the theological speculation of thinkers like Balthasar, they might have continued to lie there undeveloped. As Ivor Leclerc has so insightfully pointed out, the history of metaphysics is inseparable from, though not identical with, its content.

OBJECTION

Before concluding, I must take into account an obvious objection that must have come into the minds of many of you, especially perhaps of fellow Thomists. If this self-communicative, relational view of being is taken seriously and applied all across the board, even to God, or whatever one wishes to call Ultimate Reality, a consequence emerges which St. Thomas himself, with many other Christian thinkers, rejects. It is this: If being is intrinsically self-communicative and relational at all levels, including the divine, then it would follow that either (1) God must necessarily, rather than freely, communicate the divine goodness in creation—which Aquinas as a Christian thinker could not subscribe to; or else (2) God's own inner being must be intrinsically relational, involving more than one person—and then we have a philosophical deduction of the doctrine of God as Trinity of distinct Persons, which Christian tradition has always held to be a "strict mystery," inaccessible to any argument of natural or purely philosophical reason, and knowable in this life only by a divine revelation. St. Thomas explicitly rejects both of these positions, the first because it seems to deny the absolute freedom of God in creation, which Christian thinkers in his time were very sensitive about maintaining against the necessary emanationism of the great Islamic thinkers like Averroës and Avicenna. The second he rejects because it seems to deny the need of a divine revelation, accepted by faith, as the only way of knowing the small number of central "strict mysteries" of the Christian religion, such as the Trinity and Christ as God become man.

What are we to make of these objections? Let us take first the *freedom of creation*. Frankly, I think St. Thomas has been overcautious here, that St. Bonaventure has done better, following out more consistently the doctrine of the self-diffusiveness of the good. In his philosophical expositions, Aquinas habitually puts forward the strong interpretation of the self-diffusiveness of being, as the texts we cited earlier clearly bear witness to. Then suddenly, when he comes to the question of the freedom of creation, he pulls back and explains that in this case the self-diffusiveness of the good must be taken only in the sense of a final, not an efficient cause. That is, once God has created freely through efficient causality then he necessarily diffuses his goodness as final cause over all things.[22]

[*Author's Note*: The reader should take note that my response to this objection is here completely rewritten and significantly different from the text of the original article as published in *Communio*.]

St. Thomas does have a partial good answer to this difficulty, although I am not sure it is fully adequate. His first move is to distinguish between the orders of efficient and final causality in the self-diffusiveness of the good. There is no doubt that in the original Platonic and

Neoplatonic doctrine this self-diffusiveness was taken in the strong sense as including active efficient causality, as well as final causality, since the Good was the highest reality, above "being" itself, from which all other realities emanate. St. Thomas prefers to distinguish the two orders, restricting the diffusiveness of the good as such to the order of final causality, where its influence works necessarily on the things drawn to it, once efficient causality has begun to work. The order of efficient causality, on the other hand, can be free.[23]

This enables him to distance himself from the Neoplatonic and Arabic emanation doctrines, with their connotation of necessity, as opposed to the Christian doctrine of the freedom of creation. He has indeed incorporated the whole Platonic dynamism of the good into his own metaphysics, but he prefers to describe it consistently as the "self-communication of act," or of existence (*esse*). Thus he says, in a text quoted earlier, "Communication belongs to the very meaning (*ratio*) of actuality."[24]

But this distinction, legitimate and more technically precise as it is, only pushes the difficulty back one step. What about the self-diffusiveness, the innate tendency toward self-communication, of the act of existence itself? How does this apply to God, which it must as the supreme exemplar of being itself, without denying the freedom of creation? Here St. Thomas makes a second and truly creative move. Calling on the Christian revelation of God as Triune in his inner life, he points out that there already exists in God a supremely perfect and complete self-communication in the inner life of God, where the Father pours out his entire divine nature as gift to the Son, and both together to the Holy Spirit, in an infinitely intense self-diffusiveness of the divine being and goodness. And this self-communicating love, which is the very nature of God, of being at its fullest, is of its nature necessary, i.e., not a matter of free choice. Once this necessary self-communication is present, eternally so, in the inner life of God, then the further self-communication in the creation of a finite world is no longer necessary but can be a purely gratuitous, free overflow, since the basic law of being as self-communicating has already been taken care of with infinite perfection.[25] This is a perfect example, to me, of what it means to have a properly *Christian* philosophy, where one can draw when necessary on a higher revealed source of truth to illumine and help to solve a problem incapable of adequate solution on the level of a metaphysics of purely natural reason.

This is indeed a brilliant solution—and one which Hegel should have paid more attention to, since it would have rendered unnecessary the need of his God to create a finite world in order to express himself and come to know himself through an Other. This was already achieved in the Trinity.

St. Thomas makes another contribution to the solution by proposing a strictly philosophical argument, without reference to any theological doctrines, why creation of *this* finite world *must* be free. One can say first that the creation of any *particular* finite world by an infinite cause must be free. For, given a cause of infinite perfection, as God must be, it is impossible to deduce from it by any logical argument—by any necessity of reason, to put it more broadly—the existence of any *particular* finite effect, or system of effects: for given an infinite cause, an infinite number of other effects is always possible. So the appearance of any one particular finite order must pass through the selection process of intelligent free choice, otherwise nothing definite will emerge at all. There can be no necessary connection between a source of infinite power and any finite effect, only a contingent one. Thus whatever finite created order exists must be the result of a free choice on God's part. This is enough, I think, to satisfy the requirements both of sound theistic metaphysics and Christian theological tradition.[26]

But the further question now arises: Is it necessary that the self-diffusiveness of the divine goodness manifest itself in *some* finite universe, although any particular one would have to be freely chosen? This is a considerably more difficult question. St. Thomas would say "No." I think one should say "Yes," with some reservations. Given an infinitely good and loving personal being, it seems to me one can say it is *inevitable* that it will pour over in *some* way to share its goodness outside itself, though one cannot predict just how. This inevitability, or "necessity," if you will, is not any external compulsion or blind metaphysical force, but the very "logic," the special logic, of a loving nature, that it will spontaneously pour over to share its goodness in some way, if it can, with a spontaneity that is at once lucidly and consciously free, uncompelled by anything but love, yet inevitable, "out of character" for it not to happen. Thus in the case of God, as Hegel and others have well said, in a certain sense freedom and necessity come together in a transcendent synthesis, proper only to the nature of love. Even on our own human level, in fact, if we know a habitually generous, loving, and compassionate person, we can predict with practical certainty that if someone needy comes her way and she is able to help without obstacles or conflicting demands, she will certainly do so, though freely. The rationality of love is a unique kind of rationality transcending the limits of logic (though not contradicting them).

After I had written the above, my attention was called to what seems to me the best and most thorough treatment of this whole question of the self-diffusiveness of the good, with the most abundant textual grounding, of any I have seen. This is Chapter IX: "The Creative Diffusion of the Good," in the recent excellent study by Fran O'Rourke, of University College, Dublin, entitled *Pseudo-Dionysius and the Metaphysics of St. Thomas* (Leiden: Brill, 1992). The author's exposition of Aquinas's position seems to me quite solid and well backed up. But he ventures further to make the very interesting suggestion that the principle of the self-diffusiveness of the good, or of existence itself, which he joins closely together, is not some ultimate necessary law of being itself but is the reflection in creatures of the radical *free* decision of God to share the divine goodness out of pure generous liberality beyond all necessity. This radical liberality of God *is* the ultimate mystery of creation, beyond which we cannot go for any deeper explanation, and God wishes creatures to reflect this divine liberality in their own expansive, self-communicating acts of existence.

I think he has it right about St. Thomas, who consistently opposes the procession of creatures from God by nature or by necessity to procession by a will decision based on the pure generosity of God's goodness. But in the author's metaphysical explanation he leaves out what seems to me a key element in the whole picture: the infinite, eternal self-communication of the divine goodness not by free choice but by the necessity of God's own divine nature, in the Trinity of Persons within God. Since this is the very nature of being at its highest, it would seem to me that the principle of the self-diffusiveness of the good and being does not originate in God's free decision to create out of pure free generosity, but is anchored in something deeper in the divine nature, hence in the nature of being itself, and it is this aspect of the divine nature itself, expressed by the divine will in its free act of creation, that creatures are imitating in the metaphysical "law" they exhibit, that every being, insofar as it *is* in act, is self-communicative, expansive, self-sharing. And I suspect this may be a little closer to the position of Pseudo-Dionysius.

St. Thomas himself seems also occasionally to hint at something a little more than a purely contingent free decision by God, when he speaks, in texts quoted with admirable honesty by O'Rourke, of creation not as being due by any necessity or relation of justice, but as somehow "befitting," "appropriate to" the divine goodness (*per modum cuisdam condecentiae; decet bonitatem ipsius*).[27] Could we not say, then, that it is the very nature of God to be self-communicating out of love, and that the fitting expression of this inner nature with respect to creation is a further free self-sharing? But here the categories of free, inevitable, natural all converge together so that God may be said to transcend their differences in a way beyond the reach of our concepts. In two remarkable texts Thomas actually suggests something like this:

> For God to will something of those things that he does not will out of necessity is not a natural act; neither on the other hand is it unnatural, or against nature; but it is voluntary.[28]
>
> For the divine will is to be understood as existing beyond the order of beings, as though a cause that pours forth the whole of being and all its differences. But the possible and the necessary are differences of being; and therefore from the divine will itself necessity and contingency in things take their origin . . . all depend on the divine will as on the first cause, which transcends the order of necessity and contingency.[29]

Perhaps we should leave the matter there in mystery, insisting only that God's free generosity in creation is itself a reflection of a deeper inner "law" of self-communicating love that is the very nature of the Supreme Being. It is free, but in a manner that is also somehow fitting, appropriate to divine goodness, hence also in a sense "inevitable."

Let us come now to the *second main objection* noted earlier: Are we not deducing from natural reason the need for some kind of *interpersonal relationship on the divine level itself*, thus deducing the philosophical necessity of something like the Trinity of Persons in God, which is supposed to be accessible only through divine revelation accepted through faith, according to orthodox Christian tradition? The question is not an easy one, but I do not think we are forced into an either/or confrontation between faith and reason. Already in the twelfth century, Richard of St. Victor proposed a kind of deduction of a suasive argument from natural reason showing why, if God is personal at all, he-she must have some other person to relate to in love, since the very meaning of person and loving implies an interpersonal term of relation. He also tried to show why there must be not only some plurality of persons within the divine life, but precisely three and no more.[30]

Aquinas and the later scholastics rejected his argument as not meeting the rigorous requirements of the newly discovered Aristotelian rules of argumentation. But there is much wisdom and cogency in Richard's analysis, as Ewert Cousins has tried to show, although a strict rigorous argument cannot be framed. It would seem to me that one could hold there must be *some* kind of interpersonal relation on the divine level, following from the analogy of the terms person and love, but one could not deduce with any certainty just what form this would have to take or *how many* persons it would have to involve: why not two, or four, why necessarily only three: If one leaves the latter point open, it would seem that one has not deduced from reason the precise Christian mystery of God as *Triune* in persons.

Conclusions

Thus the way seems open to me to work out a philosophically—and theologically—viable "creative completion" or retrieval of St. Thomas's metaphysics of being and the person. This retrieval which would first highlight the intrinsically expansive, self-communicative, and therefore relational dimension of existential being as such, then apply this to the person as the fullest realization of what it means to *be.* Thereby would be generated a metaphysics of the person as intrinsically self-communicative, relational, and therefore interpersonal, whose natural self-expression on the highest level would be love.

Is the above analysis a purely philosophical, or a theologically guided one? I think it is one of those not infrequent cases in Western thought (also found in most Eastern traditions in an analogous way) of a basic metaphysical concept that as a historical fact received its first stimulus and illumination from a theological source, but once "unveiled" can become a self-sustaining philosophical insight, recommending itself by its superior explanatory power.

Notes

1. *Summa Theologiae,* I, q. 29, a. 3.
2. Josef Ratzinger, *Introduction to Christianity* (New York: Herder & Herder, 1970), pp. 132, 137; "Concerning the Notion of Person in Theology," *Communio,* 17 (1990), 438–54.
3. W. Norris Clarke, "Action as the Self-Revelation of Being: A Central Theme in the Thought of St. Thomas," now chapter 3 in this collection.
4. *Summa contra Gentes,* I, ch. 43.
5. *Sum. c. Gentes,* II, ch. 7.
6. *De Potentia,* q. 2, a. 1.
7. *Sum. c. Gentes,* III, ch. 64.
8. *Sum. Theol.,* I, q. 19, a. 2.
9. *Sum. Theol.,* I, q. 105, a. 5.
10. *Sum. c. Gentes,* III, ch. 113.
11. Etienne Gilson, *Being and Some Philosophers* (Toronto: Pontifical Institute of Mediaeval Studies, 1952), p. 184.

12. Gerald Phelan, "The Existentialism of St. Thomas," in *Collected Papers* (Toronto: Pont. Inst. of Med. Stud., 1967), p. 77.
13. Jacques Maritain, *Existence and the Existent* (Garden City, N.Y.: Doubleday, 1957), p. 90.
14. I have developed this formula at length in my article, "To Be Is to Be Substance-in Relation," in *Metaphysics as Foundation: Essays in Honor of Ivor Leclerc*, ed. P. Bogaard and G. Treash (Albany: SUNY Press, 1993), 161–83—reprinted as chapter 6 in this collection.
15. Josef Pieper, *The Truth of All Things*, reprinted in *Living the Truth* (San Francisco: Ignatius Press, 1989), pp. 83, 82.
16. The first part of the quotation is from Jacques Maritain, *Existence and the Existent*, p. 90; the second part from Maritain, *Challenges and Renewals* (Univ. of Notre Dame Press, 1966), pp. 74–75.
17. Josef Pieper, *Living the Truth*, p. 83.
18. *Sum Theol.*, I–II, q. 114, a. 2 ad 1; cf. the rich metaphysical grounding of this in Mary Rousseau, *Community: The Tie That Binds* (Lanham, Md.: Univ. Press of America, 1991).
19. Norbert Hoffman, *Toward a Civilization of Love* (San Francisco: Ignatius Press, 1985), pp. 237–38, quoted in the suggestive and stimulating article of Robert Connor, "Relation, the Thomistic *Esse*, and American Culture: Toward a Metaphysic of Sanctity," *Communio*, 17 (1990), 455–64.
20. O'Hanlon, *The Immutability of God in the Theology of Hans Urs von Balthasar* (London: Cambridge Univ. Press, 1990).
21. Taken from the preparatory article nicely summarizing his book, "Does God Change? Hans Urs von Balthasar on the Immutability of God," *Irish Theological Quarterly*, 53 (1987), 161–83, at p. 171.
22. A key text of St. Thomas is *De Veritate*, q. 21, a. 1 ad 4. Cf. also Jules Péghaire, "L'axiome 'Bonum est diffusivum sui' dans le néoplatonisme et le thomisme," *Revue de l'Université d'Ottawa*, 2 (1932), 5*–30*; M. J. Nicolas, O.P., "Bonum est diffusivum sui," *Revue thomiste*, 55 (1955), 363–76; Norman Kretzmann, "Goodness, Knowledge, and Indeterminacy in the Philosophy of Thomas Aquinas," *Journal of Philosophy*, 80 (1983), 631–49; and the valuable collection, *Being and Goodness: The Concept of the Good in Metaphysics and Natural Theology*, ed. Scott MacDonald (Ithaca: Cornell Univ. Press, 1990).
23. E.g., *De Veritate*, q. 21, a. 1 ad 4.
24. Note 7 above.
25. Cf. *De Potentia*, q. 3, a. 15, and the illuminating article, developing in detail this whole point, by Gregory Reichberg, "The Communication of the Divine Nature: Thomas's Response to Neoplatonism," *Proceedings of American Catholic Philosophical Assoc.*, 66 (1992).
26. *De Potentia*, q. 3, a. 15; *Sum. c. Gentes*, II, ch. 81–83.
27. *Sum. c. Gentes*, II, ch. 28, n. 13; I, ch. 86, n. 5.
28. *Sum. Theol.*, I, q. 19, a. 3 ad 3.
29. *Expositio in Libros Perihermeneias*, I, lect. 14, n. 197.
30. Cf. Ewert Cousins, "A Theology of Interpersonal Relations," *Thought*, 45 (1970), 56–82.

ABOUT THE AUTHOR

W. Norris Clarke, S.J., Professor Emeritus of Philosophy of Fordham University, is the author of many articles as well as three previous books: *The Philosophical Approach to God: A Neothomist Perspective; The Universe as Journey*; and *Person and Being*. He was the co-founder and Editor-in-Chief of the *International Philosophical Quarterly*, 1961–85, and is a past president of the Metaphysical Society of America, the American Catholic Philosophical Association, and the Jesuit Philosophical Association. He received his Ph.D. from the Université Catholique de Louvian, Belgium, and is the recipient of an Honorary Doctor of Laws from Villanova Univesity and an Honorary Doctor of Humanities from Wheeling Jesuit College. In addition to more than thirty years of teaching at Fordham University, he has taught at many Jesuit colleges and universities throughout the United States.

www.ingramcontent.com/pod-product-compliance
Lightning Source LLC
Chambersburg PA
CBHW031252230426
43670CB00005B/156